RAISE YOUR GAME

RAISE YOUR GAME

GAME

*High-Performance Secrets from
the Best of the Best*

ALAN STEIN JR.

with Jon Sternfeld

Foreword by Jay Bilas

CENTER
STREET

New York Nashville

Center Street
Hachette Book Group
1290 Avenue of the Americas, New York, NY 10104
centerstreet.com
twitter.com/centerstreet

First edition: January 2019

Center Street is a division of Hachette Book Group, Inc. The Center Street name and logo are trademarks of Hachette Book Group, Inc.

The publisher is not responsible for websites (or their content) that are not owned by the publisher.

The Hachette Speakers Bureau provides a wide range of authors for speaking events. To find out more, go to www.HachetteSpeakersBureau.com or call (866) 376-6591.

Library of Congress Cataloging-in-Publication Data

Names: Stein, Alan, Jr., author. | Sternfeld, Jon, author.
Title: Raise your game : high performance secrets from the best of the best /
    Alan Stein Jr., with Jon Sternfeld ; foreword by Jay Bilas.
Description: First edition. | New York : Center Street, [2019] | Includes bibliographical
    references.
Identifiers: LCCN 2018034534| ISBN 9781546082866 (hardcover) | ISBN
    9781549171345 (audio download) | ISBN 9781546082873 (ebook)
Subjects: LCSH: Success in business. | Success. | Performance.
Classification: LCC HF5386 .S8559 2019 | DDC 650.1—dc23
LC record available at https://lccn.loc.gov/2018034534

ISBNs: 978-1-5460-8286-6 (hardcover), 978-1-5460-8287-3 (ebook)

Printed in the United States of America

LSC-C

10 9 8 7 6 5 4 3 2 1

Luke, Jack, and Lyla . . . I love you more than words can express.
You inspire me to raise my game.

CONTENTS

Part I: Player

Part II: Coach

Part III: Team

FOREWORD

I first met Alan Stein Jr. at a Skills Academy for high school basketball players. It was essentially a camp for many of the best prospects in the country, players who would soon populate the NBA draft and be some of the biggest names in the game. Alan was introduced to me as an expert in athletic performance training. I soon learned he was much more than that.

From the very beginning of the Skills Academy, Alan was never on time. He was always early. He didn't speak in meetings unless he had something important to say. He listened intently and took notes purposefully. He was always available, and no task at the camp was too small for him. He was, to use a term that has become almost cliché, a servant-leader. In my view, however, Alan was something more valuable. He was a great teammate. He did his job and helped others do theirs.

To me, that is an important aspect of Alan's character. He has ambition to move up and succeed, just as any motivated person would, but, rather than concentrate on "networking," Alan was resolute to do the job in front of him and look for any way to add value to the jobs being performed by others. If a player was in the gym early, Alan rebounded for that player. If someone was needed to jump into a drill, Alan was right there to do it. If there was something on the floor, Alan picked it up. If the floor had not been swept from the day prior, Alan swept it.

It was not done to impress; it was done because it was needed. But, it did impress. It impressed everyone. General Martin Dempsey, former chairman of the Joint Chiefs of Staff, once said that leadership is a journey, not a destination. If you ever think you have it right and have nothing else to learn about leadership, Dempsey continued, you are making a serious mistake. To me, Alan embodies General Dempsey's three key principles of leadership: character, competence, and humility. Alan is a man of great character, a man with a moral firmness that does not bend to any prevailing wind. He is an expert in his field and continues to study and learn as the game and technology change. And, Alan is humble enough to listen, learn, and work as if he is dirt poor.

Alan has risen in his field and is held in such high esteem by the best players and coaches in the game because of the consistent excellence in the performance of his job, and because he is constantly getting better and making his team better. Alan brings positive energy to everything he does, the positive energy that comes not from cheerleading but from the inspiration of doing hard things well. Alan does those hard things, and others join in willingly because of the example he sets.

An example of his example: several years ago, I started a basketball camp in Charlotte, North Carolina, for high school players who wish to get better and young coaches who wish to develop their skills. I believe I started this camp and continue it every year for the right reason: to give back and help others the way that so many helped me along the way. When the camp started, it was low budget and fledgling, and I mentioned it to Alan. Immediately, he said he would be there to work the camp. Frankly, the camp was far below

Alan's level. Yet he was there from the first coaches' meeting to the last moment any player was on the floor. He was, literally, the first person in the gym and the last person to leave.

Although Alan would shrug this off, the example he sets for these young high school players is invaluable. And the role model he is for young coaches is unmatched. Alan brings a technical expertise to the camp that few camps around the country can match. But he brings an inspirational presence that no camp anywhere can match. That is how important he is.

Both Alan and I are products of team sports, and I believe we both understand and value how the lessons and principles we learned in team sports can be applied and used in academics, business, and countless other pursuits. For many reasons the principles that make one successful in team sports resonate with people and reach them on a different level, one that lessons from other endeavors seemingly cannot.

In basketball, my team always had an opponent. We had a talented, athletic, and unified group of players actively and physically trying to stop us from executing the actions we intended to take. In school and business, I may have had competitors, but I never had an opponent.

Never once in my career as a lawyer or broadcaster did anyone actively try to stop me from executing the actions I intended to take. The only one that could stop me was me. This book will help you get out of your own way and free you up to achieve without fear of failure. It won't motivate you, because you don't need motivation. It will inspire you.

I have spent the last twenty-six years as both a lawyer and a broadcaster. I can confidently state that I have not worked a single day without consciously using the lessons I learned from a coach or a teammate I have been around or from the books I have read in my field. This book will provide you with those lessons and principles of success that translate across boundaries of sport and business.

I am so pleased that Alan has written this book. He has learned from the best, and as a result, he is the best. And I am profoundly lucky to have him as a friend.

—Jay Bilas ESPN

INTRODUCTION

In 2013, USA Basketball invited me out to Las Vegas to work at a camp alongside some of the best college coaches in the world, giants like the University of Kentucky's John Calipari, the University of Florida's Billy Donovan, and Gonzaga University's Mark Few. The first day was dominated by shooting drills and scrimmages before the coaches conducted a formal draft, led by CBS's Bill Raftery and ESPN's P. J. Carlesimo, to select the teams. But as I looked out onto the court, I wasn't watching college stars or future NBA prospects. No, the players were all middle-aged men with lots of disposable income, a willingness to hustle, and an undying love of basketball. USAB was getting into the sports fantasy camp business, a booming industry. Incredibly successful men will pay serious money to run up and down the court for hours, shoot hoops, and get yelled at from the sidelines by their heroes. That's their dream.

I worked this camp for several years, and it's a fantastic experience. The participants may take their private jet to Las Vegas and get chauffeured to the gym in a Bentley, but they are almost universally down-to-earth guys. They are just incredibly driven and enormously successful. The glamour of being a multimillionaire and Fortune 100 CEO drains away as they pant up and down the court with their headbands, gym shorts, and for some, beer bellies. But this doesn't diminish them in my eyes—not at all. In fact, it elevates them. I love how seriously they take the games, how intensely they prepare, how they get out there early to do foam rolling and stretching, how they scream their heads off at the referees after a blown call.

During breaks in the day, they're making calls, conducting deals, and running their businesses. Then the games start up and they're on the court again, boxing out and hustling back on defense. They're hypercompetitive. It's how they got where they are in life. And that competitive element is not a switch they can turn on and off—it's in their nature, part of who they are. Athletic skills may not transfer from the boardroom to the court, but the approach, fundamentals, and attitude most certainly do.

Sport is the great equalizer, and these guys know it. Everyone might "yes" them all day—waiters scurry to find them the best wine, valets hustle after their car—but deep down they want someone who will get on them for a poor shot or swat their layup into the stands. They want to *earn their buckets*. They know that you get strong by going uphill. And there's nothing like a basketball game against other fierce competitors to see what you're made of.

Vasu Kulkarni, CEO of sports analytics company Krossover and CourtsideVC, has made basketball the frame around which all of his businesses revolve. He gets incredibly enthusiastic talking about basketball and wears his love for the game on his sleeve. "The court brings out your true colors," he told me in an interview. "A lot of times what you see on the court is what you get off the court. So many people I do business with, I try to bring them to a court."

A game of hoops is a shared experience. It's intense, it's exhausting, and you get to experience the highs of victory and the lows of defeat with others who care about the outcome. "I find basketball to be a great way to forge relationships and build bridges with people," he said. Vasu is taking his perspective from one of the all-time greats. Hall of Fame legend Larry Bird reportedly said he knew everything he needed to know about someone based on how that person behaved on the basketball court.[1]

The link between the sports and the business worlds is a natural one. It's not a coincidence that the top coaches do double duty as leadership and motivation experts. John Calipari of Kentucky and Jay Wright of Villanova write business leadership books, Duke coach Mike Krzyzewski works as a motivational speaker in his free time, UNC coach Dean Smith was invited to give lectures at management schools in far-off places like Switzerland.

Institutions, companies, and regular people just trying to get ahead will cough up serious money, sacrifice weekends, and travel substantial distances to hear what a top coach has to say. And they're not taking notes on zone defenses and how to execute the pick and roll. Some attendees may not even follow sports, but they understand the jewels of wisdom that these coaches carry. The coaches' lessons are universal, and their results are concrete and inarguable.

College coaches also have to start over from scratch every couple of years or so, with a new crop of talent and new strengths and weaknesses. The coaches—and the programs they develop—are the consistent factors, so a college team's long-term success is a testament to their leadership. They understand the basic priniciples of success because they have to continue to execute them year in and year out.

It's an important reminder: Success is a result of what we do *all of the time*. The highest performers in all walks of life have embraced this fact; they have taken full ownership and have chosen to create and implement positive habits. They understand that you can't be selective when it comes to excellence. As the saying goes, how you do anything is how you do everything.

Most of my career has been spent helping elite basketball

players improve their athleticism and their mind-body connection. I've worked with the likes of Kevin Durant and Victor Oladipo and watched superstars like Kobe Bryant and Steph Curry in their private practice routines—and two things stick out. One, they stick to the basics. They study and practice the basics to the point that they're automatic, as if the actions are doing them. Two, they work harder than anyone else. They might lose, but they simply will not be outworked.

I've been a basketball performance coach since I graduated from college in 1999. Major companies from all over the world now hire me to teach, train, and consult on effective leadership and teamwork because the principles of achievement on the court parallel the principles necessary to succeed in any industry. I believe in the fundamentals, and I preach the fundamentals. I've seen people fail or succeed based on their commitment to the unsexy, the unpopular, and the unglamorous. "Success is neither magical nor mysterious," wrote one of my heroes, Jim Rohn. "Success is the natural consequence of consistently applying the basic fundamentals."

I want to teach you how to live present in a distracted society so you will be a more connected, productive, and influential leader and teammate. Monumental change occurs only with the accumulation of the little things. Never forget: it's what all the big things are made from.

Success isn't something that happens to you. It's something you attract, you choose, and you create. Successful people do the little things better than everyone else. This is what makes the best the best. World-class performers and the uber-successful amassed their achievements by sticking to the fundamentals and doing the little things—every single day.

We can look to athletes and businesses because they are masters at willing a certain outcome into existence. LeBron James can visualize himself catching up to an opponent on a fast break, see when and how that player is going to go in for the layup, and then time his movement to smack the ball against the glass. He saw it before it happened; he willed the result into existence. The great athletes like LeBron do that all the time—but so did Steve Jobs and Bill Gates.

I've spent the past fifteen-plus years working with the highest-performing athletes on the planet. I now teach people how to utilize the same strategies in business and life that elite players and teams use to perform at a world-class level. My goal for this book is simple—to educate and inspire readers to take immediate action to improve their mind-set, habits, and value.*

The very first step to raising performance is learning how to *live present*. The happiest, most influential, and most successful people I've ever met are able to put their full attention into the present moment. They have learned how to focus on three things:

1. The next play
2. The controllables
3. The process

In my quest to help organizations run more efficiently, I've befriended, learned from, and interviewed successful CEOs, executives, entrepreneurs, and leaders. In doing so, I've found that the traits that are needed to be a successful player, coach, and teammate are the same characteristics that are used to run some of the biggest and most significant companies in the world. The parallels are eye-opening. I've been fascinated by how these aspects of culture, commitment, and teamwork transcend industry.

---

* Note for Readers: For simplicity, I've chosen to use the pronoun "he" throughout this book. Consistently saying "he or she" is clunky, and alternating pronouns is confusing. I believe in being direct. Just know that effective leadership and elite performance know no gender—every word of this book is equally applicable to males and females.

The tools required for success are available to everyone. They're shared openly by countless individuals who have made it to the top. Everything we need to maximize our happiness, fulfillment, confidence, influence, and success is readily available. But it's up to us to put these strategies into practice, make them habits, and live them out daily. And that's the reason I wrote this book.

You need to *make the choice* to act—to apply the information here and become a more influential leader, and teammate. You need to *make the choice* to close the gap between what you know and what you do. Because the choices you make today will determine where you are tomorrow.

This book will help you drill down on your answers to these vital questions:

1. What sacrifices do I need to make?
2. What skills do I need to acquire?
3. Whose help would I benefit from?
4. What challenges should I expect?
5. What habits do I need to change?

This book will be the initial spark to raising your game, in every area of your life. It will provide you with the tools, concepts, stories, lessons, and actionable tasks that I've learned from a variety of high performers. Along the way I will share the meaningful and impactful conversations and observations I've been so fortunate to have gained from countless high achievers. But the real work is up to you. After all, you can't pay someone else to do your push-ups.

I was taught at a young age that knowledge is power. But that is actually incomplete: Knowledge by itself is useless. The power is in the application. Knowing without doing is the equivalent of not knowing at all.

So it's not necessarily about knowledge. The vast majority of people know what foods they should eat, how much sleep they should get, and what they should do for their physical fitness. Yet obesity has been on the rise for years. Why? Although people know what they need to do, *they just don't do it.*

When it comes to improving performance—in any area of life—the most basic and effective strategy is to close *performance gaps.* These are the gaps between what we know we are supposed to do and what we actually do. Everyone has performance gaps, but the world's highest performers and achievers have found ways to eliminate or reduce them in the most important areas.

We live in the information age. Thanks to technology, we can find quality information on just about anything in a matter of seconds. Not knowing something is hardly ever the reason our performance suffers. The reason we get stuck, frustrated, and exhausted is not from lack of knowing—it's from lack of doing. This book will help motivate, inspire, and guide you to start closing your most pressing performance gaps.

HOW THIS BOOK IS ORGANIZED

The book is divided into three parts: "Player," "Coach," and "Team," which correlate in business to employee, manager/CEO, and organization. Each part contains the five characteristics required to be successful in that specific role.

All three parts flow into each other like this:

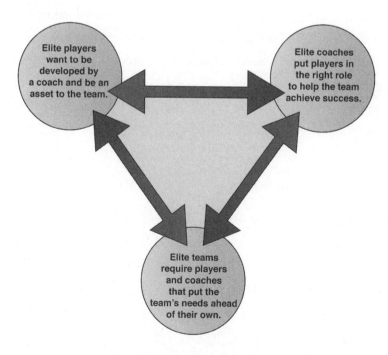

*graphic designed by Jeremy Stein

It's important to note that none of these parts are mutually exclusive and each section has valuable characteristics applicable to everyone. The key traits for a coach can be utilized by a player now (or later, if he plans to become a coach)—and vice versa—and a team works only if the players and the coaches are fulfilling their roles.

I intentionally divided this book into three parts to take a closer look at each vantage point and perspective, as every one of us fulfills the role of player, coach, and teammate throughout our lives. Regardless of your age or vocation, I guarantee you are constantly flowing from one of these titles to another (and are often serving as two or three of them at once).

Part I: Player

A *player* is any individual who is part of a team, company, or organization. This section is divided into five chapters, each focusing on a single quality that is necessary for an individual to have (and work on) in order to succeed. Each characteristic builds on the previous one, and the final one—confidence—is a result of the previous four working in harmony.

Chapter One: Self-Awareness

This is what everything else in this book is built from. Making "you" your business. Self-awareness means having and developing an understanding of who you are, and what you can and can't do. If you don't know where you're starting from, then it is impossible to develop the tools to move to the next level. It all starts here.

Chapter Two: Passion

This is hard to teach but monumentally important to emphasize and tap into. It's the possession of a love for what you do and the inner drive to pursue your goals. It's a willingness to do what needs to be done—even the unpleasant stuff—because the outcome matters that much to you. It's about having heart and putting yourself—all of yourself—into your work.

Chapter Three: Discipline

Discipline is about developing the routine, structure, and habits to achieve your goals. It's about doing what others aren't doing, investigating how to get ahead, and understanding that talent alone is never enough. This is the system that the self-aware and passionate put into place and repeatedly develop, adapt, and hone.

Chapter Four: Coachability

Successful people are open to learning. The best never stop, and it's their commitment to finding their gaps and filling them that brought them to where they are. It's also what keeps them moving up. They possess the humility to understand that good enough is never good enough. If you aren't coachable, you will never progress. Coachability is about having the right attitude and approach toward self-improvement.

Chapter Five: Confidence

This is the accumulation of the first four. Confidence, *earned* confidence, is about outlook and attitude. It's knowing that you will succeed because you have put in the time, effort, and learning into mastering what it is you do. It's the face you wear out in the world because the mechanics on the inside are solid and humming.

Part II: Coach

A *coach*, for our purposes, refers to someone who has been given authority over others. This could be a CEO, a director, a manager, a supervisor, a coach, or a parent. It can be someone who has one direct report or can be someone who has a thousand. Part 2 is for anyone looking to improve their ability to lead, impact, and influence others.

This part is divided into five chapters, each focusing on a single quality that is necessary for a *coach* to have—and develop—in order to succeed. As in part 1, each characteristic builds on the previous one, and the final trait—empowerment—is a result of the previous four working together in harmony.

Chapter Six: Vision

A coach must work to stay ahead of the competition and see what others don't or can't. In order to move yourself and those you lead forward, you must envision what you want to create and take the steps to make it happen. Vision is carrying a map to the future, and it includes how you communicate that map so that others are inspired to get behind you.

Chapter Seven: Culture

A coach is only as strong as the environment he creates. It should be a place of safety, motivation, and inspiration. Culture includes the physical space where you work, the manner in which everyone interacts, and the rules and values the coach instills, encourages, and rewards. A coach should build a work environment where everyone is able to achieve both their highest selves, as well as what is best for the team. The right culture will convince everyone that these are one and the same.

Chapter Eight: Servant

True leaders serve their people, not the other way around. Leaders make themselves available and accessible to those they lead. Being a servant leader is about understanding your people's desires and responding to their needs. It is an antidote to the brute force management style that is outdated and ineffective. A servant leader empathetically listens, remains open and adaptable, and is willing to get his hands dirty in the service of the vision and the culture.

Chapter Nine: Character

Character refers to who the coach is as a person, even when there's no reward involved. It's about being someone of honor and integrity whom others can trust and get behind. No one wants to work for a liar, a jerk, or a cheater. Having character means you are the kind of person *you* would work for. Though the short-term may occasionally reward those who take shortcuts, the long term always rewards high character.

Chapter Ten: Empowerment

Empowerment is the culmination of the first four coaching traits. It's the final step because it is about leaders letting go, allowing their people the freedom and support to become leaders themselves. To empower is to make your people feel valued and valuable. A leader trusts his team in a way that lets the members know they are each integral parts of the whole.

Part III: Team

A *team* is any group, business, or organization that collectively works together to accomplish a shared vision and mission. Like the previous two parts, this is broken down into five characteristics, each building on the previous one. Once again, the final characteristic, cohesion, is the culmination of the previous four.

Even if you work for a nontraditional company or by yourself, you are part of a team. No one achieves success alone. While you may have to do most of the heavy lifting, everyone needs and receives help in some way, shape, or form. All of us are a part of something bigger than ourselves—in our work, our families, and our communities. We all depend on teammates whom we count on and those we need to serve and support. In ways big and small, we are all teammates.

Chapter Eleven: Belief

Belief is the first trait in this part because it is the groundwork that enables any team to be successful. It refers to the underlying attitude that a team has about itself. Believing means having the conviction that the team can succeed and carrying a commitment that what they are trying to do is valuable. It's how a team knows they can trust each other: Each member is "all in," gaining strength from knowing this fact about one another.

Chapter Twelve: Unselfishness

Selfishness will destroy any team. Every member of the team needs to be unselfish and genuinely care about his teammates, coaches, and mission—not just his own success, advancement, or credit. Each member must be willing to put the team before his own agenda and desires and acknowledge that he is simply part of a whole. Unselfishness means recognizing collective achievement is the primary goal.

Chapter Thirteen: Role Clarity

Role clarity is a key aspect of how a team operates and interacts with one another. Each member understands his specific place in the whole and where others fit in. Successful teams know that every member matters, that they are a puzzle made up of different interlocking pieces. The whole doesn't work or make any sense without each piece fulfilling its part.

Chapter Fourteen: Communication

Communication is the glue that keeps the team together. It's about having the openness to talk and listen with respect, purpose, and attention. It's not just about the verbal, but body language and tone as well. This trait is applicable across all industries, relationships, and organizations.

Chapter Fifteen: Cohesion

Cohesion is the accumulation of the previous four traits discussed in part 3. It is the natural result of all members understanding their individual role, communicating with the others, believing in the mission, and being unselfish in the execution. To cohere is to operate successfully as a whole, which is stronger than the sum of its parts.

PART I

PLAYER

CHAPTER ONE

Self-Awareness

> Embrace the people who tell you you're full of crap.
>
> —Gary Vaynerchuck

Here's a foundational argument for the rest of this book: the single most important thing a person needs for success is self-awareness. This includes who you are, what you can do, what you can't do, where your value comes from, and where you need improvement. Nothing I teach or preach in this book will matter if you don't start here.

Self-awareness is not just the most important quality; it's the hub of all the others. In today's business world, recognizing your edge and your deficits is *the* go-to skill. What to capitalize on, what to hone, where to build, where to delegate—it's all part of that pool of self-awareness.

Self-awareness is not something you just do as a once-in-a-while inventory thing—at the start of a project or job or at the end of the year. It's far too important for that. It's a habit that you have to cultivate and sharpen every single day. Remember that: *Practicing self-awareness is a habit.*

When Houston Rockets general manager Daryl Morey, a pioneer in advanced statistics, was asked what things he wished he could forecast about his players, he answered, "Do they have the self-awareness of where they're not as good as they need to be, meaning do they understand there's a gap between them and Chris Paul or James Harden or any of these great players in the league? And then...what are their habits to improve that gap?"[1]

Self-awareness is like the arrow on the Google map—you start there, figuring out where you are. Then it's about the commitment to do what needs to be done to get you where you want to be. "The best performers observe themselves closely," business journalist Geoff Colvin wrote in *Talent Is Overrated: What Really Separates World-Class Performers from Everyone Else.* In the book, Colvin looked at what distinguishes top performers in all arenas and found, "They are in effect able to step outside themselves, monitor what is happening in their own mind, and ask how it's going. . . . Top performers do this much more systematically than others do; it's an established part of their routine."[2]

I've given many corporate talks around the country, and I would argue that most people are sleepwalking through their work routine or, at the very least, comfortably on autopilot. Be honest: How often do you take this kind of inventory of yourself? Is it a daily habit? If not, ask yourself how you can make it one. It will be a game-changing decision and will lead to growth on a variety of different levels.

Self-Test

1. What do you do really well?
2. What do you need to improve on?
3. What is your plan for addressing No. 2?

Meeting *the* Gary Vee: The Whole Ball Game

Gary Vaynerchuck is booked down to the second. When I called his office for an interview for my podcast, his assistant said, "The next time he'll have a thirty-minute window is three months from now."

"I'll take it," I said, because I'm not stupid.

Serial entrepreneur, marketing expert, and investor Gary Vaynerchuck is already a legend. He's like a flash of light, a meteor across the media landscape whose effect is still being felt. But his beginnings were incredibly humble.

Gary is the son of immigrant parents from the Soviet Union. When he was growing up, his father owned a wine store in New Jersey where Gary worked from a very young age. In 2006 Gary started a wine show on YouTube, back when that was still called a webcast and people were just figuring out what YouTube even was. In just five years, he helped his father grow a $3 million retail store into a *$60 million* online wine business. Not resting on his laurels, he then parlayed that into VaynerMedia, which is now a $300 million consulting business and one of the world's hottest digital agencies.

Along the way, Gary became a prolific angel investor and venture capitalist, investing in companies including Snapchat, Facebook, Twitter, Uber, and Venmo, and co-founding the VaynerRSE fund. One day he'd like to buy the New York Jets. Unlike most people, this is a totally realistic goal for him.

Three months after that phone call, I was at VaynerMedia, in Gary's New York office. It was surprisingly small given that it's *his* company, but Gary doesn't come off as the kind of guy who cares about pomp and circumstance. The walls and shelves were covered in sports memorabilia, mostly Jets and Knicks, along with framed pictures of his book covers and photographs of Gary with various celebrities and big-time influencers.

His office had a comfortable sports bar feel to it, a place you can imagine killing an afternoon in. It was designed for function; there was a stand-up desk with a computer and a small conference table with four chairs for meetings. One wall was floor-to-ceiling glass with no blinds, so everyone could see into his office 24-7. The whole vibe was approachable transparency, just like Gary.

At 9:00 a.m. on the dot, he walked in, passionate and fully present, telling me he was fired up after hearing my podcast's opening theme music. Gary has this rapid-fire intense way of talking that just ropes in his audience. It's hard to focus on anything else when he's in a room. He is who he is, and he doesn't pretend or apologize.

"Self-awareness is the *game*," Gary told me. "I think self-awareness is the single most important drug in society." He admitted that it might not be the sexy thing, but it is undoubtedly the most important. "When you know yourself, you win," he said. "In business, the reason I've been successful is I know what I'm good at and I know what I'm not good at." He later added, "If you BS yourself, you never excel."

This is the essence of self-awareness: swallowing hard truths and recognizing the real version of you that is staring back in the mirror. Not the you that you wish you were or the you that you'd like to present to the world. The you as you actually are, right here and right now.

Despite his enormous success, Gary doesn't shy away from admitting there are things he doesn't know and isn't good at. In fact, his willingness to recognize these is what gives him a competitive edge. I'm sure that many guys who grew up working class and are now worth almost $200 million wouldn't bother to search for those gaps or admit to them even if they did. But Gary knows he didn't just stumble into success. He carried a commitment to self-awareness that brought him to where he is. And he continues to preach and teach the value of self-awareness.

For instance, Gary's a competitive guy, but that's not why he won't let his kids beat him in one-on-one in basketball. The reason? He wants them to understand what it takes to beat him. Letting them win would give them a false sense of accomplishment. Because of this, when one of his kids got old enough to genuinely beat him, that victory "tasted delicious." (Side note: I completely agree with Gary and even take this a step further—I won't let my kids beat me in *anything*. I think the everyone-should-get-a-trophy mind-set damages self-awareness.)

Gary knew he had thirty minutes with me, but he never once looked at his watch or phone to see what time it was. Despite having a packed day, he didn't just go through the motions. Gary demonstrated why he's successful; he was fully invested in what he was doing at that moment, looking me in the eye, and giving me pure, honest, and direct answers. The whole conversation was hyperfocused and present. If he was like that for a podcast interview, I could only imagine how locked in he is during a meeting or business call. It's how he approaches everything, and it taught me a great deal about why the successful are where they are.

Who You Are and What You Do

Understanding who you are and what you can offer puts you a step ahead of everyone else. It tells you what to capitalize on and what to improve, and sometimes, what to avoid. Self-awareness offers the needed element of perspective: the clarity of the big picture and your place in it.

The most dangerous people in the world are the ones who don't know what they don't know. Taking a bad shot is one thing. Not knowing it was a bad shot? Now you have a problem. "I'm always shocked by how many people don't seem to have that self-awareness,"

Krossover CEO Vasu Kulkarni told me, "knowing your limits, knowing what you're good at, most importantly, what you're not good at." It seems so fundamental, but that doesn't mean it's common. In fact, like all in-demand skills, the reason self-awareness is so valuable is *because* it's so rare.

Figure out what separates you from everyone else. If you don't know who you are and what you do, how is anyone else going to know? Without self-awareness, you're not going to be able to maximize your potential. And potential is not rare. Look around. The world is full of people with unused, wasted, or lost potential. They fill the seats of arenas around the globe. You have to acknowledge that you have more to learn. It's not humility for its own sake, or to be more likable; it's humility as *a path to self-awareness.*

Self-Test

1. What specific thing do you do at a very high level?
2. If I polled the people closest to you, what would they say you do really well?
3. How many opportunities do you have to do this thing?

Clear Eyes

Confidence is important and it is the focus of chapter 5, but self-awareness requires that you avoid the pitfall of arrogance. Arrogance prevents us from seeing our flaws. Humility gives us 20/20 vision and allows us to stay open.

Too many people do not own up to their mistakes and are constantly trying to hide their flaws and shortcomings. I think this is alpha dog nonsense and a recipe for self-destruction. It is a short-term strategy that will cause long-term problems. "Own your weaknesses at work," Adam Galinsky and Maurice Schweitzer wrote in *Friend and Foe: When to Cooperate, When to Compete, and How to Succeed at Both.* "Be powerful with them, be the first to admit them, and what follows may surprise you."[3] The experts suggest that one of the key ways to improve your self-awareness is through listening.

Think about all the conversations and meetings where you've just been waiting to talk. What could you have missed? Do you honestly think you're the only one who has anything to offer? You should be *least* interested in what you have to say; you already know what you know.

As counterintuitive as it sounds, a key step in acquiring self-awareness is to ask those who know you best. This is your inner circle—trusted friends, family, and colleagues who you know love you, challenge you, push you, support you, and want what is best for you. If you ask your inner circle if you are an empathetic listener and they all say "no," then it doesn't matter what you think: you are *not* an empathetic listener. You will have reached a high level of self-awareness when your evaluation of your strengths and weaknesses is aligned with your inner circle's.

> Don't worry about them. Let them worry about you.
>
> —John Wooden

Control the Controllables

Self-awareness is about knowing where your control begins and where it ends. Often, understanding where that line is determines your chances of success. Something I say to my players, to my colleagues, and to my audiences all the time is *control the controllables.*

There are only two things in this world that we have 100 percent control over, 100 percent of the time. That is our effort and our attitude. Coming to this epiphany was a tough pill for me to swallow, as I've always skewed a tad toward being a control freak. But it's true. Granted, we can dictate our mind-set, enthusiasm, and preparation (all vital ingredients in performance)—but these are all just branches of effort and attitude.

Spending our time, focus, and energy on things outside of our control is a poor use of resources. Face it, you have minimal control over your boss, your coworkers, your employees, your colleagues, your customers, your spouse, your friends, or your children. So don't waste your mental, emotional, and physical currency on them! Instead, focus on the two things you actually have control over. You can absolutely impact and influence many of the events and people in your life—but you do not control their behavior, their decisions, or the outcome. So let it go. Invest that energy internally. You'll feel better.

I remember my parents telling me as a young kid, "You don't control what other people do or say, but you do control how you respond and react." As a father of three young children, I have said this exact statement on countless occasions. And it's not only true for children—it's true for all of us. Learning how to control the controllables is imperative to maximizing performance. When you get distracted by things you don't control, your performance suffers. We have limited energy, attention, and resources—so put them where they can actually make a difference.

One of the things that separates elite basketball players from average players is this ability to focus on their own effort and attitude. Average players worry about what their coach is doing, what their teammates are doing, what their opponent is doing, even what the referee is doing! Great players process feedback from each of those domains. But they spend each play and practice session focusing on what they're doing and how they process what is happening. They work on their *effort* and *attitude*.

We decide how we view things and what we do about them. That's it. Everything else is out of our hands. If you don't get that promotion or new client, you can stew on fault, fairness, and blame. You can spend weeks swimming in that—lots of people do it! Or you can work on what you do. Which of these options is most likely to lead to that next promotion or client?

The Lessons of Socks and Shoes

Controlling the controllables also comes down to basic preparation: being ready when and where others are not. John Wooden won ten National Championships with the UCLA Bruins, including a record seven straight titles, a record that is so eye-poppingly insane that I would wager it will never be broken. How many schools even go back-to-back? (Only Florida and Duke have done that since UCLA's streak ended in 1973.) Wooden is an icon and a legend, but let's not get confused. He was not a wizard. He worked on what he could: he managed the basics.

Every season at UCLA one of the first things Wooden would do in the locker room was teach his players how to correctly put on their socks and shoes to alleviate chaffing and blisters. Most eighteen-year-olds would laugh off such an instruction, but Wooden had a reputation, so his players trusted him. They knew his record so they did what he said.

Because of this little, seemingly insignificant—almost childish—thing, Wooden's players almost never got blisters. By the end of the game, when the other team's feet were aching like blazing coals, Wooden's guys were as fresh as they were at tip-off. Socks and shoes are as basic as you can get, but Wooden understood that the players' game started there. If they couldn't stand up, if they couldn't run, they couldn't execute a single thing he taught them. *Start with what you can control.*

Any time spent on something outside of your attitude or effort is wasted, because it's energy and time *away* from what you can control. Most people waste a tremendous amount of time and energy complaining. What do they complain about? They complain about everything outside of their control. No one ever seems to complain about their own attitude or effort. It's always someone else's that they find fault with.

"Complaining is like throwing up," my friend Jon Gordon likes to say. "It makes you feel better, but it makes everyone else feel worse."

Focus on your attitude and your effort and do so consistently.

That's how you win.

Self-Test

Rate yourself on a scale ranging from 1 (strongly disagree) to 5 (strongly agree).

1. I have high expectations for myself and my team.
2. I constantly ask questions to my close friends, family, and colleagues.
3. I work on my craft daily and am constantly learning and growing.
4. I handle pressure well and embrace adversity.

5. I am focused on the right things, and my schedule is aligned with my priorities.

6. I am an active and empathetic listener.

7. I communicate clearly and effectively.

8. I encourage feedback and questions, and I accept criticism well.

9. I openly admit when I am wrong and accept responsibility.

10. I have a healthy way of dealing with disappointment, anger, and frustration.

Put all your eggs in one basket, and *watch that basket.*

—Andrew Carnegie

One Thing Well

Focus on who you are and what you do well. That is how you succeed. NBA sharpshooters like Kyle Korver and J. J. Redick get paid absurd amounts of money to do one thing: catch and shoot. That's it. Catch the ball and shoot the ball. And I don't say that to diminish them. But that is what got them to where they are, and it's where their greatness lies. Well rounded is overrated. Use your self-awareness to double down on what you do best. *Find the one thing you do better than anyone else and continue to pour into that.*

That is a dying idea. Simon Sinek, bestselling author and leadership consultant for Microsoft, Disney, and Airbnb, believes that we've lost the desire—and ability—to excel in one thing. "Giving a lot of one's self to a small number of things," he wrote, "seems to have been replaced by giving a little bit of one's self to a large number of things."[4] *Own your space.* Turn yourself into someone invaluable:

make it so no one else can do what you do. Self-awareness is the key to getting a competitive advantage; it leads to a pattern of utilizing your strengths and managing your weaknesses. It's how you become great, singularly great, at anything.

A Gallup poll of thousands of organizations showed that when an organization focused on an employee's strength, the level of that employee's engagement was nearly 75 percent. And when they didn't? It was 9 percent.[5] If people don't feel like they're being utilized well, if their strengths are not being tapped, then they're just going to feel like they're being wasted. And they withdraw. Another study of top business executives found that self-awareness was both the highest predictor of performance as well as the least utilized criteria. That pattern emerges again and again: self-awareness is so basic and yet so exceptional.

Be Willing to Close the Store

Self-awareness is not just in the knowing but in the *adjusting* and the *correcting*. On a Tuesday afternoon in 2008, Starbucks CEO Howard Schultz, who had recently taken over a second time at the company he founded, closed every single one of its stores in America. That's over *7000* stores. The cost? Twenty-three million dollars. The reason? The espresso just wasn't good anymore. That's it. No disease outbreak or food poisoning or lawsuit. It was that simple. The coffee wasn't good. What Starbucks was known for, where its value came from, had become subpar. And Schultz decided to do something about it.

Every Starbucks barista in America had to be retrained, so Schultz did what he felt he had to do: he closed all the stores. Now, Schultz probably could have staggered the training in a series of sessions, and I'm sure his publicity team and accountants wanted him to, but he wanted to make the statement that they had been failing and they were going to correct it. He wanted the public to *know* they were closing all the stores. The sign out front of every closed Starbucks even admitted that's what the retraining was for, opening themselves up to a slew of negative press and comments. But Schultz insisted on doing it this way.[6]

Soon after, Schultz flew in 10,000 Starbucks managers to a single arena—at a cost of $30 million, to break some bad news to them. He told them that Starbucks was on the verge of closing within the year because their "Success [had] bred laziness and sloppiness."[7] He spoke to all of them openly and honestly and clearly laid down the dire path the company was on if the negative trend continued.

The Starbucks experience, the thing that Schultz had built, was vanishing. He needed to bring it back. Schultz became aware of the problems in his organization and took action to stem the tide. Ten years later, Starbucks is again one of the biggest companies and most popular brands in the world. Schultz's self-awareness, regarding himself and his company, is what saved it and helped it thrive.

Know Thyself

Self-awareness—especially in hypercompetitive fields—requires stepping outside your bubble. It means understanding yourself the way your competitors do. All campaigning politicians do opposition research on their opponents, and the smartest ones want to get their hands on their opponents' opposition research on them. It's gold because it tells them what they need to work on, where they are vulnerable, and where they are likely to get hit. (That's exactly how Eminem's character won the final rap battle in *8 Mile*!) This type of awareness is key: it helps you see how you size up to the competition and gives you insight into how they might defeat you. *Close the holes in your game*, whatever your game is.

Some people don't like to look at their weaknesses—either because they're so focused on self-esteem or because they don't want to admit that their weaknesses exist. But those who do, those whom others might think don't have any weaknesses, are the ones who have worked like crazy on improving them. But it's important to note that we are only talking about applicable weaknesses. Weaknesses that matter and weaknesses that affect performance. It's okay if Kyle Korver and J. J. Redick are weak rebounders. It's okay if Starbucks doesn't make world-renowned bagels. That isn't what makes them who they are.

Work with what you have. Find your competitive advantage. You're dealing with a much larger pool than those in the past. Not too long ago workers were only competing with potential employees who lived within commuting distance from the office. Those days are long gone. Now, in the information age, the pool is the entire globe. Good enough is no longer good enough. Self-awareness will be your edge: securing that interview, beating out a competitive pool, getting that promotion, or launching that startup. Remember: *if you don't know what you do well, no one else will either.*

Mile 17

Self-awareness tends to develop with age. It's not that it automatically arrives as the years pile on; it's just that the young don't seem to have much use for it. It's funny how maturity works. In my twenties, I thought I knew everything. Now in my forties, I realize how much I didn't know then as well as how much more I still need to learn.

In 2002, a few years after graduating college, I signed up to run my first marathon. It had always been a goal of mine; running 26.2 miles just seemed to be the most physically challenging thing a normal person could do.

Plus I was trying to impress a girlfriend who was really into running.

I played college basketball, which was incredibly demanding, and had a fairly decent understanding of proper training, but I didn't know a lick about preparing for a marathon. Basketball is an interval-based sport, meaning everything is short duration and high intensity. The whole concept of pacing myself for 26.2 miles was foreign to me. It was apples and oranges. So my preparation and marathon training program was grossly insufficient. My youthful naïveté simply thought, *A few years ago I was a college athlete, I'll be fine.* I was blindly stepping off a ledge figuring I knew how far the drop would be. But I had no clue.

At the start of a marathon, runners are staggered based on their predicted mile pace. You can't have everyone pushing their way to the starting line when the gun goes off—it's impractical, there's no room, and it would make a mess. When I arrived to line up that morning, I had no frame of reference for what my pace would be. I ran a 5:03 mile in college (when I was in the best shape of my life), but I wasn't delusional—I knew I couldn't keep that pace for the whole race. So I ventured back to the 8-to-9-minute mile pace and took a look around: I saw middle-aged soccer moms and guys in their sixties with gray hair and outdated clothes. *No way*, I thought. *These are old people. I don't belong here.* So I inched my way up to a group I thought looked more like me, which turned out to be the 6-minute-per-mile-pace group. Satisfied, I took my place among them.

When the race started, it was like I was shot out of a cannon. With my adrenaline pumping, I started off at a lightning-fast pace that would be impossible to sustain. I didn't know at the time that the effects of distance running were a little bit like doing shots of tequila at a bar: You feel pretty good after two or three shots, but that fourth one will smash you. Everything feels fantastic until the moment you fall off the cliff. The problem is, you rarely see the cliff coming. You just fall. Your senses drain away, you feel sick, and you lose control. It silently creeps up on you, and then it pounces. That's how the marathon was.

At mile 8, I felt great.

At mile 12, I felt okay.

At mile 17, it all...unraveled.

When I met Jesse Itzler, entrepreneur and co-owner of the Atlanta Hawks, he told me that every single one of us has this little voice inside of us that's full of self-doubt. When things start getting tough in our lives—physically, mentally, emotionally—that voice gets louder and louder and the negative self-talk begins. It's a self-preservation mechanism; if you're putting yourself through grueling physical pain, your mind is trying to get you to stop. That's what it's there for. Its job is to save you.

At mile 17, my little voice started whispering, and I could not shut it up. I'm an all-around positive guy, confident and optimistic in my day-to-day life, but I just didn't have the energy to ignore that voice. Plus, it sounded so *reasonable*. With every step I took, the voice got louder and louder. My mind and body started shutting down. Feeling immensely defeated, I started walking. Prior to that race, I would've bet someone a million dollars that I wouldn't have to walk at all, much less the last nine miles. It was dejecting and humbling, and I felt like a failure.

Though part of me would rather ignore what happened next, it's too important, so we'll return to my marathon debacle later in this section.

Markelle and the Power of Self-Awareness

I have seen self-awareness make or break people in sports, in business, and in life. It is often the difference maker in whether or not someone rises to the top of his field. For six years, I was the performance coach for the DeMatha Catholic High School basketball program, a national powerhouse located just outside of Washington, DC. The school has six national championships, thirty-nine conference championships, and has produced fourteen NBA players. It holds an iconic and prestigious position in the rarefied world of elite high school basketball.

As a quiet and skinny thirteen-year-old, Markelle Fultz attended one of our summer camps. He was a polite and respectful young man who showed signs of potential, but he was well below the level of player we usually recruited. When he expressed interest in attending DeMatha, Coach Mike Jones was direct and honest: *we'd love to have you, but don't plan on making the varsity anytime soon.*

Markelle decided to come to DeMatha anyway, which says a great deal about him and his commitment to the game. He probably could've gone somewhere else, gotten it fully paid for, and been the big dog, but he chose to go with the best, playing for a coach that guaranteed him nothing. This was exceptionally rare: young players tend to go where they're recruited, but Markelle came to us.

Most recruited players expect to at least start on junior varsity, so they can jump to varsity as soon as possible. But Markelle had the humility—and awareness—to know his level, so he began on the freshman team. He didn't get down or dejected because he was starting at the "bottom." He respected the process, worked on his game, and made it up to JV the next year.

Of course, people were buzzing in his ear, "You should be on varsity," or "You should play at another school," all the noise that comes with coming into your own. But Markelle had the self-awareness to block them out. He kept on track, going to the gym, working on his game, and finding a way to raise his level. Self-awareness almost always leads directly to humility; when you know the things you don't do well, you become humble and driven.

Markelle put in so much work after his sophomore year that he jumped to varsity and became one of the best players in the conference, then in the DC area. But even then, after he made it to the top of this prestigious group, he didn't stop. Instead of resting on his laurels, he improved even more from junior to senior year, becoming an All-American and accepting a full scholarship to the University of Washington.

It's called "self" awareness but the people you choose to surround yourself with play a part in that. A self-aware person is going to invite healthy criticism, and one way to do that is not to shy away from hearing the truth. It's important to have supportive people who aren't afraid to tell you the things that you need to hear instead of the things that you want to hear. The people in Markelle's circle helped reinforce his own sense of self.

In 2017, Markelle was the number 1 pick in the NBA draft. I wasn't surprised at all. He didn't lose the work ethic, the drive, and the self-awareness—even as the accolades rolled in at college. He stayed focused, even with all the hype and attention that comes when you're projected to be a top pick. Part of being in the NBA is knowing your part in the whole. Most players can't immediately dominate an NBA court like they did in college—so they have to have awareness of what their place is among the other four guys in the same color jerseys.

Unfortunately, a disappointing thing happened to Markelle during his NBA rookie season with the Philadelphia 76ers. A shoulder injury before the season began sidelined him for a month. Then two months. Then it looked like he'd be out for most of the season. Then grainy cell phone video came out from the Sixers practice arena showing that he had changed his jump shot. People were alarmed. Something just didn't look right.

Then the tweeters and commentators had a field day—a Markelle watch—where week after week of the number 1 overall pick sitting on the bench brought theories and criticisms. There was talk of him losing his confidence. There was talk of him being the biggest bust in the NBA draft. It was an unprecedented amount of speculation and scrutiny. But Markelle stayed quiet.

Then on a regular season game in March of his rookie season, he returned. And you know what? He was fine. Better than fine. He was great. A month later he recorded a triple double—double digits in points, assists, and rebounds—the youngest player in NBA *history* to do so.

I watched Markelle grow each step on his journey, and I know his career will soar exactly as the scouts first predicted. He has the self-awareness to make it in a business where a lot of talented players just don't pan out. He knows who he is, and even with the basketball world watching, he will not get rattled.

Self-Test

Despite the "self" in self-awareness, to ensure accuracy it is important to solicit intentional and purposeful feedback from those who know you best (your inner circle).

As comedians know, there's only one measure of whether or not a joke is funny: Does the audience laugh? It sounds simple, but there is real depth to that concept. You may believe you possess the necessary humility, but if the five people closest to you feel otherwise, then guess what?

Identify three people that you feel know you the best. They can be friends, family, or colleagues. You need to create a safe environment for them to share their honest thoughts and feelings: Ask them to share the truth as they see it. Explain what it's for and that you'd appreciate constructive criticism. The more honest the feedback, the more helpful and impactful this exercise will be.

Ask them to rate you on the following questions on a scale of 1 to 10 (1 being low and 10 being high):

> **Do I communicate well?** Do I effectively convey my message?
> **Am I courageous?** Am I unafraid to take risks?
> **Am I disciplined?** Do I commit to the process of doing things?
> **Am I focused?** Can I block out distractions?
> **Am I generous?** Am I a giving person?
> **Do I show initiative?** Do I start things on my own?
> **Do I use sound judgment?** Do I know what is truly important?
> **Do I listen?** Do I hear others, or only hear what I want to hear?
> **Am I optimistic?** Do I choose to see the good in every situation?
> **Am I a resolver?** Do I just identify problems...or actually fix them?
> **Am I responsible?** Do I hold myself accountable?
> **Am I secure?** Do I trust those around me?

Once you've collected their feedback, see how it compares to the other people you gave it to. See how it compares to how you see yourself. Look for trends and patterns. Identify your top strengths and your most glaring weaknesses.

What sticks out?

It is important not to jump to conclusions or judgment.

Remember, this is simply feedback. The results themselves are neither positive nor negative. You decide whether or not to use them in a way that serves you and moves you forward or to use them in a way that hinders you.

> We can't change what we don't notice.
>
> —Tony Schwartz, author and journalist

The Fogged-Up Mirror

There's a contradiction at work when we talk of self-awareness. You have to notice if you have it, and that ability is the very thing you're looking to build! Because of this catch-22, I don't think you can ask people if they are self-aware and ever get any other answer than yes. That's the tricky thing about it. They can't see their own blind spots.

In fact, 95 percent of people, when surveyed, claim to be self-aware.[8] Virtually no human on the planet would admit to not being self-aware, but the vast majority are not. I think this comes from a lack of understanding of what self-awareness means. There is a phenomenon called the Dunning-Kruger effect, which put simply is: *we can't know everything that we don't know.* (Dunning and Kruger were two Stanford researchers who found that the subjects who did the worst on their tests were regularly the most confident.)

There's an emotional aspect, too—a type of denial at work. Just about everyone can rattle off what they're good at, but then there's the lurking stuff no one wants to address: the things that scare them, that challenge them, that might keep them up at night.

We tend to look away from what we can't do; we avoid digging deeper and uncovering how to do something about them. It's easier to ignore them or blame outside forces. We live a lie that we keep telling ourselves, so our level of self-awareness is weak, or even nonexistent.

That's where the real hard work comes in—being able to look in the mirror and know what we're scared of and what we're insecure about. We are taught to suppress or avoid our adversity and pain, but we have to look at that if we're going to get anywhere. It's where we all have to start.

Key Point: Learn your strengths and weaknesses, inside and out, because self-awareness makes everything else possible.

Remember:

☞ If you don't know who you are and what you do, nothing else you know or learn will matter.

☞ *Control the controllables.* Don't get caught up in things outside your frame of influence.

☞ Recognize what you can contribute—where your value is—and others will notice. And they will reward you for it.

☞ Avoid the arrogance that blinds you to areas in which you need to improve.

CHAPTER TWO

Passion

> No balls, no babies.
>
> —Mark Cuban

If you have the love for something, then all the work that follows is easier. In fact, "work" wouldn't even be the right word. If you consider work a "grind"—a word I hate—then it will remain so. Sure, there are things we have to *grind* out, and no one loves every aspect of his job, but if your heart and soul are not in it, if you are not committed to the larger goal and purpose, then find something else to do. Get out of there. You're no good to anyone. "You don't have to love the hard work," NBA trainer Tim Grover wrote. "You just have to crave the end result so intensely that the hard work is irrelevant."[1] It comes down to heart, or what some people call passion.

Now, I'm not naïve; I know work is work. I'm an up-early-dominate-the-day-satisfyingly-wiped-out-at-night kind of guy. But viewing work as a grind will not just make you miserable, it'll lead to poor performance. An effective mind shift that I use is turning a "have to" into a "get to." I don't *have to* go work out, I *get to*. I don't *have to* call this client, I *get to*. I don't *have to* write this chapter, I *get to*! Putting in work is a privilege. If you instill your work with passion—with all of yourself—the necessary hustle will naturally follow. You will have a built-in motivator, an automatic engine, to power through.

Think of your passion as energy you carry around, energy that hasn't been used yet, energy just waiting to be fed into something. It's up to you find what that is. Lately the word you hear a lot is "grit," which I think of as *putting your passion to use*. Talent alone will never be enough because it's not rare. Innate skill is overrated and it rarely gets the job done. What you put behind that talent: that's where the difference comes in.

Amplifying Yourself

Passion is the engine that carries you through the hard times, through the early years, through the days where you have no idea if things are going to work out. The passion, in many ways, will be the first thing to come. It'll let you know what you should be pursuing in your life. It's up to you to listen. And then it's up to you to act.

With apologies to a certain beer company, Jesse Itzler is arguably the World's Most Interesting Man. He's an NBA team co-owner, serial entrepreneur, philanthropist, and endurance warrior who has written books about training with a Navy SEAL and living with Tibetan monks. I'd wanted to meet him for almost a decade and was fortunate enough to be invited to speak at a retreat that he and his wife, Spanx founder Sara Blakely, held at one of their homes in Connecticut. It was an incredible weekend: part inspirational, part business, part human connection, part fantasy camp.

As financially set as the two of them are, Jesse and Sara are the most humble, generous, and authentic people you will ever meet.

They both have unwavering self-belief and confidence in them-selves. They bet on themselves big time when no one else did, and it paid off. "Money just amplifies who you are," they both like to say. If you're an a-hole, money makes you a giant a-hole. If you're a gen-erous person, then money allows you to do more good in the world. And that's apparent in how they live their lives. Their Live Life for a Living retreat was one of the most transformational experiences I have ever had. It was about the basics of old school connection—people actually kept their phones buried for the entire weekend.

Jesse isn't afraid to be vulnerable and put himself out there. He preaches how self-doubt is the number one success killer and how you can either sit around and wait for an opportunity or you can create one yourself. His daily mantra? *I didn't come this far to only come this far.*

Jesse started as a music artist. He recorded his first rap demo on his answering machine, playing an instrumental beat on a boom box and rapping the lyrics onto a mini-cassette tape. The only window of stu-dio time he could get was from midnight to 7:00 a.m., so for months he rode his bike 20 miles a day to spend all night in the recording studio, only to ride it back in the morning to his job as a kiddie-pool attendant. In 1993 he rocketed to fame after writing "Go New York Go," which became the infectious New York Knicks theme song at Madison Square Garden. After a successful music career, he moved into entrepreneurship, founding Marquis Jet, a private plane credit card service before selling it to Warren Buffet's Berkshire Hathaway. Then he partnered with Zico Coconut Water before selling it to Coca-Cola. Suffice it to say, he never has to worry about money ever again.

But nothing's changed because Jesse was never motivated by money. As he wrote in *Living with a SEAL: 31 Days of Training with the Toughest Man on the Planet*, "Any success I have ever had in my life usually occured when I was not chasing the money but was doing things out of passion."[2] And I believe it. I know Jesse, and he is an inspiration to me in my own work. He puts his passion into everything he does, and applies it to giving back to the world.

> We spend far too much time at work for it not to have meaning.
>
> —Satya Nadella, Microsoft CEO

Staying on It

Do you give yourself to what you do? *All* of yourself? In what ways are you holding back? Why? Could it be the reason why you're not where you want to be?

My friend Jon Gordon, author of many bestselling books on leadership in sports, business, and life, shared this fantastic word with me: *meraki*. It's a Greek word that means "putting yourself in what you do." I wish we had a word in English for that, but we don't. I fear that the reason we don't is that our culture puts less value in the idea.

Superstar trainer Tim Grover, who has worked with everyone from Michael Jordan to Kobe Bryant, told an amazing story about Charles Barkley in his book *Relentless*. There was a period during Barkley's playing days when he was having rehab on his knee and was given strict instructions not to go on the court. Of course, Barkley didn't get to where he was by following the rules so he got on Grover, insisting and insisting until Grover did what most of us would do. He gave in. Grover said Barkley could practice shooting as long as he didn't step down on the injured leg, which was still in a boot.

"No problem," Barkley said, and Grover handed him the ball.

Grover then watched in awe as Barkley, with his booted foot never touching the ground, stood under the basket and dunked ten times a row, on his good foot. *On one foot from a standing jump.* That's how much passion he had to get back on the court.

Talent alone is a part of the equation, sure, but if it's not activated, it'll just sit there. Unused, untapped, and ultimately, unknown. As two-time NBA MVP Steve Nash has said about resilience: "That's a muscle that needs to be developed. You can be born with great grit and resilience but you have to continue to develop that muscle as well."[3]

I can't teach you to have passion. No one can. All I can advise is to find what brings it out in you and then channel the hell of it. And don't let up.

Some call it resolve or perseverance or persistence. Whatever we call it, we know it when we see it. It's Barkley dunking on one foot. It's Kobe coming back from a nearly career-ending injury. It's a fifteen-year-old Michael Jordan working his tail off to make his high school varsity team after getting cut the previous year. It's a thirty-two-year-old Jordan coming back after retirement to win another three championships in a row. It's about putting a realistic goal in front of you and stretching to accomplish it. What is it for you?

From the Bottom

Starting out, Mark Cuban didn't have anything handed to him. He began selling everything from garbage bags to powdered milk to franchises for a TV repair shop. Cuban then made his way to a job at a software store, opening up in the morning and sweeping the floors at night. Even at that early stage, Cuban had the perspective not to see any work as a drag, but rather as an opportunity. And he didn't waste it: on his own time, he read all the computer manuals lying around until he knew how each machine worked.

"In every job, I would justify it in my mind," he wrote in his book *How to Win at the Sport of Business*, "whether I loved it or hated it, that I was getting paid to learn and every experience would be of value when I figured out what I wanted to do."[4] As a young man, Cuban had the passion to succeed. It allowed him to translate the grind, or the boredom, or whatever you want to call it, into opportunities. Not everyone sees those so-called dead-end jobs as openings but Cuban did. I don't believe there is such a thing as a dead-end job. Create the opening yourself by making sure it leads somewhere. Cuban did and he ended up a billionaire and icon.

Jason Stein (no relation), CEO of media agencies Laundry Service and Cycle Media, started out in a similar way: he responded to 200 Craigslist media jobs *a day* in order to land just one.[5] Phil Knight began Nike by driving around selling sneakers at track meets out of the trunk of his car. The first investor to say yes to Whole Foods' founder John Mackey regarding his idea of opening a natural food market in Texas was not moved by his idea. He was moved by Mackey's enthusiasm.[6] In the 1990s Google co-founders Sergey Brin and Larry Page were committed to creating the world's best search engine, and they "could figure out the money stuff later."[7]

None of these people were driven by money—they couldn't be. The money was so far off and nowhere near a sure thing. But so many of their imitators failed and continue to fail because they pursue the money as its own end rather than giving their passion the keys and letting it take them there.

Why would someone spend the countless hours it takes to get good at something? What keeps them there and coming back for more? Only passion.

Late Nights in the Film Room

Success is built on the backs of long hours, solitary commitment, and sometimes what appears to be "menial" work. No one starts out with the flashy job. The only people who end up landing those jobs are those who are willing to do all the unflashy things that build toward it.

Bill Belichick, who has a record seven Super Bowl rings,* was not a coaching prodigy. Despite his stellar reputation as among the most knowledgeable NFL coaches ever to put on a headset, he was—and remains to this day—a workhorse. He rose through the coaching ranks by becoming an expert at a skill that no one else had mastered, the one that everyone else hated: watching film.[8]

When Belichick started out, as a twenty-three-year-old assistant on the Baltimore Colts' coaching staff, he offered to watch and analyze film—for free. (He was paid only $25 a week for his regular duties.) Of course, it was a lot of extra hours, some of it eye-watering and mind-numbing, and he never got credit for any insight that was used on the field. That was for his superiors. But that didn't matter.

Let's stop and go over that again: *He took the worst job for no pay and got no credit for it. And he asked to do it.*

Belichick "thrived on what was considered grunt work," Ryan Holiday explained in *Ego Is the Enemy.* "[He] strove to become the best at precisely what others thought they were too good for."[9] Once Belichick established himself as not just an expert at breaking down film, but someone who wanted to win badly enough that he would become an expert at breaking down film, other coaching staffs took notice. The rest is literally history.

---

* Belichick has five rings as the Patriots' head coach and two from his time as the New York Giants' defensive coordinator.

Other big-time coaches began as video guys, doing the grunt work to make themselves indispensable. Among these were Erik Spoelstra of the Miami Heat,[10] who spent countless hours breaking down film early in his career until years later he looked up and he was calling plays for LeBron James and Dwyane Wade. Holiday simplifies the Belichick and Spoelstra approach this way: "Find what nobody else wants to do and do it."[11]

Jeff Van Gundy is the epitome of passion. As the New York Knicks head coach in the early '90s, I loved watching him screaming his head off, never sitting down, just locked into the game in a way that his players must have loved. I particularly remember him backing up his players in high-tension situations: getting head-butted by Marcus Camby after Camby took a swing at one of his players and grabbing for dear life on to seven-foot Alonzo Mourning's foot during a Knicks scuffle. (YouTube these. Trust me.)

Van Gundy is a huge advocate of the get-on-the-ground, scrappy player who doesn't care what his stat line looks like. As a coach, he did what he could from the sidelines to practice what he preached.

Nowadays Van Gundy is an NBA broadcaster who also gives smart and inspirational talks to players and coaches alike. "Want to be an *uncommon* player?" he asked at one of his talks. "Box out. Take charges. Dive for loose balls. Make the extra pass. Those are all things everyone can do, yet very few actually do."

I've met him a few times and interviewed him for my podcast. He is an engaging and knowledgeable coach who has a powerful way of cutting right to the heart of the matter. When I asked him as a coach whether experience or instinct was more important, he told me he saw them as two sides of the same coin. "Experience *gives* you instinct," he told me on my podcast, "if you pay attention." It's not the accumulation of your years or games or even victories alone that matters. It's what you do with them.

Self-Test

Stop for a moment and think about your job. There's what you're assigned to do, but there are other things that need to be done, right?

Are there skills or knowledge that would be invaluable if they existed inside one employee? Of course there are. If you don't know what those are, find out. Once you do, become the master of them. Make it so no one can do what you do.

Create Your Own Opportunities

It's up to you to be ready for the moment. Your opportunities may be few and far between. You may not know when they're coming, so it's best to always be prepared.

In 1990 Tim Grover was a young trainer with a master's degree working at a health club in Chicago. One morning he read an article in the newspaper about how Michael Jordan was tired of getting roughed up by the "Bad Boy" Detroit Pistons, who were consistently eliminating the Bulls in the playoffs. Grover's eyes lit up. He saw his opening.

Though Jordan was by then already the NBA's best and most visible player, Grover was not intimidated; he took the ball and drove toward the hole. After some hustle and a good dose of fearlessness, he secured a meeting with the Bulls' doctor and trainer. "What were the chances they would advise their superstar player to work with this unknown trainer who had never trained a professional athlete?" he wrote. "None, everyone said. Forget it. Impossible."[12]

But it wasn't. In fact, that's exactly what happened. Jordan and the Bulls hired Grover, who stayed with Jordan for the rest of his career. Once Grover worked with—and succeeded with—Jordan, Grover became a known quantity and rose to the top of his profession. He is now a legend, and it all goes back to a single decision. That day in the health club, Grover didn't spend time going over all the reasons it wasn't going to happen, why Michael Jordan and the Bulls wouldn't hire someone like him. He *made* it happen. Those opportunities are not as frequent as we'd like them to be, and they almost never appear in the way that we imagine they would, but none of that matters. *Find the door. Open the door. Step through the door.*

When They Call Your Number

Passion is necessary to get you through the time periods when the opportunities just aren't there. It's what drives you to be ready when the time comes—and you never know when that will happen. It's funny how few people remember who Tom Brady used to be. Brady was an unknown sixth-round draft pick, a backup quarterback, watching New England Patriots' games from the sidelines.

One Sunday in 2001 Patriots' franchise quarterback Drew Bledsoe went down with a devastating injury and Brady got the call. He put on his helmet and ran onto the field. Seventeen years later Brady is still at it, and few would argue that he isn't among the greatest ever in his job. When the moment presented itself, he was ready. Of course, he couldn't wait until Bledsoe went down to prepare himself or else he wouldn't have been able to capitalize when it happened. He got himself ready and trusted that his moment would come.

Brady's "moment" has lasted almost twenty years. His career will go down as one of the most impressive longevity stories in the history of professional sports. He is currently forty-one years old and talks about playing another five years, an impossible feat for a football player, much less a quarterback, to achieve. How has he done it? Passion for the game, of course. But not just that.

He hasn't forgotten that lesson from that Sunday in 2001. He's getting himself ready because he cares enough to do it, becoming a trailblazer in the areas of health and wellness. "Outside of playing football," Tom Brady told an interviewer, "the one thing I love to do is to prepare for it."[13] He's actually passionate about the *preparation*. Think about how hard it is to beat someone like that, whose passion extends to the most grueling part of the work. We'll return to this idea in the next chapter, when I talk about meeting Kobe Bryant.

Competition Is Good for Your Health

Passion is indeed an inner drive, but it can also be brought out through external factors. One of the most effective ways to bring out passion is through competition, to tap into our desire to win. The root of the word "competition" in Latin is "to strive,"[14] and in that striving we get better. It's why great teams compete with each other every day. The starters compete to keep their jobs, and the reserves and role players compete to take their jobs. A healthy competition is good for the workplace, just like it is on the court. At DeMatha, Coach Jones ends every practice with inter-team competitions, in order to tap into that competitive instinct. Competition is a powerful and intense energy source that should be utilized as a force for good.

Psychologist Adam Galinsky and business professor Maurice Schweitzer wrote in *Friend and Foe* about the value of competitiveness in work and life. Setting us up in a head-to-head matchup, in a situation that we may lose, is constructive because "disappointment can be turned into motivation."[15] When we *feel* the loss, we internalize the need to get better. We are driven to return stronger and get a win. This is why so many workplaces now look to sports to teach everything from motivation to teamwork to discipline. The court is like a testing lab for what works and what doesn't.

For instance, statistics show that basketball teams that are down by 1 at halftime win more often than teams who are up by 1. It seems strange until we think about it, but then it makes perfect sense. The team that is down by 1 has that extra motivation that comes from being down, which fires them up.[16] Think about being in a race— would you rather be slightly ahead or slightly behind? The runner who is slightly behind has a visual of where he needs to get to and the tangible motivation to get there, while the runner slightly ahead does not. A wide-open track in front of you may be exciting but it's not the motivator that another runner's back can be.

There's a reason why kids play games, not just practice, when they start a sport. Long before they know what they're doing, they enjoy the boost, the energy, and the passion that comes from competition. The main reason sports are central to the youth experience is because of the intangibles that arise out of practicing, competing, and being on a team.

Teaching children the importance of competing is why I don't let my kids win at anything. No, I am not an egomaniac. I do this to teach them about life. By definition, it's not an accomplishment unless it is earned. I want my kids to earn everything in their lives. In games of skill, strength, or speed, where I clearly have a formidable advantage, I will often handicap the rules (e.g., give them a significant head start in a race) to give them better odds. However, I still do my best to beat them.

When they do win, I congratulate them and tell them how proud I am of their effort. I intentionally recognize how hard they worked, how much they practiced, and how they never quit. It's important to acknowledge the process, not the outcome. I don't make a big deal when they win or lose, but rather highlight the role their effort and attitude played. And regardless of the outcome, I make sure that whoever wins does so with humility and graciousness and whoever loses does so with class and grace.

Obstacles

Passion goes hand in hand with courage—whether on a large or a small scale. Maybe the most amazing personification of courage I've ever heard of is Aron Ralston. Ralston has since become an icon and well-known adventurer since a movie was made about his life, but on April 26, 2003, he was just alone and screwed.

While hiking by himself in Utah, Ralston stepped on a boulder that jarred loose and landed right on top of his arm, pinning it—and him—to the side of a canyon wall. For six days Ralston was stuck there in a standing position, his arm trapped, with little food or water or chance of being rescued, drinking his own piss and freezing. But he refused to relent. Of course, what people talk about now was Ralston's decision on day 6 to *break and then cut off his own arm*, but remember, he had to make it to that point. He spent 126 hours under circumstances none of us can imagine before figuring out not just how to do that, but bringing himself to a point where he mentally *could* do that. He spent the last hour doing what almost none us could imagine ourselves doing. Today, Ralston—prosthetic arm and all—still continues to climb and has become a motivational speaker. It's nearly impossible to complain about your circumstance after listening to this guy's story.

Fortunately, none of us has to face Ralston's horrifying situation, but his story is an inspiration wrapped inside a lesson. In *The Obstacle Is the Way*, Ryan Holiday looked at the great achievers of history—from all arenas—and found that they all shared one characteristic: pushback. "Like oxygen to a fire," he wrote, "obstacles became fuel for the blaze that was their ambition. . . . Every impediment serves to make the inferno within them burn with great ferocity."[17]

The truly ambitious, the passionate ones who rise to the top of their fields, feed on the obstacles. They don't see them just as things to avoid—those are rich energy sources.

Remember that the only difference between seeing something as a problem or an opportunity is your attitude. Here are four keys to overcoming adversity:

1. Stay honest.
2. Stay positive.
3. Stay insulated.
4. Stay confident.

Self-Test

Think about the current obstacles in your work and life. Write down your three primary obstacles, which is a helpful way to see them for what they are. In what ways can they be motivators? How can you turn them into fuel?

> When you stop growing, you start to decay.
>
> —Mike Krzyzewski

Your Comfort Zone Is a Cage

As human beings, it is wired in our DNA to crave comfort. To subconsciously make things as easy as possible. But that's not how we grow. We grow through *discomfort*. We grow through stretching, through challenge, through adversity. Low performers crave comfort; high performers don't just tolerate or do well in discomfort, they *seek it out*. They keep raising the degree of difficulty so they're forced to strive and stretch and improve. The discomfort isn't where they stop; it's where they start.

Passion allows you to drive through the type of discomfort that would cause most people to quit. That's why you must condition yourself to be *comfortable being uncomfortable*. How many times have you heard that you need to work hard to be successful? Probably more than you can count. But no one really defines what hard work is or what it means to work hard. Here is my personal definition: *Hard work is intentionally leaving your comfort zone with purpose.* That's how you grow.

If I asked you to put down this book and start doing push-ups right now, what would you do when it got tough? You'd stop, right? Once your chest and shoulders and arms were on fire and shaking, you'd stop. That just seems natural. But what if I told you that it's the reps after that point which actually make the difference? Those are the ones that make you stronger.

In the spring of 2018 a trend started happening online with professional gymnasts. They were all posting videos of themselves, which were going viral. Gold medal routines? No. Personal high-light reels? Hardly. They were all posting their most epic fails, falls, and crashes. It happened after an Italian gymnast posted her own and started the hashtag #GymnasticsFallChallenge, and it took off, with over a thousand professional gymnasts posting their own.[18] Why? Because these professionals understood that they were only publi-cized for doing well. Maybe that selective editing gave the wrong impression about how hard they worked and how difficult their events were. The public lapped up the videos. True, we all have the juvenile impulse to laugh when people wipe out, but we also like to see that these professionals are human. The videos illuminated that they are people who have worked their tails off, building their failures into something else. The failures weren't sidetracks; they were the stepping-stones to their success.

The same is true in business. It's only after the no's, the letdowns, the misfires, the doubts, and the resistance that the best ideas surface. *Failure is learning.* Billionaire investor Warren Buffett is a big proponent of studying failures because he knows that those stories are where the gold lies. He doesn't just preach it either. He has "made it a habit for years to write down the reasons why he is making an investment decision and later look back to see what went right or wrong."[19]

It's not a coincidence that adversity is a key part of so many success stories. From Oprah to Steve Jobs to Tony Robbins, it's rare that you find someone who achieved greatness who didn't face huge adversity. Those obstacles got turned inside out.

> Happiness can be defined, in part at least, as the fruit of the desire and ability to sacrifice what we want *now* for what we want *eventually*.
>
> —Stephen Covey

Common Denominators

Be open to failure. Invite failure. As long as you're failing differently each time, in the long run you're actually not failing at all. The most successful people I have come across—from players to coaches to entrepreneurs to CEOs—do not fear failure. They trust the process and do not worry about the outcome. This goes for virtually all the success stories we see on the news or read about—including in this book.

According to former PayPal executive VP and LinkedIn cofounder Reid Hoffman, whose first digital venture flamed out, "If you tune it so that you have zero chance of failure, you also usually have zero chance for success."[20] As someone already worth over $3 billion, Hoffman is still a proponent of failure. Failure, especially tough losses, is beneficial because "you learn to keep a certain amount of humility [and] you learn to keep a certain amount of objectivity." That doesn't mean they're easy—it just means there's something worthy at the other end.

This goes for companies, and it goes for individuals. Is it a grind, or is it a journey? That's up to you. When Sir Edmund Hillary and Tenzing Norgay became the first men in history to summit Mount Everest, they celebrated. They took it all in: *for fifteen minutes*. Then they climbed back down.

Stop seeking out your comfort zone, consciously or unconsciously. It's your enemy. It makes you soft and complacent. You have to consistently step out of your comfort zone and challenge yourself. When Bill Gates was starting Microsoft, he always promised more than he could deliver. He just said yes, and then he would figure out how to do it afterward. Steve Smith, his marketing director, said, "Virtually everything we sold was not a product when we sold it. We sold promises."[21] Follow that: sell promises. You'll be amazed what you can pull off when it's time to produce.

There is no reward for always playing it safe. The most successful people in any industry thrive in discomfort. Why? Because temporary discomfort leads to permanent improvement. No one will hand you anything. You have to earn and deserve success. You have to have the courage to sacrifice your immediate contentment. Embrace the process required because you want it badly enough. Dig into your passion and let it be your guide.

Key Point: Passion is the engine that powers us through what we have to do. If you know what yours is, tap into it as much as you can. If you don't, commit yourself to searching and finding it.

Remember:

☞ Passion is what will separate you from others and your life's work from anyone else's.

☞ No one makes it by coasting on talent; skill alone rarely gets the job done.

☞ Your attitude and approach determine whether it's a "grind" or a journey.

☞ Care about the result so much that you are willing to do what it takes to get there.

☞ Use your passion as a guide to what you should be doing.

CHAPTER THREE

Discipline

> Luck is the residue of design.
>
> —Branch Rickey

I don't believe in luck. I think unhappy and unsuccessful people use luck as an excuse. What most people call good luck is actually the expected collision between preparation and opportunity. In order to be lucky, you need to be ready for when opportunity knocks. Was Tom Brady lucky? Not at all. A hundred other guys could've been Drew Bledsoe's backup the day he went down. But none of them would have had the career Brady has had. It is always better to be prepared for an opportunity that never arises than unprepared for one that does.

We know we should be prepared, but do we look closely enough at what that means? *How do you prepare?*

You need to *be* ready in case you don't have time to *get* ready. How do you do that? Work on your craft every single day. Do what others aren't doing. Read, watch, and listen to everything you can in your chosen field. Spend time on it that others are spending in front of the television or sleeping in. The resources are there. Find them. Use them. And then, if you want to be lucky, you need to be in the right place at the right time. But instead of waiting for that to happen, you can *make* that happen. How? Create value in everything you do, everyplace you go, and every person you connect with.

Ask yourself this question: Are the actions you take today on par with the dreams you have for tomorrow?

How to Be Prepared

1. Read.
2. Study.
3. Observe.
4. Evaluate.
5. Reach out.
6. Risk.

> Good habits are hard to form and easy to live with. Bad habits are easy to form and hard to live with.
>
> —Mark Matteson, author and speaker

Deep Dive

We all live in a highly distracted society; it's hard to find the time to develop the focus to sink into our work. Computer science professor Cal Newport, who wrote an entire book called *Deep Work*, thinks it's a dying skill. According to Newport, going deep into our work is "a crucial ability for anyone looking to move ahead in a globally competitive information economy that tends to chew up and spit out those who aren't earning their keep."[1] Translation: The future is going to value those who can get lost in their work, who can block out all interruptions, who can focus even among the onslaught of distractions that characterize life in modern society. If you can't do this, you're in trouble. If you know you can't do this, start addressing it.

How long can you work at your computer, drafting table, or whatever your canvas is without seeking out a distraction? How long can you go without checking your texts? Or Twitter? They might seem like short detours, little blips in your day, but they add up. All those little moments that break the flow of your work have a huge effect on your overall productivity. They prevent you from going deep. When he was in grade school, young Jeff Bezos would get so lost in his assignments that teachers had to pick up his chair with him in it to get him to move to the next task.[2] Even back then, no one had to teach Jeff Bezos how to go deep into his work.

Every researcher who has looked at multitasking has come back with the same conclusion: it's a myth. We don't do two things at once; we move back and forth *between* two tasks, never getting into the flow of either, each task feeling like a distraction from the other. We like to think we can multitask but we're just *half-tasking two things at once*. Be suspicious of anyone who claims to be a great multitasker; I guarantee you important things are getting missed.

The future will be run by those who know how to go deep into their work. That's when it will become a secret weapon. As Newport wrote, "Depth will become increasingly rare and therefore increasingly valuable."[3] He offers this equation, which he calls The Law of Productivity:

High-Quality Work Produced = (Time Spent) X (Intensity of Focus)[4]

Time is, without question, our most precious resource. The moment we are born, our hourglass gets flipped over. That means that our most valuable currency is our attention. It shows what we truly value. Unfortunately, a huge portion of our time is being spent doing things that we're not paying attention to. In fact, according to a Harvard study, "People spend 46.9 percent of their waking hours thinking about something other than what they're doing."[5] That's nearly *half the day* of not being where their feet are.

Where you put your attention determines whether or not you are wasting, spending, or investing your time. Be *present*. It sounds so simple but just look around. It isn't. It might be the hardest thing for us to regularly do. And it's only getting harder.

I can't help but think of one of the many mind-blowing moments from LeBron James's career. But this one was not on the court, it was behind a microphone. After his Cavs lost the first game of the 2018 Eastern Conference Finals, a reporter asked LeBron, "What happened in the fourth quarter?" Partly as a tongue-in-cheek response and partly as a peek into how his mind works, LeBron took the question literally. He preceded to give a detailed blow-by-blow of the entire sequence of plays from the start of that quarter until his coach's time-out. There was a light laugh in the room, and LeBron gave a little smirk when he was done, but it shone a spotlight on how his gifts are not just physical. Imagine the focus of being able to do that.

Two games later he did it again, describing at the post-game press conference, in perfect detail, three different passes he made in the game, where other players were on the floor, and how he executed them. His mind is so locked in to what he is doing that even with everything that comes with being the best player on the planet in a playoff game situation, those details were easy for him to just rattle off.

Self-Test

Productivity Audit:

- What are your three most important work-related responsibilities?
- What do you actually do every day at work?
- Compare lists.

Note: If you aren't investing at least 80 to 90 percent of your time on your primary three responsibilities—then you are not being as efficient and as productive as you are capable of. Shift your energy and time so your priorities are treated like priorities.

The Swish Standard

To be disciplined is to carry incredibly high standards for yourself. It's making those lofty standards your baseline, meeting them, and then trying to exceed them. Years ago I got an up-close look at a player who would eventually become arguably the best shooter in NBA history—and a peek at how he got there.

At a skills camp eleven years ago, I had the pleasure of meeting and working with Steph Curry. At the time he was a rising sophomore, an undersized college player out of Davidson College, an under-the-radar school in the Southern Conference. Actually, it was Curry himself who would bring Davidson to national attention, significantly raising its profile in subsequent years.

I was the camp's performance coach, and Steph was one of the camp's counselors. He had just completed his freshman year and wasn't on the map yet—not even at the college level. But I was struck immediately. If you had the eyes to know what to look for, you'd have seen it, too. This kid was something special.

It began before it even began. At the start of each session, Steph made sure that he was always the first guy on the court. While others were lounging around with headphones and flip-flops on, lackadaisically stretching or joking around, Steph was already laced up and going through a structured shooting routine.

By the time the actual workout started, he had already made a couple hundred shots and was in a full sweat. Later, waiting on drill lines, while others were looking bored or chatting it up, Steph was studying the moves. I watched him closely and could see his focus. While he was on line, he was pantomiming his footwork for a variety of finishes around the basket so that when it was his turn, he could execute them correctly.

As a coach, someone who is trained to look for these kinds of things, I couldn't keep my eyes off him. If Steph did something correctly, he then made sure to repeat it and repeat it by himself, cementing that muscle memory. If he did something incorrectly, he would go and find the nearest coach and ask for personal instruction. Then they'd go off to the sidelines to make sure he had his footwork down or whatever it was he needed to do. Remember, this was not a tryout. No one was scouting him, and he wasn't raising his draft stock or any kind of rating. That's not why he was doing it. He was building a monster. Just nobody knew it yet.

Later that day, Steph grabbed me while I was picking things up from the court. "Hey, do you mind rebounding for me?" he asked. "I'm not leaving until I swish five free throws in a row."

As I stood under the basket and rebounded for him, I was in awe of this standard of excellence. Making five in a row at all is hard enough, especially at the end of a grueling practice, but that wasn't his routine. He needed to swish them. (A swish doesn't touch the backboard or rim; it's named for the sound it makes.)

The thing is, you can't really concentrate on swishing. If you focus on that, you're focusing on the wrong thing. It has to be completely automatic. Most people would say a made shot is a made shot, but that just wasn't Curry's standard. You can't make a shot any more perfectly than swishing it.

A few times he swished four and made, but didn't swish, the fifth, and started over. Now, no one would've cared if he'd called it a day, but he was committed to reaching his standard. These days Steph Curry is considered the best shooter in the league, maybe the greatest shooter of all time. It didn't come out of nowhere—it started with the discipline he had to meet that high standard in those gyms when no one was paying him any attention at all.

Steph's father, Dell Curry, was an NBA player, a great shooter, and Steph saw firsthand that if you want to be great at something, you put the time in and put the work in. Most kids only see ESPN highlights and YouTube clips. Steph saw the boring early mornings and exhaustive practice routines. He saw what it took and *decided* it was worth it.

Unseen Hours

My good friend and colleague Drew Hanlen is an internationally renowned NBA strategic skills coach. He has coined a phrase that I absolutely love: *unseen hours*. It refers to all the time and effort the public doesn't see that lays the foundation to the success they *do* see. It's the work they put in when there are no TV cameras, no fans, and no cheerleaders. It's the baskets they make that don't count, the passes that don't show up on instant replay, the hustling that never gets them any shout-outs. It's what happens when the gym is empty and the hour is insanely early or insanely late. Those are the unseen hours. That's where the heavy lifting happens, and the average spectator doesn't even think about it. Drew would know, having worked closely with many of the NBA's youngest stars, from Bradley Beal to Joel Embiid to Andrew Wiggins to Jayson Tatum, during their unseen hours. Their work is so much deeper than the time we see them on the court.

There's a famous story about Pablo Picasso that epitomizes the value of the unseen hours. Picasso, in his later years, was sketching in a park when a woman walked up to him. "Excuse me," she interrupted, "do you think you could sketch me something?" She offered to pay him for his time.

He agreed, quickly dashed off a sketch, and handed it back to her.

"That will be five thousand francs," he said.

"What?" the woman asked, dumbfounded. "How could you charge that much for something that took you five minutes?"

"Ah, but madam," he said, gesturing to the drawing, "*that* took me my whole life."[6]

Self-help icon and bestselling author Tony Robbins is a guy who has become as successful in his arena as anyone I can think of. He has Leonardo DiCaprio on speed dial and calls the former British prime minister "Meg" Thatcher. In 1998, the night before Bill Clinton's impeachment proceedings were about to begin in Congress, Robbins got a call at his home: it was the president, seeking his advice.

Robbins is famous for saying, "People are rewarded in public for things they practice for years in private." The stuff we do see, that we admire, the moments we hang up a poster of or tell each other stories about? That's literally the tip. It's all about that iceberg underneath.

At one time my friend Babe Kwasniak was the sales director for Ameripath, a cancer diagnostics company. When that company was sold to Quest for a couple billion dollars, he left business and decided to pursue his passion: coaching basketball. Coach Kwas, as he's affectionately called, is one of the best basketball coaches I've ever been around.

"Ever see a duck floating on the water? Most graceful thing ever," he told me in an interview. "In business or on a team you should be the same way, classy and professional. Ever see a duck swimming under water? Ugliest thing you ever witnessed. What we do when no one is watching is rarely graceful."

Discipline comes down to a simple choice.

1. Decide exactly what you want.
2. Determine the price you have to pay.
3. Choose whether or not you are willing to pay it.

That's it. Go through three steps and move on. You'll save yourself a lot of heartbreak and time if you get this out of the way first.

Blackouts with Kobe

Discipline is not sexy and it's not glamorous. It's an ethic and it's a belief system. It's the groundwork on which you build anything worth building. The human brain wants to work as efficiently as possible. In order to tap into that efficiency, we need to create good, consistent habits. Collectively these translate into discipline.

In 2007 Nike flew me to Los Angeles to work at the first ever

Kobe Bryant Skills Academy. They brought in the nation's top high school and college players (Arizona State's James Harden among them) for an intensive three-day mini-camp so that the players could learn from the best in the world.

Few would argue that at that time, Kobe was the best player in the game. Jordan was the past, LeBron was the future, and Kobe was the guy. There had always been urban legends about what his workouts entailed. Word around our circles was that Kobe used to call them "blackouts" instead of workouts.

Since I was staff and might never again get the chance, I asked Kobe if I could watch him work out. That's how it is in my business. Everyone can see the game, but to really learn the secrets, you have to watch the practice. It's the difference between buying Jay-Z's album and sitting in the studio watching him write and record one.

"Sure," Kobe said. "I'm going tomorrow at four."

"But don't we have a camp session at three thirty tomorrow afternoon?" I reminded him.

"I know," he replied. "I'm working out at four *a.m.*"

Okay then.

I figured if I was going to be there anyway, I might as well try and impress Kobe. I might as well show him how serious a trainer I was. So I planned to *beat* him to the gym. When my alarm went off at 3:00 a.m., I quickly jumped up, got dressed, and grabbed a taxi. I got to the gym around 3:30 a.m., so of course, it was pitch black outside. But as soon as I stepped out of the cab, I could see the gym light was already on. And I even heard a ball bouncing and sneakers squeaking. I quietly walked in the side door, and Kobe was already in a full sweat. He was going through an intense warm-up *before* the real workout started. I grabbed a seat, didn't say a word to him or his trainer, and just watched.

For forty-five minutes I was shocked. For forty-five minutes I watched the best player in the world do the most basic drills.

I watched the best player on the planet do basic ball-handling drills.

I watched the best player on the planet do basic footwork.

I watched the best player on the planet do basic offensive moves.

Granted, he did everything with surgical precision and super-hero intensity, but the stuff he was doing was so simple. I couldn't believe it.

Later that day I went over to him. "Thanks again," I said, "I really enjoyed watching your workout this morning."

"No problem," Kobe replied.

Then I hesitated, not wanting to sound rude—or worse—condescending. "You're the best player in the world. Why do such basic stuff?"

He flashed that gleaming smile of his. "Why do you think I'm the best player in the game?" he asked. "Because I never get bored with the basics."

He knew that if his footwork was not razor sharp, then the rest of the move would never be as good as it could be. And he knew that the only way to do that was through sheer repetition. Kobe had such an understanding of building things step by step, brick by brick; he worshipped at the altar of the basics. If someone at Kobe's level needs to commit hours to practicing the fundamentals, then so do all of us. Kobe taught me a pivotal lesson that morning. The basics are *simple*, but not *easy*. If they were easy, everyone would do them.

Everything a player does starts at his feet—every shot, every pass, and every defensive slide. Footwork is the foundation of their entire game. Proper footwork provides a player with more options both offensively and defensively. It improves movement efficiency, speed, quickness, and agility. Proper footwork makes average players good,

good players great, and great players elite. It's why Kobe spent so much time working on this. Until you have that down, you can't really execute or else you're building off a weak foundation. Learn the basics. Know the basics. Master the basics. Ask yourself: What are the basics of your business?

As a consultant, speaker, and author, I recognize that there is some debate about what the basics of my business are. Many believe the most basic component of my business is sales. I have to sell my services to clients; once I'm hired, I have to sell my message, beliefs, and strategies. But I choose to dig deeper than that. What is a basic of sales? Communication. What is a basic of communication? Listening.

When I break it all down, I believe the most basic component of my business, or any business for that matter, is *active listening*. Active listening is listening to learn, not listening to respond. It's listening to connect, not listening to reply. It's listening empathetically—which is the ability to try to see the world through another person's eyes and trying to respect, appreciate, and understand their perspective. Regardless of a company's size or industry, if they want to be elite, they must learn to master the fundamentals of active listening (to both their employees and their customers/clients). Active listening is the "footwork" of business.

Against the Hack

We live in an instantly downloadable world that encourages us to skip steps and circumvent the *process*. We are taught to chase what's hot, flashy, and sexy, and ignore the fundamentals. We are lured into "hacking" this or that, finding a way to skip the line. But the basics work. They always have and they always will.

A hack is a shortcut. A hack is a data breach. A hack is what people call a lame comedian. I don't believe in any of these. I believe in efficiency, not shortcuts. Skip the hacks. Do the work. Earn your success.

My friend Jay Bilas always talks about how his father was all about the process, whether that applied to sports, life, or yard work. "Jay," he'd say, "the only way you can get to the top of any ladder is step by step, rung by rung." Bilas's father emphasized that you cannot skip steps on a ladder. If you miss one, you'll fall all the way back to the bottom. It can take you an entire lifetime to build up your reputation, and you can do one boneheaded thing and lose it instantly.

Our culture encourages us to skip steps because we think we can get the glory without getting down the basics. It's why twelve-year old kids are spending their practices heaving half-court shots. Because that's what Steph Curry can do. In my day they were working on their in-the-air moves because of Michael Jordan.

The kids today aren't thinking about why Curry can do that. He has built his skills to the point where making it from that distance is an extension of his natural shooting. Nailing a three-pointer at the buzzer in the NBA is as glamorous as it gets. But being alone in the gym at dawn shooting a hundred free throws in a row? Those are reps. That's just work. People like Steph Curry and Kobe Bryant never forget that's where their whole game begins.

> Discipline is easy. Sustained, consistent discipline is hard.
>
> —Jesse Itzler

The Five Steps to Mastering Any Skill

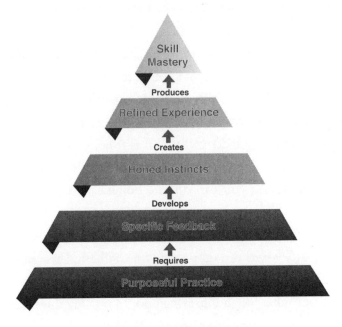

Skill
Mastery

Produces

Refined Experience

Creates

Honed Instincts

Develops

Specific Feedback

Requires

Purposeful Practice

*graphic designed by Jeremy Stein

Future You

Passion might be the why, but discipline is the how. As a society, we might have the energy to get going, but not to keep at it. The numbers don't lie. Ninety percent of all startups fail.[7] According to researchers, "Ninety-five percent of those who lose weight on a diet regain it, and a significant percentage gain back more than they originally lost."[8] The numbers on New Year's resolutions, company reorganizations, and post–heart attack changes are also wildly depressing. The reason? There's too much attention to the initial promise and not enough to laying the groundwork in order to actually execute and sustain it.

Preparation is a controllable competitive advantage. It's setting up your future self for success. When I asked Mark Cuban about what skills transfer from sports to business, he told me, "Preparation, preparation, preparation." He prepares relentlessly to ensure that he is the most knowledgeable person in the room. *Any room.*

Cuban is constantly looking to improve on what he doesn't know, which he calls a "knowledge advantage." When I met him, he told me, "That's the thing with technology. If you put in the time, you can keep up with anybody." It's all out there. *You* control your knowledge advantage. Cuban firmly believes that most people don't bother with the effort or time to gaining one, and he passed a lot of those people on his way to the top.

Starting out in the computer business, Cuban bought every book and magazine he could, making educating himself his number one priority: "Anyone could buy the same books and magazines," he wrote in his book. "The same information was available to anyone who wanted it. Turns out most people didn't want it."[9] They might want the end result, but they don't want to do what it takes to get there. Cuban did. He still does.

Success is like a loose ball. It's out there. It comes down to one simple thing: Who wants it? Learn to find it easy to do the things other people find it easy *not* to do. Successful people find it easy to read, to work out, to eat well, to be attentive, to set standards, to find a mentor, to attend seminars, and to network. As Jim Rohn would often say: Unsuccessful people find it easy *not* to do these things.[10] Circumstance and fortune certainly play their part, but you can control how ready you are when the opportunity comes, or when it comes or how it comes. I know for a fact that preparation trumps pressure. I've seen it so many times, in all kinds of settings. *Control the controllables.* Don't focus on the outcome, focus *on the process.*

I want you to close your eyes for a second and picture a brick wall.

Got it?

Okay.

If you're like me, you picture a wall where every brick has been laid perfectly. There aren't any bricks missing or any sticking out. Which means someone took the care and precision to lay every brick *perfectly*. And if you have the discipline to lay each brick perfectly, the end result will be a sound, sturdy wall. Nothing else is even possible.

When you focus on the process, the outcome will take care of itself.

Over time, by putting in the work—by having the discipline to put in the work—you set yourself up for success. Experience isn't about your former titles or your résumé. Experience is the unseen hours, the early mornings, the late nights, everything that happens when no one is watching. When you have accumulated enough of those, your skills will come out of you as naturally as your breath does.

When No One Is Watching

My longtime friend Dave Bollwinkel is a scout for the Chicago Bulls. When Syracuse came to DC to play Georgetown for a 4:00 p.m. game many years ago, Dave texted me. He said he was coming to town to scout a couple of players on each team and invited me to come. *Meet me outside the arena at 11?* he texted.

11? I replied. *The game's at 4. Why do we need to be there five hours before tip-off?*

Because that's my job, he wrote back.

It was Dave's job as a scout to watch players when they didn't know someone was watching them. Dave didn't care so much about the game itself; he had already watched hours of film on these guys. He needed to watch them before the game, to see how they interacted with their teammates and coaches, how they talked to the building's service staff, what routines they put into practice and were executing in their free time.

He wanted to see how they prepare. Are they clowning around and throwing up hook shots from half-court, or do they go through a structured, specific routine? When the strength coach is taking them through their warm-up, are they just as dialed in as they are at tip-off or are they goofing off?

Dave and I sat up in the stands—the only ones watching these private shoot-arounds—and he took page after page of notes. Even though I don't have Dave's keen eye, it was still crystal clear to me which players knew how to prepare and which ones didn't. In one shoot-around, two or three players drastically raised their stock in Dave's eyes and two or three drastically lowered their stock. And here's the thing: *none of them had any idea.*

Dave was writing down notes that would actually impact these players' futures and they didn't even know it, based on things they probably didn't even think were important. The lesson? Someone is always watching you, and everything you do matters. If you don't think your pregame preparation matters, then on some level you won't play as well once the stands are full. We all have off days, but the habits of preparation are going to reveal so much more than how we do on one day.

It's why in high school, Larry Bird shot 500 free throws before school every morning, even during the months he had a broken ankle and was likely to miss the rest of the season.[11] "If you cheated…in the dark of the morning," heavyweight champion Joe Frazier once said, "you're getting found out now under the bright lights."[12]

Our Choices, Our Stories

In 2010 Amazon founder and CEO Jeff Bezos gave the commencement speech to Princeton University's graduating class. He talked about how our lives can be summed up as a story of our choices. When we are old and sharing our story, "the telling that will be most compact and meaningful will be the series of choices you have made," he said. "In the end, we are our choices."[13]

Each and every day, you have a choice to make. You can choose to work hard or you can choose to *not* work hard. And remember: *not working hard is actually a choice.* It doesn't feel like one but it most certainly is. In fact, it's often the easiest choice available. That's why so many people make it.

If you want to be successful, you need to decide to work hard consistently. You must choose to get better every day, even when no one else is around, and even when you don't feel like it (especially at those times—because that's how you get a leg up on everyone else). Merely wanting it is not enough. Just about everyone wants it. Make the sacrifices necessary to make it happen.

Key Point: Create habits and structure that will give you an edge in your business. Discipline means having, maintaining, and refining a system in place to work on your game.

Remember:

☞ There's no such thing as "finding" success, as if you stumbled upon it. You create success by building the habits to reach it.

☞ It's the consistent habits that make the best the best. Build a schedule and a structure of habits that put first things first.

☞ Knock out distractions. Consider how to spend your time wisely and efficiently. Be ruthless in trimming the "fat" from your day.

☞ Use your unseen hours. Make the most of your time—those at the top do not waste a second. Focus on what matters.

CHAPTER FOUR

Coachability

It's what you learn *after* you know it all that counts.

—John Wooden

Feedback is the sound of the world responding to us. Ignore it at your own risk because it is absolutely instrumental to improvement. If you don't know—and aren't willing to discover—how you need to get better, you will forever be stuck where you are. An ego might prevent you from wanting to hear it, but those who have a thick skin and an understanding of the big picture crave it. As discussed, self-awareness is the necessary foundation, but true feedback needs to come from an outside source. Those who are willing to heed it are what I call coachable.

If you are not coachable, you are closed to development and, ultimately, success. Winners want to know the area where they are losing and how they are losing—so they can win there as well. It's the only way to patch up errors, close those holes, and make yourself a force to be reckoned with. Drop the ego and stay open. You'll be surprised how many things you can do something about and how many things you can influence.

How we choose to process feedback determines whether or not we progress or regress. The world's highest performers and achievers make the decision to use all feedback in a manner that moves them forward. We have the choice in how to process feedback—the feedback itself is neither positive nor negative. It's neutral. It's sterile. It's unbiased. It becomes positive or negative only when we choose to attach feelings and emotions to it. It doesn't matter if it is a coach correcting a player's footwork, a manager offering suggestions on a proposal, or an audience rating a speaker.

In the world of athletic performance training, I was raised on a philosophy called high-intensity training, an incredibly intense training methodology that calls for you to take every set to the point of MMF (momentary muscular failure). You push the weight until you can't push it any more. Because of this, I am conditioned to push for failure, every set of every workout.

Think about it: If a basketball player does a thirty-minute ball-handling workout and never loses the ball, then he did not get any better! All he did was replicate what he was already capable of doing. In order to progress, he has to push past his current limits. *If you're not losing the ball, then you're not getting any better.*

Coachable Business

Of course, the concepts of coachability go far beyond the gym and the court. As the business advice has it: "Your worst customer is your best friend."[1] You learn through your failures, through those who reject you, turn you away, and want nothing to do with you. Don't be afraid to hear them out. They will become your greatest teachers.

Arthur Blank, cofounder of Home Depot and owner of the Atlanta Falcons, claimed he built his business on finding holes he needed to fill. And he continued that mind-set as he worked his way up. "When I was running Home Depot," he said, "I'd always stop the customers who walked out of our stores with nothing. They were the ones who taught us the most."[2] We know that the ones who best adapt are the ones who survive. High achievers are always going through this process: *learn—unlearn—relearn.*

Look at Domino's, which owned the pizza delivery market for years. At some point along the way, they got complacent and then sloppy. Once competitors started cutting into their market share, they asked for customer feedback. The overwhelming response? "Your pizza sucks!" (I'm paraphrasing.) They took this feedback to heart—even running an advertising campaign admitting to it!— and took aggressive steps to make their pizzas healthier and tastier. They called it the "pizza turnaround" and their sales have improved dramatically, surpassing their competitors for the first time in years.[3]

In *Mindset: The New Psychology of Success,* psychologist Carol Dweck compares two kinds of people: those with a fixed mind-set, who assume that they are where they should be, and those with a growth mind-set, who are always pushing. She calls this stretching. "People in a growth mindset don't just seek challenge, they thrive on it," she wrote. "The bigger the challenge, the more they stretch."[4] Her research shows conclusively how those with the growth mind-set are more likely to bounce back from challenges, put in that extra effort, and become successful.

How we react to our failures is going to be one of the most crucial aspects of our game. We all run into failures—some are our fault, some are the way of the world. But what separates the successful from the rest is how they *use* those failures. In fact, those with a growth mind-set don't treat them like failures at all. They're just opportunities to learn. This is what distinguishes the truly successful. They don't stop when they reach a level of success, and they definitely don't stop when they hit a wall. The wall is actually when they really start pushing.

> Coachability breaks down into three parts:
>
> - **Trust:** full confidence from coach to player, player to coach, and coach/player to team
> - **Openness:** the humility, trust, and desire to welcome instruction and guidance
> - **Execution:** the ability to precisely carry out a desired course of action

KD and Knowing What's Good for You

Coachability is understanding the gap between where you are and where you want to be—and committing to doing what it takes to get from one to the other. When I first met Kevin Durant in 2004, he was a skinny high school junior who didn't say much beyond *hello, good-bye,* and *thanks.* If you think KD is skinny now, you should have seen him then. He'd need a cinder block in his lap just to keep the seat down at a movie theater! Don't get me wrong—he was unbelievably talented and had a killer work ethic, but he needed to get stronger and add muscle if he wanted to succeed at the next level. So I stepped in. After some hustle and convincing on my part, his wonderful mother, Wanda, finally let me take him through a workout.

And I crushed him. I was the hammer and the nails. At the end of a brutal full-body strength workout, Kevin was literally lying in a heap on the floor. Because he was so quiet, it was hard for me to get a read on what he was thinking and feeling about it.

When we were done, I walked over to him. "Hey, young buck," I asked him, "You like that workout?"

He looked me in the eye, dead serious. "No," he said. "But I know this is what I need to do to play in the NBA. When can we meet again?"

Even at fifteen years old, KD had the maturity to know what he needed to do to get where he wanted to go. He had that special something. When elite guys find something they can't do, they step into it. That's what makes them who they are.

I saw an HBO documentary on Durant's off-season, and it was unbelievable how much work he put in just during his *vacation*. Just watching his routine was exhausting. "He's working as if he's still trying to get to the NBA," his friend said. It didn't matter that he had just been named the league's MVP! He was still pushing like he was that fifteen-year-old kid trying to make it. When he came on to my podcast during the off-season, it was the same exact thing. I talked to him at the end of a practice day that had started at 8 a.m. The off-season is "the real season," he told me. "It's where you get better."

Actually, it's not when everyone gets better. Only those who are willing to be coached do.

Durant's coachability sets an example for others. He told me he recognizes the influence he has over rookies and bench players and makes a point of getting to practice early to work on his game, knowing that others will follow his lead. If you think you already know enough in your field and don't need to be coached, keep in mind that even Kevin Durant is not at that point. And he will never get to that point. That's just who he is. You think you are better at what you do than Kevin Durant is at what he does? Enough said.

When Michael Jordan was first spotted at a summer camp as a teenager, it wasn't his athleticism that impressed the scouts. It was his ability at a young age to take coaching.[5] The best are coachable. Their drive for greatness means they have an insatiable desire to improve. They're never satisfied with where they are, and they refuse to stop learning. Though it would be extremely easy for them to do so, they don't rest on their laurels or accolades.

In his book *Eleven Rings: The Soul of Success*, former Chicago

Bulls and Los Angeles Lakers coach Phil Jackson discusses a ritual he would engage in with his players at the start of each training camp. He would line the players up on the baseline and ask them if they were willing to accept his coaching for the upcoming season.

Jackson, one of the winningest coaches of all time, understood the necessity of this exchange. Maybe some players thought it was hokey or didn't understand why they had to do it every season, but Jackson knew: he solidified that bond because it laid the groundwork for everything that would come after.

> The people who have taught me most in my career are the ones who pointed out what I didn't see.
>
> —Sheryl Sandberg, Facebook COO

Sniffing Around

Are you a curious person? Are you interested in learning more about your business and the world around you? Is one of your engines the desire to know more? If not, I got some bad news for you.

At the *New York Times*, Adam Bryant interviews successful CEOs for a living and studies them across all industries. The common denominator? "Passionate curiosity,"[6] he wrote. We don't always see that side of them, he explained, because their public faces are those of cool, collected leaders.[7] They have to be. But talk to any of them one on one, as he does, and you'll find they are "eager students who devour insights and lessons, and are genuinely, enthusiastically interested in everything going on around them."[8] When I read this, I flashed back to Mark Cuban. These are people at the top of their game, the absolute pinnacle, but they are still driven to know more. That's how they stay up there.

Look at all the twenty-first century's big ideas, and you'll find curious people at their core. Airbnb co-founder and CEO Brian Chesky, who turned a lark of an idea about sharing floor space and air mattresses into a $30 billion behemoth, is defined by everyone who knows him as having a "near pathological curiosity"[9] and "an obsession with constantly absorbing new information."[10] And here's the key. He's *still* like that. Sara Blakely, billionaire founder of Spanx, is the same way. "When I see a problem," she told an interviewer, "I just start asking questions. I am looking for a gap."[11]

CEOs who have gone through the fire and come out the other end are looking for those who remind them of themselves. They value the risk takers, the ones who are brave enough to try and humble enough to learn, to fail, and to try again. The take-no-prisoners jerk who acts like he knows everything? Nobody wants that guy. There's nothing to teach him and nothing he can offer. The ones who are open? Willing to listen and be coached? Every team could use more of those. Make yourself invaluable. Become a sponge. Be willing to listen and learn. *Stay coachable.*

When the San Antonio Spurs' season ends each year, Gregg Popovich takes each player aside, individually, and thanks them for allowing him to coach them.[12] It's a powerful message: not just because of the gesture of gratitude, but because it reminds the players that it's a two-way relationship. No one can coach you without your consent. Make sure you are open to it.

Bring on the Fail

Every single ladder to success has rungs of failure on it. They are not pit stops or anomalies. They are a key part of the journey. We don't know how to do anything until we screw up at it enough times. "Never flinch at failure," legendary UCLA coach John Wooden wrote. "I was taught not to fear making a mistake if it was the right kind of mistake. My college coach at Purdue told us that the team that makes the most mistakes usually wins."[13] Once we get past the ego aspect of the equation, we realize how valuable failure is. We learn far more from it than we do from success.

It's an idea that has spread to the business world as well. Sara Blakely makes a point of celebrating "Oops" moments around the Spanx office so employees can see how the mistakes can become teaching moments. She credits her father for this philosophy and approach. At the dinner table when she was growing up, he would ask what she and her brother had failed at that week.[14] She internalized the idea and continues to ensure that failures are treated as the lessons they are.

The Lessons of the Untalented

P. J. Carlesimo is a coaching legend—at all levels: at Seton Hall, in the NBA—for four teams, including two Spurs' championship teams—and most impressively, for the 1992 Dream Team who won Olympic gold in Barcelona, the most-talented team ever assembled. However, when I interviewed him for my podcast, he surprised me by not discussing the elite players he worked with. "You learn a lot more when you have a team that's not very talented," he told me. "You learn a lot more when you lose, particularly early in your career, which is something that I went through. . . . It's a great teacher." Carlesimo understood that failure is really just the word we give to all those previous reps that got us to where we are now.

Some academics have begun putting a "notable failures" section on their résumés. I'm a fan of this trend. It opens up the idea that we are not all progressing in a straight line. Scrubbing our career trajectories of our setbacks doesn't serve anything but our egos. Let's make a point to dig in on them—not to dwell, but to explore.

An overpowering fear of failure may be a generational issue as well. According to a recent study, 40 percent of millennials carry a fear of failure, more than any other age group.[15] If I had to guess, I imagine that growing up in a social media culture, a world where every little thing is shared, has created this side effect. No one wants to mess up because it's so public and embarrassing. But failure is a built-in motivation and teaching system—if you're smart enough to embrace it. "Failure is so valuable," says researcher James Prochasksa, because "it forces us to learn, even if we don't want to."[16]

> Sometimes life hits you in the head with a brick.
>
> —Steve Jobs

How Strong Is Your Bounceback?

The reason I'm so passionate about embracing failure is that I used to shy away from it. In fact, it wasn't until I was in my early thirties that I changed my mind-set to accept my mistakes as valuable, as a necessary part of the process. No one gets it right every time. So the question isn't whether or not you will fail, as everyone inevitably does. It's how you respond. How you deal with failure determines your ultimate happiness and success. Let's call it your bounceback.

Apple's Steve Jobs will forever be hailed as a visionary genius, but the story about him that gets told most often is how he was fired from the company he built, only to return and save it twelve years later, turning it into one of the most successful and important brands on the planet. To his credit, Jobs didn't bury that part of his biography; he often retold the story himself, because he understood it was the foundation of his future success. Failure only becomes positive or negative based on how you frame it and how you personalize it. The exact same failure can inspire you, motivate you, and teach you, or it can crush you, debilitate you, and paralyze you. It is a matter of choice.

Failure is about walking headfirst into "no," into adversity, into discomfort. We must condition ourselves to embrace it and thrive from it. I'm grateful to have gotten a lot of yeses in my life. And almost all of them have come after countless nos. As a professional speaker, I hear no on a daily basis; I think of it as just part of my workday. But I have always felt that every "no" gets me closer to a "yes." If you are constantly getting yeses, then you aren't pushing hard enough. *If you didn't lose the ball, then you haven't learned anything.*

It's up to you how you choose to feel about and perceive your misses. It goes back to the growth mind-set. Those who see failures as walls will do nothing to get past them. Those who see them as doors will do the work to get them open.

Be Ready to Receive

An important part of being coachable is being open to lessons from anywhere and anyone. Former Ultimate Fighting Champion Frank Shamrock was once pound for pound the deadliest man in the world. He is an extremely fit, handsome man with a powerful presence and energy. Though Frank speaks with authority, he's actually quite reserved, the perfect mix of confidence and humility. He knows he could beat any human to death in six seconds, but he carries himself in a way that neither celebrates nor hides this fact. I got to spend quality time with Frank at a retreat recently. When I spoke with him, he was open about all the mistakes he has made in his personal life and how hard he has worked to correct them and move forward.

The first twenty-one years of Frank's life were brutal. He suffered abuse as a child and he was in and out of the foster care system and then jail. After making the choice to turn his life around, he began his fighting career, which he approached differently than he had anything in his life up to that point. Frank took a very scientific and cerebral approach, which was unheard of at the time. He studied his opponents' weaknesses, leverages, and fighting styles, developing a clear advantage as soon as he entered the Octagon, the UFC ring. He constantly evolved as a fighter, never wanting to become predictable. "Everything works, but nothing works forever," he told me.

Frank lives by a system he calls the +, =, − system:

+ (plus): He finds someone ahead of him and learns from them.

= (equal): He finds someone equal to him and exchanges with them.

− (minus): He finds someone he is ahead of and shares with them.

I love this system for many reasons, but one is that it recognizes that ideas, help, and motivation can come from anyone and anywhere. Frank doesn't see some people as worth the time and some not. Everyone has value. Lessons are all around us.

You need to carry a readiness to receive instruction and be open about where you get ideas. On Amazon.com, the idea of other web pages—even homemade ones—having an Amazon button? It came from a customer. Bezos has built Amazon into a goliath, partly because of "a willingness to jump on new ideas that come from any source."[17] It takes humility and openness to accept ideas from anywhere and everywhere. New results require new behaviors. If nothing changes, nothing changes.

In the early 1980s the rock band Metallica was on the verge of becoming huge when they kicked out their first guitarist. They held auditions and hired an unknown kid, Kirk Hammett, to become their new guitarist. The first thing Hammett did after getting the job of lead guitarist for what was about to be the biggest band in the world?

He hired a guitar teacher.

Times of Transition

Growth, development, and improvement must be a continuous process. How long is it acceptable to be in the third grade? One year. At that point, you are not only expected to move on, you are forced to! Why don't employees feel compelled to do the same? Many employees stay at the same level year after year.

Growth comes only from transition. Your happiness, performance, and success are predicated on your ability to manage these transitions. Sometimes we initiate change, and sometimes it is forced upon us. Either way, we must adapt. You must expect transition; always be ready for it because it won't always announce itself and you may not have time to get ready. Life is filled with transitions; our ability to anticipate them before they arrive and embrace them when they do is what allows us to get a leg up and rise to the next level. Along the way, you'll be amazed what you can accomplish as long as you remain coachable.

Key Point: It's a journey, not a destination. The successful ones never stop growing. Accept that you have more to learn, and be willing to get it from anywhere and anyone.

Remember:

☞ You control your "knowledge advantage."

☞ Never quickly judge who or what is worth paying attention to. Be open.

☞ Great ideas are in the air all around us. Train your eyes to recognize them.

☞ Embrace failure for the teaching tool that it is.

☞ Feedback is the sound of the world responding to us.

CHAPTER FIVE

Confidence

> You can't possibly become better than me because you're not spending the time on it that I do, so I already won.
>
> —Kobe Bryant

Confidence is the last chapter of part 1 because it is the sum total of all the previous qualities. Do you have self-awareness? Are you passionate? Are you willing to do disciplined work? Will you remain coachable? The natural result of all this is confidence. Earned confidence. Grounded confidence. *Authentic* confidence.

When you go into a situation prepared, confidence can't help but arise. It's no different than Steph Curry confidently swishing his free throws when the game is on the line and millions are watching. He knows they're going in, because he's made thousands of them when no one was there.

The Smartest Guy in the Room

There are some people you meet, who are at the top of their game and after five minutes talking to them, you understand how they got

Self Awareness
+ Passion
+ Discipline
+ Coachability

Confidence

*graphic designed by Jeremy Stein

where they are. They just exude a kind of earned confidence in what they do and what they know that comes from years—decades—of investing in themselves.

A few years ago, my *Hardwood Hustle* podcast team and I booked flights down to Dallas to meet with one of the most confident people in the worlds of sports and business: Dallas Mavericks owner, *Shark Tank* star, and renegade billionaire Mark Cuban. Our flights were delayed so we showed up in Dallas on no sleep, but that didn't matter. I was psyched; being in Cuban's presence was like having an IV drip of caffeine. He's just an inspiring and magnetic kind of guy.

Mark was at the top of my must-meet bucket list, so sitting across from him and getting to talk shop was a phenomenal experience. He was a total gentleman, easy and hospitable as he granted us full access to his private suite at the American Airlines Center. His office is in the bunker underneath the stadium, decked out with several big-screen TVs, leather couches, Mavericks memorabilia, and a full bar. It was the ultimate man cave.

Cuban's an extremely busy guy, but he ended up giving us a couple of hours—and we had a blast. He was on a schedule and he had somewhere to be, but he never made us feel like it. What I like and respect most about Mark is his confidence. "We all doubt ourselves at one point or another," Cuban told me. "Confidence gives me the ability to push through that doubt. Confidence has helped me in every presentation I have ever made in my life." Cuban is a living example of the power of confidence—he's a self-made man who has, through force of will, become a powerhouse. He is brilliant, innovative, and fearless, the very definition of a maverick. And his confidence is *earned*.

Talking to Cuban, who was lounging casually in a T-shirt and track pants, his knees up and feet on the table, I was struck by his authenticity. As he pounded Red Bull, he spoke as casually as if we were buddies drinking beers and watching a game. He didn't seem like a billionaire or an icon or any of it. There was no calculation about how he wanted to sound. He offered no talking points or branded sayings that he'd said a billion other times. Mark Cuban was *real*.

I've met enough big-time sports, media, and businesspeople to know that this is rare. Cuban is a guy who knows who he is and what he wants, and he's not too concerned about how he comes off. He has strong opinions, and he's not afraid to share them. It's just who he is. Cuban knows self-confidence is not just a result, it's also a cause. It's a self-regenerating process.

Mark's first company, Micro Solutions, began humbly, with a $500 job from his first customer. In 1990, he sold that company to CompuServe. Today he's worth over $3 billion, and his businesses are still growing. When he took over the Mavericks, they were the worst team in the NBA. In fact, they were voted worst professional sports franchise of the 1990s. The very first thing Cuban did as their owner was upgrade the players' locker room and travel accommodations. Why? Most executives might think that's the last thing you should do for a losing team: that'll just make them more comfortable and encourage their complacency. But Cuban isn't most executives. He knew that once the players felt valued, they would value each other and their game more.

On the other side of the locker room door, he got his hands dirty. He put his desk on the ticket sales floor and set up shop there, making sales calls alongside the agents. Cuban worked to directly convince the people of Dallas to come out and support a team that was playing to an empty stadium—and losing—all the time. And it worked.

Cuban doesn't get hampered by obstacles; in fact, they get him going. He told me that he was *motivated* by taking over the worst team in the NBA. "You can use fear as a roadblock or as motivation,"[1] he wrote in his book, and his life and career are a testament to which choice he makes, over and over again.

When I asked him his definition of success, he answered immediately: "Waking up every morning with a smile on my face knowing I'm going to make this a great day." It was only when I was relistening to our interview that I realized how profound this was. Not that it was going to be a great day, but that he was going to *make* it one—that's the key. It's in his hands. That's the power and reach of confidence.

"I love to compete. When I was younger, I liked to prove to everybody that it didn't matter how old I was," he told me. "I was twenty-two, twenty-three starting a business. I'd kick your ass no matter what. Now that I'm older…I don't care if you're eighteen, twelve, or fifty, I'm going to kick your ass. You can work hard and I'm just going to outwork you, and outgrind you, and do whatever it takes."

Cuban often talks about how his goal is to always be the most prepared and most knowledgeable person when he sits down in a room. He preaches the gospel of knowing your stuff. "I get my confidence from knowing that I outwork everyone and read more than anyone," he told me. "Knowing I put in the time to give myself a competitive advantage is where I get my confidence from." If he loses out on something, it will never be due to lack of knowledge or lack of preparation. He's a master of the unseen hours and that's why he's successful.

Cuban believes confidence is misunderstood; it's not just empty self-esteem or, as he put it, giving yourself a participation medal. "It comes from experience and knowledge," he said. Confidence also doesn't mean invincibility. It doesn't mean he's never afraid. In fact, he told that me that when he walks in to convince someone to buy one of his companies, "It's always terrifying, and I'm always wary of what will happen, but my preparation and confidence get me through!" I was reassured knowing that Mark Cuban still gets terrified in high-stakes situations. It reminded me that confidence doesn't mean never being afraid—it just means being prepared and driven enough to get yourself past that fear.

What Losing Gives Us

Contrary to the old Vince Lombardi maxim, which has been quoted far too many times, winning is not the only thing. Not even close. Of course, it feels great and it's what we're all trying to work toward, but success is built on the backs of failures. That's just a fact. It's not just about overcoming fear; it's about using that feeling to drive you. The energy—even the anxiety—that comes from being afraid is something to utilize. It can be channeled into something; it can be the engine that fires you forward, even into things you are afraid of.

Of course, confidence comes from being successful. Mark Cuban is the way he is because of what he has accomplished. But we can't forget that confidence comes from going through adversity, coming out the other end, and continuing to go forward.

Confidence is also about conviction, muscling through obstacles, and withstanding heartbreak. It's holding fast to your vision even when the world isn't buying. It took Perry Chen *eight years* to launch Kickstarter from the original idea.[2] Every single investor passed on Airbnb until Silicon Valley's biggest, Sequoia Capital, didn't.[3] Think about how many great ideas and smart entrepreneurs don't end up breaking through. It takes people who resiliently believe in themselves—almost to an irrational point—to come out the other side.

Confidence comes from both winning *and* losing, which takes years of passion and discipline to build. A lot of it has to do with getting rid of the negative self-talk and replacing it with words and beliefs that keep you striving for what you want. You can change what you do by changing the way you think. It's that simple.

> Comparison is the thief of joy.
>
> —Teddy Roosevelt

A Game You Can't Win

My friend Paul Biancardi of ESPN loves to say, "You will always lose the Comparison Game." Why is that? Because it's rigged. It has no function besides enlarging self-doubt. I'm typing this chapter on board a flight to South Dakota. Among the 250 passengers on this plane, I can quickly find someone better looking, funnier, more successful, taller, more muscular, smarter. It won't take long to find someone who scores higher than me on almost any metric.

If I use these people as my measuring stick—to determine my self-worth and value—I will always lose.

I will never measure up.

I will always fall short.

I will never have or be enough.

But this is an easy trap to fall into. I still occasionally catch myself doing it.

Conventional advertising's number one goal is to get us to play the Comparison Game. To make us feel like we aren't enough, to brainwash us into believing we always need more and to magnify our insecurities. In many ways, social media has expanded this issue. We get so hyperfocused on what everyone else has and what everyone else is doing that we lose sight of ourselves.

Comparison never serves us or adds value to our lives. In fact, it robs us of happiness and fulfillment. The only thing we should compare ourselves to is our previous selves or to what we are capable of.

That is the only way you can win.

Game Face

Successful people often have routines to help access or build their self-confidence. If you don't, consider developing one—even look to the world of sports for ideas. In *Psyched Up: How the Science of Mental Preparation Can Help You Succeed*, Dan McGinn shadowed a doctor who has a specific routine he goes through before going into surgery to get him mentally ready. The surgeon happens to be a former wrestler, and he uses similar preparation techniques to the ones he once used before a match.[4]

McGinn also wrote about witnessing West Point athletes preparing for a game by listening to an actor reading their "greatest hits," highlights of successes they've had on the field. He interviewed masters of performance like Jerry Seinfeld about their pre-show routines and sat in on a Juilliard class that is exclusively about mental preparation. Juilliard students—the best young musicians in the world—have a full semester class that doesn't teach music at all. The class's sole purpose is to get the students psychologically ready for the stage and the pressures of performing in front of an audience. Professors in this class even make students do calisthenics and ask them to perform pieces immediately afterward so that they can get used to that adrenaline flowing through their bodies as they play.[5]

Confidence is the face we put out to the world. We're living in a "shark tank economy," where we're judged by important singular moments—the big interview, presentation, or evaluation—and we need to perform at our best. Without confidence, it's unlikely anyone is going to give us that account, client, job, or promotion. Even if we have the skills, if no one knows or trusts that we do, we will not be able to make the big leap.

Next Play

Confidence comes from not getting bogged down in the past. We extract what we need to improve, and then we move on. At a DeMatha game, Coach Jones will say "next play" at least a hundred times. Ref missed a call? *Next play.* You turned the ball over? *Next play.* You missed a wide-open shot? *Next play.* It goes back to what you can control: focus on the next play. The most important question you can ask yourself after success or failure is: *What now?*

The only way you can be at your best is to be fully present. It doesn't mean ignoring what happened—you need to pull lessons from that experience. It's about not sulking or getting down. It's about taking what you can from the experience and *applying* it to the next play, whatever that next play is.

> No serious physical event is a physical event...they're all mental events.
>
> —*The Selection*[6]

The Guy in the Blue Tuxedo

Okay, I've been putting it off, but it's time. Let's go back to 2002, mile 17 of my first marathon. My legs were on fire, and my body had shut down. I'd slowed down to a walk, humiliated and broken. It was the first time in my life that I allowed my negative self-talk to completely take over. I was just swimming in it: *I can't do this. I can't finish. I'm done.* I knew that it wasn't healthy or productive to go there but that voice was deafening. It was hard to block out. Every time I tried to muster up the strength to get running again, it was like my legs were full of lead. They just wouldn't move. And the voice would begin screaming again.

As I spiraled in this negative self-talk—*you suck, you can't do this, you're finished*—two people ran by me whom I will never forget. They are forever burned into my memory.

One was an eighty-year-old man in a powder blue tuxedo. He was good enough to run a marathon wearing anything. And he just sailed right by me. Like he was on a Sunday stroll. It was a vicious hit to my ego, and though he didn't mean to, he added insult to injury.

But that wasn't the worst. The worst was when a middle-aged woman ran by me who had—I am not kidding—*crapped her pants.* Her shorts were completely brown in the back. I later learned it's fairly normal when you put your body through intense physical stress for certain systems of your body to shut off. It happens; you have no bodily control. But she ran right by me, too. The one-two punch was brutal, beyond humbling. I walked the rest of the way, all the way to the finish.

Even though I finished the race, it was not the way I had planned. It wasn't on my terms. At the end, I told myself, *I will never do this again. That was the worst experience of my life.*

Years later, I still think about it. It has always been in the back of my mind, bothering me. Not so much the failing—there's no shame in not being able to run an entire marathon—but the fact that I allowed my negative self-talk to get the best of me. I use that memory as fuel and motivation to never put myself in that position again. Since then, to test myself and push past my fear, I have participated in several endurance events. Were they hard? Absolutely. But that's why they were worth it. Hell, the first person who ever ran a marathon—twenty-five hundred years ago in Athens—got to the end and promptly dropped dead.

Stratton Mountain*

I carried the marathon experience with me for fifteen years. It lingered in the back of my mind; the way my negative self-talk took over, the way my confidence wasn't earned, the way I put myself in a position to be embarrassed like that. In 2017 I took on a far more grueling activity. I participated in the 29029 Everest Challenge. The task was to ascend Stratton Mountain *seventeen* times over the course of two days, the equivalent of ascending Mount Everest. Even though we rode down in a gondola after each ascent, it was far and away the toughest thing I've ever done—way more grueling than the marathon.

Among the participants were a guy who had rowed across the Atlantic Ocean, the world record holder for climbing the highest

* A version of this section first appeared on my social media accounts.

mountains on each of the seven continents (more on him later), two former NFL players, a trainer on NBC's *The Biggest Loser*, and a woman who was preparing to run seven marathons on seven continents in seven *consecutive* days. It was an awe-inspiring group, and I was humbled just to be among them.

Of course, I hadn't forgotten the guy in the blue tuxedo and the lady who lost control of her bowels passing me fifteen years earlier. In the months before the challenge, I prepared methodically and relentlessly. I added a progressive inclined treadmill and Stairmaster program to my normal strength training routine, trying my best to simulate the experience ahead of time. Just being in shape was nowhere near good enough, and I wouldn't repeat the same mistakes. I'd have the confidence that comes from being prepared.

The mountain, with its punishing steep incline, was a beast. As a performance coach, I've always associated an elevated heart rate with high-intensity movement like sprinting. But simply *walking* up the mountain had my heart pounding, my legs burning, and though it was cold, my body completely soaked in sweat.

As physically tough as it was, climbing the mountain was actually more of a mental test. It was all about how I processed the knowledge that I was at specific landmarks. There is a difference between the mind-set of "I just got to the halfway mark!" and "Ugh, I still have halfway to go." It's the ultimate glass is half-full proposition.

There was a stark contrast between climbing in daytime, when I could see a hundred yards in front of me, and climbing at night, when I could only see as far as my headlamp would shine. Same mountain, same task, different perspective. On some ascents, I'd be all alone, and at other times, I'd go with a group. When I was solo, I was left alone with my thoughts. With others, we all worked together to support and push each other, and I was able to distract myself from the physical challenge by connecting with others.

Once I came to the humbling realization that I would not be able to complete all seventeen ascents in the time allotted, it was bittersweet. I was disappointed but it also made the pressure evaporate. When I got to that point, I could just smile, take a breath, and simply focus on enjoying the experience. I knew my twelfth ascent would be my last, and it was by far the most enjoyable. Fully present the entire time, I intentionally stopped at several landmarks to take in the view and reflect on the event and my experience.

Though I didn't finish the challenge, I knew that wasn't the point. I've never felt more satisfaction from not reaching a goal than I did at the end of that weekend. I had a transformational experience, learned a lot about myself, and was able to stay present over an extended period of time. The point was to challenge my soul, push my physical, mental, and emotional limits, and connect with extraordinary people. And I did all three.

Before, during, and after, my perspective on the whole experience was remarkably different from that marathon fifteen years ago. I didn't allow negative self-talk to bombard me when it got rough—and believe me, it got rough. Despite the pain in my legs, the exhaustion pummeling my body, I attacked the challenge with confidence and optimism. It was like I was a different person. Because I was.

Seven Things I Learned on Stratton Mountain

1. Complacency is the enemy of growth. You must take off the "cruise control" and intentionally push your limits as often as possible.

2. Physical discomfort creates emotional connection. You will make your best friends outside of your comfort zone.

3. Successful, smart, driven people want to spend time with successful, smart, driven people. Like attracts like.

4. You aren't competing with anyone else—in life or in business— you are always competing with yourself.

5. Breaking challenges into smaller pieces makes them manageable. Take things step by step.

6. View life as a series of privileges, not obligations. Change your "have to's" to "get to's." I didn't have to climb a mountain. I got to climb a mountain.

7. The climbs I did with others felt much easier than the ones I did by myself. The engaging conversation and mutual support made a huge difference. Challenges are not meant to be tackled alone.

Hardest-Working Man in the Business

"If everyone in the league worked as hard as I did," two-time NBA MVP Steve Nash used to say, "I'd be out of a job." Nash was an overachiever in the best sense of the word. He focused on the things that he could influence—like how prepared he was, which is where his confidence came from. When I met Nash, he was in his mid-thirties, nearing the twilight of an incredible career. "When you see me doing something in the game and it looks like it came out of nowhere, it didn't," he told me. "There's nothing I do in a game that I haven't done thousands of times in practice."

Nash told me that, as a point guard, his number one job is to have solutions. He needs to be a problem solver on the court. Statistically in the NBA, if the ball gets into the lane, through a pass or a dribble, the team scores at a higher percentage (even if the eventual shot is outside the lane). Once Nash gets it in there, his job is to find as many options as possible.

And he practiced all of them—passing the ball with either hand, bounce pass to the big man down low, a pocket pass to a guy for a corner three, off either foot, from either hand. In a game, Nash could confidently drive into the lane against bigger, stronger, and more athletic guys, because he was going in there with eight to ten options of what he could do. The preparation gave him confidence. No matter who was going to meet him in the lane, he already had the answers.

> Be ready to catch the ball—whatever direction it comes from.
> —Sarah Robb O'Hagan, CEO, Flywheel Sports

Optimism

Confidence comes from an understanding of your own agency, your own influence, and your own ability to make things happen. Bob Rotella is a sports psychologist who has helped everyone from Michael Jordan to Tiger Woods. In *How Champions Think: In Sports and In Life*, Rotella wrote that the first essential quality of champions is optimism.[7] Think about that: Rotella is working with people at the absolute highest level of their craft, some who are the best in the world at what they do. Yet he still thinks the positive mind-set—more than anything else—is what makes them champions. "If no one thinks your goals are crazy," Rotella wrote, "you're probably not aiming high enough."[8] *If you didn't lose the ball, then you didn't learn anything.*

A positive mind-set spreads: your approach becomes more dedicated, your outlook is more motivated, and your bounceback becomes stronger. Being optimistic is not just some pie in the sky bull or rose-colored glasses or new age fluff. It's scientifically proven to work. "Optimism, it turns out, is a tremendously powerful predictor of work performance," wrote Shawn Achor in *The Happiness Advantage.* "Studies have shown that optimists set more goals (and more difficult goals) than pessimists, and put more effort into attaining those goals, stay more engaged in the face of difficulty, and rise above obstacles more easily."[9]

When we don't do what needs to be done, we launch a cycle. We feel guilty and shameful, which erodes self-confidence. That eroding self-confidence diminishes our energy and motivation. As those decline, our productivity suffers and our attitude drops. This starts the entire cycle over again.[10]

The same cycle happens for positivity. Success and confidence breed and feed each other; you have no choice but to start with the one that is in your control. One of the best examples of the power of confidence is the four-minute mile, a mark that all the experts claimed could never be broken. Even scientists said it was physically impossible for man to do. But once Roger Bannister first broke it in 1954, it just kept breaking and breaking. People believed it could happen—so it did.* Our minds have enormous power to enlarge or shrink whatever goal we focus on. We can bring our objective closer or push it farther away simply by how we think about it.

The Boston Garden was one of the most hallowed buildings in

---

* Every year an average of twenty Americans break the four-minute mile barrier. If you add in other countries—running powerhouses like Kenya—it's way more. Sure, modern training and nutrition have a great deal to do with it, but we can't underestimate the role that confidence has played in breaking the barrier.

all of sports. It was treated like a cathedral by its fans, a place where championship banners and retired jerseys hang from the rafters as a shrine to the greatest who ever walked on a basketball court. It was a holy place, and everyone thought so—even the Lakers, their most hated rivals.

You know what Celtic legend Larry Bird always called it? "The gym."

Key Point: Earned confidence is the result of knowing yourself, caring about what you do, and committing to getting better. Confidence attracts success.

Remember:

☞ There is nothing more damaging than false confidence and nothing more powerful than properly grounded confidence.

☞ Confidence is a contagious force that shines a light on your work and gives energy to others.

☞ Don't be a jerk, but make sure your confidence comes through in how you talk and do your work.

☞ Earned confidence is a magnetic force that will get you what you want.

Self-Test

Before you move on to part 2, answer these questions:

If you were fired today... how would you get rehired tomorrow?
What would you change and do differently?
Whatever your answer is... what are you waiting for?

PART II

COACH

If you are a *coach*—you need to make a commitment to being a leader. That title is not just handed to you because you hire and fire, have the biggest paycheck, and make the final decisions. True leaders have a **vision** for where their group is going and have developed a **culture** that makes everyone want to work together to get there. They have **character** and are committed to **serving** and **empowering** every member of the team. Above all, they care: about whom they're working with and what they're doing. It is only then that they have earned the title of leader.

CHAPTER SIX

Vision

A person who knows *how* may always have a job, but the person who knows *why* will always be his boss.

—John C. Maxwell

Let's talk about vision.

A great athlete sees where his teammates are going to be—instead of just where they currently are. On the football field, quarterbacks who don't do this will be throwing incomplete passes and interceptions on a regular basis. On the hardwood, the same rule applies. Point guards, the floor generals, are required to see not just where everyone is, but where everyone is headed. Even in a mass tangle of bodies, with so many other things to consider—including their own defender and their own dribble—point guards need to be hyperaware of the direction every player is moving and where each of them will end up.

The truly elite point guards have the vision to see the now—who's cutting to the basket, whose man is late getting back, who's open. But they also have the vision to see five seconds from now:

who's about to spring open, who has lost track of their man, who's about to make a backdoor cut. The ball has to be there when they get there—on time, on target—so in a sense, the point guard has to tell the future. That's vision.

Among active players, few have better court vision than Chris Paul. I met Chris for the first time over a decade ago and had the honor of working his Elite Guard Camp for several years. To Chris's credit, he wasn't just licensing his name to the camp, as some are known to do. Chris was all in and hands-on, participating in every aspect of the camp, every drill and every meal. He walked the walk and the kids noticed. I was enormously impressed.

Of course, the greats never take time off, so even though it was the off-season and Chris had a camp to run, he still had to get in his own practice time as well. He would get up at 5:00 a.m. and do his own full workout (in the weight room and on the court) before camp began each day. His drive to be the best seemed to just relentlessly push him. Chris is one of the most competitive people I have ever met. Whether playing cards, bowling, or shooting hoops, he wants to win so badly. It's just in his blood.

Developing his court vision has made Chris among the top point guards in the NBA, among the best over the last twenty years. At the relatively small height of six feet, he *has* to have great vision to make up for his lack of size. His standards are so high that, according to a reporter, "Even the ball's laces need to match the way that particular teammate likes them."[1] This is a fact that Paul confirmed. "They put the laces on the ball for a reason,"[2] he told an interviewer.

The best point guards, like Chris, have tremendous vision. And they have it in two specific ways:

1. They literally have great court vision, meaning they always position themselves to see as much of the court as possible. Basketball is a game of straight lines and sharp angles. The elite point guards use those angles to improve their vision.

2. They are visionaries in the sense that they have to think one or two plays ahead, similar to a master chess player. They have to anticipate where the defender will shift to or where their teammate will cut to.

Looking Ahead

An athlete needs to have vision off the court as well. The great players are always ahead of the game, learning and implementing what will give them the edge. Ten years ago it was strength and conditioning and nutrition; five years ago it was sports psychology, yoga, and film breakdown/analytics. Soon it will be wearable technology, virtual reality training tools, and customized nutrition and supplementation based on blood types.

Teams are now using physical analytics (for injury predispositions), psychological testing, and profiling to determine whom they will draft. Being a great player just isn't enough anymore—they also have to be great at what the game will evolve into. They have to compete against the next generation of players entering the league, the super-stars of the future, who are going to be the best-prepared generation in the history of the sport.

This goes for successful coaches and general managers as well. They have to think about their own future, and study the future of the game. All professional sports—all businesses, really—are evolving, and the successful ones are the first to understand and accept what those changes are going to be. Houston Rockets general manager Daryl Morey has changed the way basketball is played, watched, and studied because of his early adoption of advanced analytics. When some GMs were still looking at points and rebounds, Morey and his office were inventing "true shooting percentage" (which combines three-pointers, field goals, and free throws) and other advanced statistics.

It's Morey's vision that led the Rockets to the most three-point attempts in history, and to the top of the Western Conference. Now everyone in the league is copying his approach. In the memorable words of sportswriter Tim Cato, "Morey ripped up conventionality, lit it on fire, and launched it into the Gulf of Mexico."[3] Morey has had tremendous success with recent Rockets' teams, which in 2018 came within one win of the NBA Finals. Their success began with Morey's vision to see where the game was headed.

Perhaps most famously, Billy Beane changed how baseball was played, coached, and understood with the Oakland Athletics in the early 2000s (chronicled in Michael Lewis's book *Moneyball*). Scouts and other GMs were still caught in a previous era, relying on the "eye test" and other old clichés about what a real baseball player looked like. When Beane came in with his Harvard sidekick, Paul DePodesta, the old guard all laughed at the duo, with their focus on seemingly trivial statistics like on-base percentage and walks. But Beane was on to something: the future.

The Boston Red Sox won three championships after adapting Beane's system (they tried and failed to hire him), and fifteen years later, all major league teams now have a heavily utilized advanced statistics department. An important aspect of vision is the courage of your convictions—how tightly you hold on when everyone else wants to see you fail or just assumes you will. Those who have vision aren't always embraced or popular, but they end up on top, either through reputation, legacy, or icon status.

> A good player knows where they are on the court. A great player knows where everyone is on the court.
>
> —Don Meyer

The Who and the What

True leaders are magnetic; people want to follow them because they're attracted to the vision that the leader embodies. People have to believe in the who before they follow the what.

In basketball, the greats—Bill Russell, Michael Jordan, and LeBron James—are successful because they carry a vision of success. That vision informs the choices they make and permeates everything they do. Other people are scrambling to get on board because they want to join someone with vision, someone who knows what he wants and how to get there. Getting behind that leader is a way of saying, *I want to be part of bringing that vision to fruition.*

Think about yourself: Do you have a clear vision? Is it communicated? Consistently?

A famous *Inc.* magazine survey drove home how large the gap is between what the bosses think is going on and what the reality is. The magazine first asked executives what percentage of their employees could name the company's three top priorities. The executives guessed 64 percent. They had a rosy—some would say delusional—view of how well they were communicating. When researchers conducted the survey of the employees, the actual number was 2 percent.[4] Two out of 100 employees knew what the company stood for. If you stop and think about how a company's priorities are literally the reason it exists, you realize just how mind-boggling that number is.

Know your vision, and **communicate** your vision. Effective coaches have laser-sharp clarity on where they are headed and what the team can achieve. Just as important, they consistently communicate it and even "sell it" to the doubters they need on board. It's no good being able to spot the iceberg if you can't get the ship to alter its course.

Self-Test

If you're in charge, ask yourself:

- Do your direct reports know what your vision is?
- If I asked them, could they answer? Without any preparation?
- Do you emphasize why everyone is coming to work every day?
- Do you regularly communicate what they are all working toward?
- If you do, how often?
- If not, why not? Is it because you don't know? Is it because you don't think they need to know? Is it because you've never thought about it?

Answering these questions might be a sobering exercise but don't back away. Step into it. It is essential.

Scouting the Future

Vision also involves seeing talent where only potential lies. In sports, one of the jobs of coaches, general managers, and scouts is being able to see a young recruit's future from little but early signs and flashes. The truly talented recruiters can picture what the player can be, not just what he is.

In NBA history, the order of the draft has not once been an accurate predictor of who ultimately became successful in the league. That's not because people didn't do their homework. It's because what a player is now is only an inkling of what he will be. So many other factors stand between now and later. The great visionaries account for these.

Sure, Tim Duncan of the San Antonio Spurs was the number 1 overall draft pick, but the two guys who were just as essential to the Spurs' four titles—Tony Parker and Manu Ginóbli—were nowhere near the top. Tony Parker was the twenty-seventh overall pick, and Ginóbli was picked at the very end of the draft. But Spurs management saw what each of them could become, nurtured their potential, and the rest is history.

In professional sports in the twenty-first century, teams have put so much more into scouting and evaluating now than they did in the past. They know that it is worth their time, money, and focus to vet potential players as thoroughly as possible, instead of rolling the dice and risking being wrong. A poor decision can lead to disastrous contracts, no free agents, and years of last place finishes. Just ask the teams that drafted Greg Oden at number 1 (over Kevin Durant!) and Darko Miličić (number 2 over Carmelo Anthony, Chris Bosh, and Dwyane Wade). If you're scratching your head wondering who in the world Darko Miličić is... *exactly.*

Before a team risks millions of dollars and its future on a single unproven player, every area of his game gets analyzed. Every aspect of his life is probed and considered. The information is integrated together to help a team envision what that player may turn out to be.

It's not just about size, shot selection, and footwork; there are intangibles that have to be determined such as listening skills, motivation, and unselfishness.

Of course, this applies far beyond sports. It's less quantifiable when you're not dealing with athletics, but the top businesses do this, too. They try to get a clear vision of the person *before* the hire is made. Once that employee is in the company's bloodstream, he is going to affect everything else. Airbnb founder Brian Chesky took five months and hundreds of interviews before he hired his first employee—an engineer. He told an interviewer that this first hire was like part of the company's DNA, and he treated the decision with that kind of gravity.[5] A leader has to have the vision to see what an employee can contribute—or take away—before it's too late.

In Amazon's early days, Jeff Bezos used to say that "every time we hired someone he or she would raise the bar for the next hire, so that the overall talent pool was always improving," one of Amazon's first employees, Nicholas Lovejoy, told author Richard L. Brandt. "An employee should think 'I'm glad I got hired when I did, because I wouldn't get hired now.'"[6] That's a remarkable standard, always pumping in a higher level of employee. It's also important for another reason. By always raising the bar, employees never get complacent about their place in the company. It also gives the impression of forward movement—something everyone wants to be a part of.

Pete Philo is a former NBA director of scouting and the owner/president of TPG Sports Group, a renowned basketball talent evaluator. TPG runs Sports Tank, a sports business version of the popular TV show *Shark Tank*, as well as Pro Scout School, which teaches the tools, concepts, and principles of what it takes to be an NBA executive, scout, and general manager. Pete is the epitome of a leader with vision, having seen the future of scouting and talent evaluation before it became the norm. When I met with him, he told me that one of his mentors gave him some powerful advice about vision. "Think about what problems out there *can* be solved," he said, "and from there you'll be surprised how many ideas come into your head."

Climbing over obstacles? That's impressive. Not even seeing them as obstacles, but rather opportunities? That's vision.

The Future

Vision is seeing things before they happen, before people would even consider that they *could* happen. It's Netflix taking down Blockbuster, going from 1/500th the size of the video rental giant to straight up *bankrupting* them ten years later.[7] It's Zappos taking on the entire shoe industry because the company's founders knew that buying and returning shoes were a huge hassle, but if done right, with a streamlined process and top-notch customer service, the whole experience could happen through the mail.

Vision is those few people who saw the future ten years ago: in an interconnected world, people wouldn't mind—and would pay good money—to ride in strangers' cars and stay in strangers' apartments! I grew up in the 1980s and '90s, when this was literally something no one ever would have considered. *No one.* Anyone who says they did is just lying.

Now, the founders of Airbnb and Uber are called geniuses, and using their services is just considered the smart thing to do for transportation and travel accommodations. Leaders keep their eyes on the big picture, often working to get their world to match up with their vision. They aren't afraid of being laughed at, pushed aside, or isolated. If they hold fast to their vision, even against prevailing winds, they end up on top—all alone up there, the mountain to themselves.

Vision is innovative ideas like Google's 20 percent time, where every employee gets prescribed time to work on outside projects of their choosing and invention, which led to successful Google offshoots such as Gmail, AdSense, and Google Talk. *Who would think forcing employees to work less would help them accomplish more?* That's vision.

> Chase the vision, not the money.
>
> —Tony Hsieh, CEO, Zappos

The Balancing Act

Vision requires a difficult but important balancing act: a commitment to one's convictions along with a willingness to adapt. Vision is about dedication, but that shouldn't be mistaken for stubbornness. It's about having a solid foundation so that you can then improvise as needed.

Vision—or lack of it—is behind the fate of all great companies. A lack of vision is why Reebok, which as the top shoe company had its pick of any athlete it wanted, chose *not* to sign Michael Jordan. The reason? In 1984, when Jordan arrived in the NBA, the big men were the superstars. They couldn't conceive of a shooting guard shattering that mold. They were stuck seeing what was instead of what would be.

Lack of vision is why no one carries around BlackBerries anymore even though it wasn't that long ago when everyone had one—or two—in their pocket.

It's why Kodak had to declare bankruptcy in 2012 even though they had figured out digital photography way back in 1975! They chose not to pursue it because they feared it would cut into their own film business.[8]

It's why Blockbuster didn't buy Netflix on the cheap, even though the opportunity was presented to them multiple times. They couldn't see the next step; they just didn't have the vision. "Management and vision are two separate things,"[9] a former Blockbuster executive told *Variety*. Netflix could have been theirs for the relatively paltry sum of $50 million. Just to drive the point home, as of this writing, Netflix has revolutionized how we watch television and movies, has successfully begun to make their own, and is worth $150 billion. To put such a giant number in perspective, they are worth more than *Disney*—and still growing.

Vision requires an openness to exploring the new and not, like Blockbuster and Kodak, being satisfied where you are. Remember: **your comfort zone is your cage.** Protecting a lead just does not work. In sports, the teams that just try to run out the clock don't statistically do as well as they should, especially in football. In Super Bowl LI, the Atlanta Falcons went into the locker room at half-time up 21–3. Then they were up 28–3 in the third quarter. Then, incredibly, they never scored again, losing 34–28. Protecting their lead didn't work. The reason? It sucks all the motivation out of the players. There's no excitement to latch on to. Just letting the clock run down couldn't motivate Atlanta's players the same way a comeback could motivate New England's.

> Change comes from making new rules, new precedents. All the modern advances, the truly breakthrough achievements, have not been built on precedent.
>
> —David Falk, sports agent

The Power of Purpose

Vision means understanding what your purpose is, and everything you do should be tied to your purpose. As my friend and world-renowned expert on customer service Dr. Brian Williams often says, "Don't confuse function with purpose. A chair's *function* is to provide a place for someone to sit down. A chair's *purpose* is to provide comfort."

The function of your company—selling insurance, providing financial advice—is not necessarily its purpose. Its purpose may be to help people buy homes or feel secure or plan for the future. Our purpose is why we get up in the morning—it's the driving force of our lives. A company also needs to have a purpose, one that aligns with its vision. Your purpose is where you are; your vision is where you're headed.

Self-Test

Spend some time thinking about the purpose of your company or organization, especially if you never have. Step outside of what you literally make, do, or provide and dig into what you are offering your customers, your employees, maybe even the world at large.

In one sentence, could you explain what your company's purpose is? How is it different from its function?

The Same Question 2500 Times

Don Yaeger, legendary sports journalist and motivational speaker, knows what it takes to bring vision to fruition. Besides cowriting books with sports icons like John Wooden, Walter Payton, and Joe

Namath, he spent over five years digging into what made teams work, interviewing 110 different ones. His conclusion? "The number 1 teams knew their why," he told me when I interviewed him for my podcast. "They had a sense of purpose."

Vision is a way to ground you. It provides a map, a route, and a guidebook for the twists and turns that inevitably come with any career and in any business. As Don told me, he learned this very early. Before he left his house the morning of his very first day as a sportswriter, his father stopped him in the driveway. He told the young Don that as someone who was going to have the opportunity to "be in the presence of truly extraordinary people, winners," he should think in advance of one question he could ask them. The *same* question. Don followed that advice and singled out one thing: What habit has separated you from competitors?

A few decades and 2500 interviews later, when he retired from *Sports Illustrated*, Don had a deep well to draw from. And he carried that over into the business world. "Employees show up differently when they believe they are working for a cause not a company," Don reiterated to me.

Another important lesson about vision that Don taught me, which he got from Wooden himself, was to surround yourself with the people that will help you become what you want to be. "You will never outperform your inner circle," Wooden told him. "Guard your inner circle like the most valuable asset you have."

NBA player Markelle Fultz, whom I discussed in chapter 1, understood this from a young age and developed an inner circle that didn't just tell him what he wanted to hear. It's why he's now a pro. Vision is not just about ideas; it's about people as well. It means looking to the future and understanding which people in your network help you be the best you, and which are—consciously or not—dragging you down. Surround yourself, personally and profes-sionally, with those who you can envision helping you become the highest achieving version of yourself.

Strategic Vision

We all need day-to-day focus, but without the larger picture—the *vision*—we're not really aware of where we're headed. We may not be headed anywhere at all. We may just be running in circles. Even if we're running full speed, if we have no direction, nothing will come of it but exhaustion and frustration. Then we'll look up and realize we are lost. Or that we haven't gotten anywhere.

Michael Bungay Stanier is an author, motivational speaker, and the founder of Box of Crayons, a renowned coaching program that works with all kinds of businesses. We met at the Heroic Public Speaking Headquarters, a private coaching event for professional speakers and industry leaders. When we found we sailed the same waters, we hit it off. "I like to think of strategy as a visual art," Stanier told me. "You see the destination, you start seeing the paths to get there. Sometimes we get a little obsessed with the path, and we for-get the destination."

Michael understands that the long-term success of any orga-nization or team is determined by the weekly and daily "micro-coaching sessions" that take place. He believes that these brief (10 minutes or less) interactions are the foundation to high performance and a way of keeping everyone aligned with the vision. By checking in with your people often and consistently, you get a strong feel for where their heads are and if they are on course. You also show them you care—which is vital to keeping them on that path.

It's akin to making daily deposits in a bank account. These add up over time. The best part about these mini-coaching sessions is the "player" does the vast majority of the talking. As the "coach," you are simply asking them a series of questions to get them to fully open up about what is going well, what they are finding challenging, and what they need help with.

A strong vision acts like both a blueprint of what you're building and the scaffolding that supports its construction. Some entrepreneurs have ridden their vision from scratch to the top of their field. In 1994, Kevin Plank was a walk-on fullback for the University of Maryland football team. Frustrated by how his sweat weighed him down and affected his ability to remain agile, he started tinkering with different shirt materials. Though Plank had no background in athletic wear, he knew he was on to something. He had *vision* and he had *purpose*. So he did the legwork to figure out how to make his athletic shirt lighter.[10] It sprouted a business, which led to him expanding into other clothing and spreading the word. Plank spent all of his savings, put himself $40,000 in debt, and started a company in his grandmother's basement. He called it Under Armour.

Plank didn't lack for confidence either. Every year he would mail a Christmas card to Nike CEO Phil Knight that read: *You haven't heard about us yet, but you will.* I have no idea if Knight took him seriously; it's hard to imagine he did. But I think Knight has finally gotten the message. Under Armour is now worth around $17 billion and, according to some analysts, could knock Nike off its throne.[11] In 2016 Forbes voted it the sixth most innovative company in the world. Despite its meteoric rise, Under Armour retains, according to Plank, "a walk-on mentality."[12] Though his original company has skyrocketed to the top of the sports world, his vision remains: a scrappy upstart taking on the big guys through attention to detail and quality.

One-Word Vision

Vision means having a clear understanding not just of what your product or service is, but what makes it special. Does it all filter back down into one idea? Think about it: What is the common denominator in everything you do? Can you give one word that captures it?

Most of us are intimately familiar with Apple and its products. Even if you don't own one, you've certainly seen an iPad or iPhone somewhere. There's a unifying principle—a single word, actually—that runs through all their products, going back to their original Mac computers.

Think about an Apple device. Can you guess what it is?

Apple has made a commitment to one word: *Simplicity.* Simplicity is "what drives Apple to create what it creates and behave as it behaves,"[13] wrote Ken Segall, Apple's creative director. Segall is also the man responsible for naming all the "i" products. Steve Jobs was famously maniacal about his vision and had "a deep, almost religious belief in the power of Simplicity."[14] (The word is capitalized throughout Segall's book, just to drive home the point.) Jobs himself wore the same outfit anytime the public saw him—black turtleneck, blue jeans—and became a walking embodiment of the concept.

Even after Jobs's death, simplicity remained the company's watchword. As the technological world gets more complicated, simplicity becomes even more necessary and vital. Jobs's vision continues to inform Apple and its products. Considering all that the iPhone is capable of doing, there are very few buttons on it (I count four on mine). The streamlining continues with each new one (e.g., getting rid of the earphone jack), a testament to the vision of the company's founder. Job wanted to merge the idea of progress and simplicity, recognizing that technology's purpose wasn't about adding complexity but stripping it away.

Other companies have become worldwide brands built off of the vision of one person. In the 1980s marketing director Howard Schultz was working for a small Seattle coffee shop that only sold beans. On a trip to Italy, Schultz was blown away by the coffee culture there, how the shops served as public spaces, and he came back looking to re-create that idea in America. He wanted to invent a "third place" between work and home where people would choose to spend time. He brought this idea to the owners of that coffee bean shop and the rest is history. Starbucks is one of the most ubiquitous companies on earth, up there with McDonald's and Coca-Cola. And it is the result of one man's vision come to life.

Creative Spaces

Vision may begin in one place, inside one person, but it gathers, grows, and expands in the right environment. Whole Foods began in John Mackey's Texas garage, Apple in Steve Jobs's Northern California garage, Amazon in Bezos's Seattle garage. Why garages? A garage is where you can mess around and build things. A garage can accommodate failures and screw-ups; that's practically what they're there for!

Google and Facebook both started in dorm rooms—places where young idealists with more vision than sense saw what others couldn't. A dorm room is a kind of incubator, and though Facebook is a billion-dollar juggernaut, it got off the ground because of the same like-minded camaraderie that you and your college friends shared with each other. Instead of committing themselves to watching sports or finding girls or getting drunk, Mark Zuckerberg and his roommates worked on his website. He had a vision and they helped him execute it. Vision is a type of faith in yourself and those around you. When you're young and surrounded by like-minded people, it's easier to hold your vision close. Naïveté can sometimes be an asset. There's an innocence to open eyes.

Airbnb started in a living room with an idea and an air mattress: one of the founders met a guy at a yard sale who needed a place to stay. Now Airbnb has more rooms than the world's largest hotel chains. "I think you must always live and think like a child. Or have that childlike curiosity and wonder," cofounder Brian Chesky told an interviewer. "That's probably the most important trait you can have, especially as an entrepreneur."[15] His cofounder, Joe Gebbia, said that, "Great ideas start out as polarizing." People *should* either love or hate your idea—that means it matters. It moves people in some way. It shows you're not acting out of fear; you're open to taking that big swing. You might strike out—but you refuse to strike out looking.

Vision is not about predicting what everyone will love or how to become the most popular idea. It's about putting your horses behind the *right* idea. Former athlete and motivational speaker Lewis Howes has said that you need a strong enough vision that it becomes your default setting. So those mornings you're less motivated or structured, you can still see the big picture. You plug into your vision and let it take you.[16] Having vision is a built-in GPS directing you where to go or a compass always pointing you in the right direction. Without vision, leaders are just scrambling and everyone else can tell. It affects and infects the rest of the company.

Studies show that more and more employees are tuning out at work. A recent Gallup poll found that a full *two-thirds* of workers were not engaged at work. That's a staggering number. Picture it, 66 percent of American workers, parked at their desks, inside their cubicles, just tuning out. Worldwide, only 13 percent of adults are engaged in what they do.[17] A poll in 2015 also found that *70 percent* of people "hate" their jobs,[18] which is useful for all bosses and managers to keep in mind.

As a coach, your vision provides not just the road map, but the car, the available seats, and the engine to people who are looking for something to join. Make sure you're providing these things. Day-to-day work should never drown out the larger purpose. If you feel like your people are losing their way, find methods to bring your vision to the forefront. Remind them of it in meetings, e-mails, and conversations. Put them to work on long-term projects that excite them. Discuss with employees what their individual role has to do with achieving the larger vision. Seek their input on how that vision can be brought to life. All these little things will feed into the whole, giving your people a sense of purpose and an understanding of the big picture. It will also keep them connected to you and your larger goals.

> There's nothing you can do about where the pieces are. It's only your next move that matters.
>
> —Steve Jobs

Selling Vision

I don't believe there's such a thing as a "million-dollar idea." The phrase implies that all you have to do is come up with an idea and the money will start flowing in. But that's not how it works. It's never once worked like that. Vision doesn't stop with coming up with an idea; if it did, there would be way more billionaires sitting around thinking up more ideas. It's about executing that idea, and that execution requires others' help. You have to *sell your vision* by building a dedicated and tight circle that feels strongly connected to you and to it. True leaders live and die by their vision and get others to do so as well. Communicating your vision is a must. According to the Carnegie Institute of Technology, "85% of your financial success is due to your personality and ability to communicate, negotiate, and lead. Only 15% is due to technical knowledge."[19]

Vision is about carrying both the big and the small, the now and the later, the intangible concept and the tangible steps. "The most productive people push themselves to come up with big goals," wrote Charles Duhigg in *Smarter Faster Better*, "and then have a system for breaking them into manageable parts."[20] Draw a connection between what you ultimately want to accomplish, along with what you want your organization to be, and then break it all down into the manageable steps it will take to get there.

"Any vision, however far-reaching, remains only a fantasy unless steps are taken to realize it," Maury Klein wrote in *The Change Makers*, a book that profiles the greatest entrepreneurs of the last 150 years. "What separates the great artist from the ordinary practitioner is not only grandeur of vision but, even more, the ability to bring it to fruition."[21] Remember, the word "vision" in business is usually associated with predicting the future, but the word itself is simpler than that: it just means to see. No one will see exactly what you can see. Keep your eyes open.

Key Point: Vision means understanding the future of your game and your team's purpose and funneling everything you all do toward that ultimate goal.

Remember:

☞ Leaders understand big-picture thinking—how today is connected to yesterday and to tomorrow.

☞ In the day-to-day, a leader keeps eyes on the whole, through forethought, connection, and commitment.

☞ A leader doesn't chase the popular idea. He creates the right idea.

☞ Don't forget the importance of selling your vision, inspiring and convincing other committed people to get on board.

CHAPTER SEVEN

Culture

> The role of a leader is not to come up with great ideas. The role of a leader is to create an environment in which great ideas can happen.
>
> —Simon Sinek

If vision begins in the mind, culture begins on the ground. Culture is the collective values, beliefs, behaviors, and environment of a team, group, or organization. A positive culture grows organically in an environment where everyone feels inspired, safe, and appreciated. Those who are part of a successful culture feel that their contribution and role matter, that they are being challenged to grow and develop, that they couldn't just be replaced tomorrow without the organization missing a beat. If, as a coach, you create that type of environment, then you create the fertile ground for people to become the best versions of themselves.

Celtics Culture

Culture, even in the most storied organizations, doesn't just appear, and it doesn't automatically regenerate itself. It requires someone at the helm who is committed to developing and maintaining that culture. I can't think of a better embodiment of this fact than Brad Stevens.

In the span of four years, Brad Stevens went from coaching men's basketball at Butler University, a small Division I school, to two straight national championship games, to one of the most iconic role in sports: head coach of the winningest franchise in NBA history, the Boston Celtics. Oh, and he landed the job at thirty-six years old.

If Stevens's tale had ended there, it would still be a success story. However, Stevens didn't just get the highly coveted job; he has been universally acclaimed as a runaway success. Under Stevens, the Celtics are now regularly at the top of the Eastern Conference, and a legitimate contender to make the NBA Finals. Even adversity, injury, and constant change haven't stopped him.

In the 2017–2018 season the Celtics had only four returning players from the previous year. Then they lost their highly touted new player—Gordon Hayward—for the season on opening night; they went through the season with seven rookies on a roster of twelve, and were almost first in the league in total salary lost to injury.[1] Yet they were *still* a contender for the best record in their conference. Then their best player—Kyrie Irving—went down before the playoffs started. And *still* they were one win away from that year's Finals. Without taking anything away from the remaining players who worked their butts off, their collective success is a testament to the environment Stevens had developed.

When Stevens arrived, he came into a storied franchise that had fallen on tough times. However, he refused to be intimidated by the way things were done, the way they had always been done. Think about the courage that required: a college coach—from a relatively small school—gets that rare ticket to the NBA. Improbably, he is handed the keys to one of the most of iconic teams in professional sports. However, when he gets there, he doesn't bow to an entrenched way of doing things. He takes it all head-on and knows immediately what he has to do first to turn things around: change the culture.

Even with an organization like the Celtics, with its famed arenas, its history of championship banners, and its long line of Hall of Famers, building a culture requires work. Culture is a living thing; it has to be embedded in the people and those people have to *choose* to pass it on.

Think about all the laminated packets that are passed out to new hires or stapled photocopies distributed at company meetings that are tossed in the recycle bin. I'm sure whoever wrote those up and put them together felt they were communicating the culture, but that's not how it works. It's not a one-way thing. A culture isn't born when someone reads it on the page. You can't just say it aloud and expect it to exist. It has to come to life through people.

Stevens understands motivation, what works and what doesn't. I attended a talk he gave where he explained that the key to confidence is not just getting better, but rather *knowing* you got better. A leader has to find ways to show his players they are improving, through communication, feedback, and rewards. You have to care enough, be committed enough to building a culture, to give those things to your people.

When I interviewed Stevens for my podcast, he told me that he looks for assistants who are "intelligent, creative, hardworking, and humble..." Stevens understands that each addition to the team can affect, improve, or even damage team culture and cohesion. "It's silly to think that staff chemistry doesn't affect team chemistry," he said. Think about the type of people you are bringing in and the type you are letting go; each of these choices add or subtract from the team. A hiring or firing isn't just between employee and boss—it reverberates around the entire company. A true leader is hyperaware of how each decision affects the group or company at large. Stevens cares enough about the culture he's fostering with the Celtics to constantly be evaluating how his decisions fit into the team's larger dynamics and goals.

I asked Stevens how, back when he was a college coach, he would create this buy-in from his players, many of who were the best in their respective high schools. It was something he again had to do in the NBA, with players who were the best at their respective colleges. "Each player brings great strengths to the table," he told me, "and it's incumbent on us coaches to best maximize each strength." I've been around and spoken to enough people who have coached at the highest level. It's extremely difficult to keep a unified culture together with twelve guys, all with healthy egos, who are getting paid serious money just to lace up their sneakers.

Stevens has a wisdom that far surpasses his age and an ability to empathize with all the various role players on his team. He recognizes things are tough for those on the bench, and he told me he works to "help guys understand there can be great progress and growth without playing time, there can be great value added... there's nothing like winning as a team, and we can all add value to that, that's ultimately what we have to try to do."

A lifelong learner, Stevens told me he reaches out to business leaders and those in other industries because of the universal qualities that are shared between business and sports. "If you surround yourself with the right people, and you work for empowering leaders, you can always just focus on the process," he told me. With the culture Stevens has put in place in Boston, the Celtics look like they will be contenders for a long time. Even if the players change, as they are bound to do, the culture will remain in place.

How the Car Runs

Culture may be best defined as that which exists when the boss isn't around. There's a similarity with parenting—what your kid does in front of you doesn't necessarily reflect your parenting. What he does when you're not around? That's much more accurate.

When Golden State Warriors head coach Steve Kerr, suffering from a debilitating back injury, was unable to be on the bench for the 2017 playoffs, the team still brought home another NBA championship. Didn't this show that Kerr didn't matter? Was Kerr unnecessary? Actually, *the opposite*. Because Kerr had laid the groundwork with his players, he didn't need to physically be there. He developed a culture that was so strong it remained intact even when he wasn't present.

The Warriors are stacked with talent, but anyone who understands basketball knows that alone isn't enough. Kerr's role is enormously valuable, more than any single star player. *Sports Illustrated*'s Chris Ballard wrote that even if you think the Warriors are pretty much a self-driving car, "someone has to design and maintain the car."[2] Remember, they had almost all of that talent back when Mark Jackson was coach, with little to show for it.

Part of Kerr's personality is outright humility, which might make his importance invisible to the casual observer. As a coach, he goes out of his way not to make it about himself. This creates the illusion that he stays in the background. But in reality, he is the ground itself. Part of the culture Kerr has established with Golden State is that the players are the focus. He takes less credit than he deserves because that ultimately doesn't matter to him; what he cares about is how his players feel about the group. A coach who takes too much credit isn't going to have much to take credit for. His players are going to resent it, and it will affect the team's performance.

According to Warrior's all-star forward Draymond Green, Kerr has built "a culture of empowerment,"[3] which may look like players are running the show. But that doesn't mean they actually are. This is why, during the 2018 season, Kerr comfortably let his players run time-outs, drawing up X's and O's in the huddle. He could trust them because they were working within a culture he had created. Once your vision is established, culture is what you create to incubate your vision and execute it. It's how you keep the car running.

A Culture of Connection

At Duke, a place where the culture has been consistent for decades, Coach Mike Krzyzewski spends the first team meeting every year connecting each player's actions to the larger organization—how what each player does reflects on Duke basketball and the university as a whole. "Remember that whatever happens to you, happens to all of us,"[4] he tells them, and he uses that both positively (*we're a family*) and negatively (*don't screw up*). The culture Coach K has established ties everyone together.

In an interview on Paul Rabil's *Suiting Up* podcast, Jay Williams told a great story about sitting down across from Coach K as a sixteen-year-old. Coach K referred to him as "Mr. Williams," which had a profound effect on young Jay; it made him feel like an adult.[5] Coach K didn't promise Williams, a highly coveted recruit, playing time, an NBA career, or stardom. But he did say, "I promise you that by the time you leave here you will be prepared for life."

That simple message flipped a switch for the young prospect. Williams wrote in his memoir that he then understood it was "about becoming a man...being challenged to think about my future as a man would."[6] What Coach K wants for his players is so much fuller and deeper than just basketball. It's one of the main reasons he has been such a long-term success, as have his players.

Buying In

Buy-in means that the members of your organization choose to embrace, share, and maintain the culture a coach is trying to create. A culture doesn't exist because someone at the top says so. It's brought to life by being accepted and reinforced among the rest of the group. Culture requires *consent*.

In his book *Start with Why: How Great Leaders Inspire Everyone to Take Action*, Simon Sinek champions the need for businesses to build a buy-in culture. A buy-in culture defines a purpose, creates a sense of loyalty, and makes everyone happy to serve the whole. Genuine leadership means that others willingly follow you, he explains, not because they have to, but because they *want to.*

One technique a smart leader does is to get the influencers on his side, those whom he knows will trigger a wave of acceptance across the rest of the organization. If you're looking to win over a group, figure out whom to target. *Who can move the crowd?*

A great example of this is from one of my all-time favorite movies, *Hoosiers*. Outsider coach Norman Dale (Gene Hackman) comes to small-town Indiana, a place not open to newcomers, and has a rough time coaching the high school basketball squad. He knows his days are numbered, and instead of trying to recruit the reluctant prodigy Jimmy Chitwood to join the team, he makes a point of giving the kid space, leaving him be, and talking one on one with him in an empathetic manner. He talks to Chitwood about his love for basketball but never once pressures him or even asks him to join the team. This is despite the fact that the whole town is telling him it's the only way for Coach Dale to save his job. The strategy pays off big time: When Jimmy agrees to come back on the team and play—he says he will only do it for Dale. After that, the team and the whole town get in line and they start rattling off wins. Chitwood was the pressure point and Coach Dale knew exactly how to press it.

Leadership isn't about forcing others in a direction; it's about moving ahead and trusting others will follow. Trusting they will *want* to follow. If they are working within a positive culture, they will be there—and you won't even have to keep checking if they're right behind you. Create an environment where the best ideas win, where everyone feels involved, and the whole is bigger than any individual part.

> Reward thoughtful failure.
>
> —Google maxim

Google Culture

Google didn't become a half-trillion-dollar phenomenon and the home base of the Internet by playing it safe. Its culture has always been one where the bosses encourage a healthy amount of trying and failing, throwing stuff at the wall and seeing what sticks. Google has produced some winners (Gmail, AdSense) and some losers (Google Glass) but that's the culture: *swing big.* It's the embodiment of the old adage—you miss 100 percent of the shots you don't take.

"If you're achieving all your goals," wrote former Google senior vice president Laszlo Bock, "you're not setting them aggressively enough."[7] *If you didn't lose the ball, you didn't learn anything.* In fact, at X, the arm of Google that is tasked with experimenting and trying out its craziest projects, the executives give out bonuses and vacation time for teams that choose to *end* their projects.[8]

Yep, you read that right. Employees get bonuses for giving up.

The reason? Google knows that countless man-hours and company dollars are often sunk on things that simply don't work but no one wants to say so. X's strategy is to encourage people to admit their mistakes rather than, out of pride, plowing wasted time and money into them. This strategy is an integral part of Google's culture, which doesn't just pay lip service to healthy failure—it lives it.

Besides motivating employees to go big and think different, there's a flatness to Google's structure. Senior executives at the company receive the same benefits and resources as the newly hired. The top men and women don't get their own parking spots or executive bathrooms or dining rooms.[9] "As a leader," Bock wrote, "giving up status symbols is the most powerful message you can send that you care about what your teams have to say."[10] If your company doles out privileges for senior management, think about why that is. What message does it send? Is it supposed to be a motivator? A status symbol? Why do certain titles merit their own bathroom and parking space and others don't?

A strong culture keeps an organization on track—especially when things are tough—and gives employees a sense of, and a hand in, the bigger picture. A positive culture increases efficiency, effectiveness, and productivity, while a poor culture lowers morale, increases attrition, and undermines every aspect of team cohesion. If an outsider were to wander into your office and observe fifteen minutes of your company's workday, would the organization's identity be clear? What about its standards? Its culture?

Don't forget: your people are your most important tool and your primary competitive advantage. You can copy products. You can copy services. You can copy technology. It's very hard to copy culture, and that culture is supported and spread by your people. As a coach, keep in mind that how you treat your people is an important part of that culture. If they feel valued, they will help lift up the team. If they don't, they won't bother or they'll only be out for themselves.

A Gallup poll revealed that the number one cause of employee attrition (65%) is poor management and leadership. According to Robert Levering and Milton Moskowitz, who were the originators of *Fortune*'s annual Best 100 Places to Work survey, "The key to creating a great workplace was not a prescriptive set of employee benefits, programs, and practices, but the building of high-quality relationships in the workplace."[11] Building meaningful relationships is the most effective way to keep your employees grounded, connected, and motivated. It's the foundation for a winning culture.

Self-Test

Here's a weekly employee check-in to improve job satisfaction and culture.* Consider typing up a version of it to hand out to employees.

> Last week I used my strengths when...
> Last week I added value to the team when...
> Last week I did the following tasks I enjoyed:
> Last week I felt valued and utilized when...
> These are my priorities for next week:
> This is what I need help with next week:

---

* Credit goes to Dr. Brian Williams, who showed me this.

Leaders: Addressing these weekly check-ins is not extra work. It is your work!

Negative People

Culture, especially while it is first being established, can be a fragile thing. One strong personality can poke holes in it or tear it down. Part of a company's culture is how it deals with people like this—or even if these people are allowed in the door in the first place. At his department at Stanford University, management science professor Robert I. Sutton famously instituted what his team called the "no a-hole rule." It's a test he and his colleagues use when deciding whether or not they want to work with someone. They simply ask, "Would this hire violate the no a-hole rule?"[12]

I absolutely love this—it's direct, simple, and supremely effective. Negative people are like viruses, and their attitudes spread and seep into every aspect of a workplace. "They are the Fellowship of the Miserable," Sutton wrote, "and they are the killers of the dream."[13] They look for reasons why things won't work, rather than exploring why they *could* work.

In his book *The No Asshole Rule*, Sutton goes further. He doesn't just use anecdotal evidence of his own experience. Following his training, he took an evidenced-based look at "assholes'" influence in the workplace. "The damage that assholes do to their organizations," Sutton found, "is seen in the costs of increased turnover, absenteeism, decreased commitment to work, and the distraction and impaired individual performance documented in studies of psychological abuse, bullying, and mobbing."[14]

One me-oriented person has the power to bring the entire operation crashing to the ground. These types of people are enormously powerful and influential forces, as any classroom teacher can attest. The New Zealand All Blacks, a rugby team that has had more success than just about any other team in professional sports, has a similar rule with even more colorful language: "No Dickheads."[15] These are rough-and-tumble guys playing a high-contact sport, but that doesn't mean they don't require a supportive culture in which to succeed. That doesn't mean they want to play with a-holes.

Selfishness, negativity, and bad attitudes need to be kept out. If they slip in, they need to be extricated. If they remain, they become part of the culture. Leaders need to recognize that if they allow a behavior, they are endorsing that behavior. It's that simple. Remember: *Leadership is not what you say. Leadership is what you accept.*

Culture as Value

Michael Bungay Stanier, author of *The Coaching Habit*, is an expert in business leadership and what it takes to build a winning culture. When I interviewed him, he told me, "Culture can be thought of as the habits of the people who work in that organization, the things we do each day without really thinking about it that make up 'how we really care about and how we really do things around here.' So to change your culture, change your habits."

A culture is something that will eventually grow and spread. You have control in the beginning, but after that, you're at the mercy of what develops on its own. That's why the word "culture" reminds us of something growing in a dish in chemistry class. We set up the environment and then it just does what it naturally wants to do under those conditions.

Around his UCLA players, John Wooden eventually stopped talking about winning at all; he wouldn't even say the word! He claimed not to have mentioned it as a goal in the last thirty years of his illustrious career. His standard of success was defined differently than most other coaches, and he wanted a culture in his locker room that didn't overvalue winning. "A good leader is a good salesperson," he once said. "What are you selling? What is your philosophy? What is success?"[16]

Self-Test

What is *your* team's definition of success?

Is the culture in your organization based on money? Titles? Or is it something intangible?

If you recognize that your company or team's culture is unproductive or even toxic, what steps can you take—*today*—to start changing it?

Open Culture

Another important part of culture is a sense of openness. If no one shares what they think, the culture becomes one of fear, suspicion, and failure. Problems fester in an environment where everyone is afraid to tell the boss what's going on. "If you expect a culture of trust," my friend Jay Bilas wrote, "you have to build and foster a culture of truth."[17] Though cultures will vary from business to business, honesty and trust are bedrock concepts for all organizations.

It's the leader's job to create an environment where everyone feels safe enough to speak up. I once heard this Wall Street story about a lower-tier employee at an investment firm—let's call him Marc—who had misplaced $30 million. That's right—he *misplaced it*. He didn't lose the money; in the way of financial companies, it just couldn't be located right away. And it took a few days to find it.

Marc apparently worked for a real yeller, a boss who loved to make examples out of employees in a public and embarrassing way. Since Marc was terrified, he began a series of cover-ups and evasions to buy time until the money was found. After a couple of days, the money was located and everything was fine.

Then, the big boss, an executive, called Marc and Marc's immediate boss into the office. Marc was caught, and he had to fess up. As Marc told his story, the executive listened and recognized that the real issue was not the mistake, but the cover-up Marc felt compelled to engage in. Then the executive made a decision: he fired *Marc's boss*. The executive determined that the problem was not the isolated mistake Marc made, but the culture the boss had been responsible for creating.

The Zappos Experience

One of the most impressive examples of culture in action is Zappos. On a trip to Las Vegas, I took the Zappos Tour Experience, a perk that the company provides to anyone who wants to see their headquarters, learn their history, and witness their unique culture firsthand. Zappos CEO Tony Hsieh has described Zappos as a "business that combined profits, passion, and purpose."[18] And a visit to the company's operations center told me that these aren't just inert words on a page. These are ideas that the company lives.

Though Zappos is a billion-dollar company, you wouldn't think so from wandering around their office. Rather than a staid corporate feel, the lobby was colorful and inviting, with bright mosaics on the wall and tons of Zappos swag and memorabilia. The receptionists were casually dressed with huge smiles and infectious energy. On the wall behind the front desk was a collage of severed neckties.

"What are those?" I asked the receptionist.

"Anytime someone shows up to a job interview in a tie," she answered, "we whip out our scissors and cut it off on the spot. We are not a coat-and-tie kind of company!"

On the tour, I noticed that the place was designed for both function and fun. Desks were situated in big open spaces to create a sense of community and encourage open communication. Employees had permission to decorate their areas however they wanted. This promoted warmth and individualism within the confines of the group. There were plenty of indoor and outdoor common areas for lounging and snacking. Zappos' call center is decorated like an ongoing birthday party, with a general air of celebration all around. There were white boards with goals listed in fat markers and thank-you cards from customers adorning the cubicles. Everything was open and inviting. It honestly felt like a giant family.

It's not just on display for the tour. This is what Zappos is. Every employee at Zappos must memorize its ten Core Values, things like "#3: Create Fun and a Little Weirdness" and "#7: Build a Positive Team and Family Spirit." To log in to their computers in the morning, employees are asked to identify the face of a random employee and are then given a brief bio on that employee.

There's a genuine sense that the bosses at Zappos care about the employees and go out of their way to show it. Executives check in on employees' morale through surveys about purpose, happiness, and workplace community. Every year the company assembles the Zappos Culture Book—which contains employees' (unedited) thoughts on their feelings about working at Zappos. They put out an "Ask Anything" monthly newsletter, which is anonymous and, thus, actually worth reading. Think about what you could say, hear, and learn about your workplace if people genuinely felt they could speak up?

Zappos' process is the same as that of any winning sports team. They establish their identity, standards, and culture, and then they recruit top talent that fits. They make sure to have the *right* people on their team. There is no distinction at Zappos between best and right; it's the same thing. It can take up to ninety days and seven interviews before they know if an employee is suitable for the company. There's even a specific interview that is designed just to ensure that the employee is a culture fit.[19]

The Zappos attrition rate is less than 2 percent—which is unheard of. That's almost nonexistent turnover. Zappos is so committed to making sure the hire is a good fit that they put forth a seemingly insane fail-safe. After three weeks of training, Zappos actually offers each hire $4000 just to walk away, no questions asked. It's to see if the hire values the easy money or not.[20] They want to know if working for the company matters more than a quick check, and this is the best way to find that out before they begin a relationship with that person.

When he was twenty-eight, Zappos CEO Tony Hsieh sold his first company, LinkExchange, to Microsoft for a quarter-billion dollars. The reason he did it was not what you'd think: he wasn't cashing in. The company culture had become so poisonous, Hsieh admitted to an interviewer, that he "dreaded getting out of bed in the morning."[21]

In case you think Hsieh is full of it, he even walked away early after the sale, not getting the full amount of money he could have from the Microsoft purchase. That's how miserable he was. When he arrived at Zappos, Hsieh decided "never again." From that point forward he would put culture front and center.[22] That's how he built the company into a powerhouse. Their culture has become the DNA of the company. It's not just printed on the walls. Every employee lives it.

> There is only one way to get anybody to do anything. And that is by making them want to do it.
>
> —Dale Carnegie

The Power of Owning

Coaches, especially coaches of young men and women, instinctively understand how to get buy-in. With no money or advancement involved, the motivation has to be all intrinsic: the best coaches understand how to tap into this.

At Montrose Christian High School, where I served as the basketball team's performance coach, Coach Stu Vetter always used to talk about the difference in mind-set between renting and owning. When you rent something—like an apartment or a car—you view it as temporary. Because it's not yours, you don't value it as much and you don't take as good care of it. We rent things when we are young, careless, and in a state of transition.

When we're mature, we buy.

When you buy, you have ownership. Because of that connection, you care much more because it's yours. *It's an extension of you.* Those who look at a job as just a step on the ladder or a paycheck are a drag on that place's culture. They're renting their job and it shows. It is vital that you, as a leader, create and sustain a culture where everyone sees the company as an extension of themselves. That's how you get their all. They will walk through fire for the company because it's a part of who they are. That's the power of culture.

Key Point: Culture is the environment (both physical and psychological) that a leader creates to make his people motivated, committed, and secure. It is spread and maintained by everyone else.

Remember:

☞ It is the leader's job to prepare the soil that will maximize others' potential and encourage them to be as productive as possible.

☞ Leadership doesn't simply happen. You must be intentional about generating and developing it.

☞ A leader who creates a strong culture knows that it's not about forcing people to follow you—it's about making them want to.

☞ Cultures will vary, but all leaders must create a culture of respect for everyone to thrive in.

☞ A group's culture is best reflected through how members act when the boss is not around.

CHAPTER EIGHT

Servant

> Because you really listen, you become influenceable. And being influenceable is the key to influencing others.
>
> —Stephen Covey

As we dig deeper to examine what makes an effective leader, it's important that we get something straight. Whether you're a CEO, manager, coach, or good old-fashioned boss, you work *for* your people. They don't work for you.

Stop. *Read that again.*

Do you believe it?

You work *for them.*

Maybe you thought being in charge meant people did what you want, no questions asked. Maybe you figure that you pay their salary, can hire, fire, demote, and promote them, so that should be all the motivation they need. But you're wrong. If that's the only motivation you give them, you will never get their best. You will continually just get part of them, and likely not the best part.

However, when you shift your focus from yourself to them,

things will drastically change. Remember: People are not loyal to jobs. They are not loyal to businesses. They are loyal to *other people*. Effective leadership creates strong loyalty.

And loyalty creates commitment.

And commitment strengthens culture.

And as we discussed in the last chapter, culture produces results.

Now, let's look at how to serve your people and why it matters.

The Servanthood of Pop

Servanthood is about understanding what is best for your people, seeing the work from their point of view, and making sure you give them what they need. One way to do that is to make sure you always involve people in the work that affects them. They will recognize the authentic connection that you have cultivated, and then they will buy in to what you have created.

In the summer of 2017, when San Antonio Spurs forward LaMarcus Aldridge went to head coach Gregg Popovich and asked to be traded, Popovich was stunned. Pop admitted that in his twenty-plus years of coaching, which includes five championships, a player had never done that. Not once. But the coach's reaction is one of the reasons why he's an all-time great. It also ended up changing Aldridge's mind.

What did Popovich do when one of his best players asked to be traded? He took the blame.[1] He owned up to what he had done wrong and gave the player an opening to give him another chance. Pop worked it out with Aldridge, who decided to stay, and the player has since flourished with the Spurs. And because Pop is who he is, he took it one step further. He accepted the blame publicly, telling ESPN: "It became apparent to me that it really was me...total overcoaching."[2] The humility is impressive but what hits me the most is how Popovich understood that he was there to serve his players. And he had not been serving Aldridge properly.

Most coaches will tell you, *I'm not only a coach, I'm a relationship person. Basketball is just the platform and vehicle I use.* It's not about teaching how to put a ball into the basket; that's just the mechanism. It's about something so much bigger. Legendary coach P. J. Carlesimo told me during an interview for my podcast that the best advice he ever got was: "Relationships with your players is more important than your X's and O's." P. J. nailed it. Without a personal foundation, the smartest play or the best idea won't matter. It'll never get executed properly if the player and coach aren't connected on another level.

Self-Test

Be honest.

1. Think about those who work under you. If they would list— anonymously—the three characteristics that best describe you, what do you think they'd write?

2. What would you *like* those three characteristics to be?

Coach Rav's Long Arms

I've been fortunate to meet with some of the all-time great coaches, and one common thread that links all of them is that they are never the kind of people who are out for themselves. They are connectors, givers, and sharers. They are servants to their players.

Former college basketball coach and director of International Basketball for Nike George Raveling is a legend in the sports world.

His career includes time as head coach for Iowa, Washington State, and USC; assistant coach for Villanova, Maryland, and the 1984 US Men's Basketball Team at the Olympics (where he coached young Michael Jordan and Patrick Ewing); and induction into both the Professional Basketball and the College Basketball Hall of Fame.* Raveling has been labeled a pioneer, an innovator, and a trailblazer, but almost everyone just calls him Coach Rav.

Coach Rav is one of the game's most revered mentors. His "mentor tree," the list of his mentees who have gone on to have exceptional careers, is unparalleled. As the host of two basketball podcasts—the *Hardwood Hustle* and the *Pure Sweat Basketball Show*— I recorded over a hundred interviews with basketball coaches. And in most of them, either on or off air, I've asked the guest, "Who has had the most profound impact on your career?"

No joke, George Raveling's name came up about 75 percent of the time. He was that influential. I met Coach Rav dozens of times over the years and have always appreciated his presence and authenticity. He is a good man. He's known for being a voracious reader, often bringing books as a gift when meeting with someone. In his compelling talks, he always makes a point of covering all the important aspects of coaching that do *not* take place on the court.

When I interviewed him, I asked him about servant leadership, which is not as commonly understood as it should be. "The fundamental intent of an authentic servant leader is to consistently serve the needs of those who follow," he told me. "Servant leadership is inherent in us as people."

What was astounding to me was that Raveling, eighty years old

---

* Cool side note: As a young man, Raveling was working security next to the podium where Martin Luther King Jr. gave his famous "I Have a Dream" speech in 1963. When it was over, Raveling asked King for the text, and King gave it to him. He still has it.

and having risen to the peak of multiple professions, still spoke of servanthood. "Every human being was placed on Earth to serve the needs of others," he told me. "For me it is a most important priority. It affords me the unique opportunity to consistently practice kindness, humility, courage, sacrifice, gratitude, motivation, socialization, and sensitivity." It was clear talking to him why so many coaches and players look up to this man. It's because he looked up to each of them.

Coach Cal and Connection

Watching great coaches in action is another way to get a sense of how they serve their team and the overall mission of the program. Several years ago I had the unique opportunity to watch the University of Kentucky's first basketball practice of the year and their Midnight Madness event. Midnight Madness is the start of the college basketball season, which kicks off with a giant pep rally and the team's first practice. It's such a big event that it's televised on ESPN and students camp outside the arena to ensure they get tickets.

It was future superstar Anthony Davis's freshman year, and I was excited to witness the festivities. But while the Midnight Madness was for show, the practice itself was definitely not. Coach Calipari coached his players hard. He was extremely demanding, but never demeaning, and he held his players accountable for everything they did. He didn't let up once.

Calipari explained to his players that the reason he pushes them so hard and holds them to such a high standard is because he cares about them. He wants to help them achieve their dreams, both short term (winning a national title) and long term (getting drafted in the NBA, becoming better men). Coach Cal emphasized to his players, who were getting run ragged, that they should be thankful to have people in their lives who care enough to hold them accountable.

Serving his players is at the center of everything John Calipari does as the Wildcats' coach, which besides Coach K's job, may be the most prestigious in college basketball. Calipari even titled his book *Players First*. At Kentucky, he ensures the culture is player centered and player focused. Coach Cal wrote that he believes that institutions should serve people and not vice versa.[3] I agree wholeheartedly. Sometimes an organization or corporation takes on such size and influence that we forget that it's the people who are its heart. The people are the ones who matter, and the company will live or die through those people.

At the center of the billion-dollar business that is college sports, and as the leader of one of its most hallowed teams, Calipari doesn't waver from this focus. Whether it's making note of where each player wants the ball when the game is on the line or individually asking the players what their "why" is, Calipari serves their interests. By centering everything he does on their growth as players and as people, he embodies the idea of a servant leader.

I am friends with Kentucky assistant coach Joel Justus, Calipari's longtime right-hand man. When I interviewed him for my podcast, he told me, "Coaching elite talent all starts with relationships. It's 100 percent that they know we are about them." In any coaching scenario, "If that young man or woman knows that you are for them, you got a chance. That's what Coach Calipari stresses to us... these guys have to know we're about them or we can't ask them to do anything." Part of that is recognizing that everyone talks. Some people listen. Very few connect. *Be a connector.*

When Calipari recruits, he talks about the player, his family, and his dreams. "They know we're about them," Justus told me. As a consequence, in the future, when the coaches ask something of the players, "It's already been established... this guy who's telling me to do this wants the best for me." Leaders lay this foundation early and return to it often—*I am here to serve you. Let me know what you need, what your goals are, and I'll help you get there.*

When I asked Justus to tell me the biggest thing he learned from Calipari, he told me it was that "this business, if it's about anything, it's about people. It's about caring for these young people and letting them know 'I'm for you'... if a kid knows that you're for them, the sky's the limit."

The same goes for a boss, manager, or CEO. If your employees truly believe that you have their backs, that you're looking out for their best interests, that you're there to serve them, you'll never have to worry about their commitment or their effort.

Self-Test

What Language Are You Speaking?

The 5 Love Languages by Gary Chapman is one of the most influential and impactful books I've ever read.

The premise is basic: We all feel, process, and interpret love differently. How I receive love is going to be different from how you receive love. You may need quality time, whereas I may need words of affirmation. Someone else may need acts of service, physical touch, or actual gifts. The result of these various languages is that if you don't speak your partner's primary love language, they won't feel the love you are offering. You might as well be speaking to them in Mandarin.

This is a powerful lesson, but it goes outside romantic relationships into our other relationships, including those in the workplace. It's helpful to swap out the word "love" for "appreciation." Think about your Appreciation Language at work. If you are in charge, do you know the primary Appreciation Language of those who work for you?

Are you rewarding a job well done with a Starbucks gift card, even though that person would prefer an afternoon off? Are you giving them an afternoon off when all they want is to be praised in front of the team? Are you praising them in front of the team—even though that embarrasses them—when all they really want is a tangible reward? As a leader, you need to know what motivates your people, where they find purpose, what their strengths are, what they enjoy, and how they most feel appreciated.

A Gallup poll verified that the number one motivator in the workplace is recognition and appreciation.[4] So if you want to see performance and morale increase, learn to speak each person's Appreciation Language.

The Alpha Servant

Serving others is not an act of charity or sacrifice. It's not about giving yourself up, bottling your own desires, or being walked over. It's about providing for those who need to work with you so that all of you rise to your highest level—together.

A few years ago, when Kevin Durant was beginning his rise to the elite level of the NBA, the basketball and media community were trying to put a nickname on him. All the greats have one: MJ, Magic (we forget his name is Earvin!), Larry Legend, Sir Charles, the King, the Answer, the Splash Brothers, the list goes on and on.

When someone asked Durant what nickname he'd give himself, he surprised a lot of people by saying he wanted to be called "The Servant." *The Servant?* People were confused. And what usually happens when people don't understand something is they laugh. They mock. They insult. *Why would the alpha dog of a title contender call himself a servant? What is this guy talking about?*

But I know Kevin—and he had it exactly right. True leaders serve others, and they serve the mission. A servant leader puts others' needs ahead of his own. He commits to adding value to everyone and everything he comes in contact with.

In the summer of 2016, when Durant decided to join the talent-stacked Golden State Warriors, the talking heads on ESPN and the chirpers on social media thought he was taking the easy path. They thought he was selling out, that he lacked leadership. I saw it much differently. I believe KD sacrificed his own prominence for a larger goal. In a league dominated by players making sure "I get mine," seeking out places where they can get endorsements, star status, and max contracts, it was the ultimate servant move. Because of that, Durant has been able to take on a leadership role. His coaches and teammates recognize what he's in it for. He has already proven it.

The concept of service is intimately connected to strong leadership. A leader ties his own needs and desires to the team's in order to create a unified purpose. It comes from a place of compassion and empathy. A company straps itself to the needs of its employees first: *serve them and they will serve you.* Once that agreement is firmly in place, then you focus on serving the customers.

As a leader, think about the language you use, because it reveals so much about your thinking. If you use "I" and "me" more than "us" and "we," you are creating a gap between you and your team. That gap will grow into a barrier, which over time will become impossible to remove, lessen, or cross. Communicate that you are "we" driven, not "me" driven, and others will respond. Don't focus on what you want *from* your employees. Focus on what you want *for* your employees.

My friend Babe Kwasniak—the outstanding high school coach and former business leader—is also an Army veteran. "The Army taught me leadership is everything," he told me. "Soldiers would rather be in Baghdad working for someone they respect and they know cares for them than in Hawaii for a jerk who doesn't." The facts back Babe up. Surveys show that "65 percent of working Americans would prefer a new boss to a pay raise."[5]

Think about how revealing that is—more people care about that relationship than their salary. Don't forget: a boss/employee relationship *is* a relationship, not a transaction. Great bosses know this and work to build that relationship.

Self-Test

One way to serve your employees is by committing to their improvement and goals. *Take tangible action.* For instance, leaders should check in regularly on whether their people are fulfilled, productive, and effective. Ask questions like:

1. What did you do this week that you want to do more of?

2. What did you do this week that you want to do less of?

3. How did you use your strengths today?

Calling Out Errors

Serving others sometimes means guidance and instruction. Tread respectfully and carefully when addressing an employee's mistakes, errors, or misjudgments. Instruction is always going to work better than criticism because it's forward-thinking. It focuses not on what was done, but on what *can* be done. Remember that people respond to things they can do something about. If they want to improve, they will take it to heart. If they just feel like they're being told what they did wrong, they will tune out.

Also, it's important for a leader to focus feedback on a person's actions, not on his character. If someone feels that his mistake is internal—part of who he is—he will be less likely to solve the problem. Why? Because he feels like the problem can't be solved. It's just who he is. Personal criticism is a confidence destroyer and, thus, an ineffective approach to addressing an issue.

Don't forget that a big part of serving people is building their confidence. This is something that great coaches know. It's not coddling. It's energizing. "Provide frequent recognition and encouragement," wrote researcher Shawn Achor in his book *The Happiness Advantage*. It will directly translate into productivity. According to Achor, "One study found that...when recognition is specific and deliberately delivered, it is even more motivating than money."[6] *Recognition and praise are more motivating than money.* Let that sink in for a while. Then put it to use at the office.

> Clients do not come first. Employees come first. If you take care of your employees, they will take care of the clients.
>
> —Richard Branson

Investing in People

Great leaders understand that underneath the profits, spreadsheets, and meetings, companies are about people. Everything else is subservient to the people who make up the company and, by extension, to the customers and clients. Starbucks was the first company in the United States to give health benefits and stock options to even part-time employees.[7] Founder and CEO Howard Schultz believed that serving his employees was the best way to create a sustainable business, one where that feeling of being taken care of would transfer from employee to customer. Sometimes when I'm stuck on the phone with a company—car insurance, health care, power company—and I can hear the misery in the customer representative's voice, I think about the person in charge of that department. I wonder if that boss knows what is trickling out to the customers. I wonder if *his* boss knows.

Recently, Starbucks went one step further, announcing that they would begin paying *full tuition* for its employees to go to college. Now, I'm sure some number crunchers determined that's a waste of money. If you just think of it as a perk, then maybe it is. But it's not a perk. Schultz believes, "It wasn't charity because investing in people is how we grow." Even when Starbucks was in financial trouble in 2008, Schultz held tight to this commitment and refused to give it up.[8]

What's important to remember is that Schultz doesn't run a charity—he cares about growth, profits, and market share. He just knows the best way to raise the level of his company is to build up his employees. "Take love, humanity, and humility and then place it against a performance-driven organization; these are in conflict to the naked eye," Schultz wrote. "But I believe that performance is significantly enhanced by this kind of leadership."[9] He doesn't just provide lip service to the idea; he backs it up with action.

The great companies make sure their employees are taken care of first. Continental Airlines created loyalty from its people by actually treating them like team members. When the company met its target goals for the percentage of planes that arrived on time, every employee—from baggage handlers to ticket agents—got bonus checks.[10] It's hard to quantify the effect, but I'm sure that Continental employees passed that appreciation and spirit on to the customers. Simon Sinek offers a piece of wisdom that all businesses would be wise to heed: "Customers will never love a company until the employees love it first."[11]

Jimmy Wales, CEO of *Wikipedia*, believes you should treat employees like volunteers. Because of *Wikipedia*'s business model, Wales also deals with many literal volunteers, and he credits years of interacting with them with teaching him a valuable lesson about motivation and management. "You can't just tell them what to do," he told *Fortune* magazine. "A good manager knows the same is true with employees. If you have the right people, and you're organizing things sensibly, there shouldn't be a lot of telling people what to do."[12] It's a good thought experiment: if your employees *were* volunteers, how would you get them motivated, involved, and connected to the mission?

> People don't care how much you know until they know how much you care.
>
> —Unknown

The Death of "Do What I Say"

The days of managing through intimidation, fear, and brute force are long gone—and thankfully, they're not coming back. Kim Scott has been CEO advisor for Twitter and Dropbox, and worked for both Apple and Google, among many other industry leaders. "Authoritarian bosses tend to be particularly weak persuaders; they don't feel a need to explain the decision or their logic..." she wrote. "They fail to establish credibility because they expect people to do what they say simply because they're the boss."[13] It hasn't been political correctness or workplace sensitivity that has phased out the authoritarian boss. It's about ineffectiveness.

Google serves its employees by making work as pleasant a place as possible, with nap pods, gyms, free food from eleven different restaurants, and snacks in kitchens all around its campus.[14] If you're thinking, *Well, they can afford it,* keep in mind that they've been doing things like this since day one. Even though Google's bottom line certainly sags under all these amenities, serving their employees has paid off in the long run. Incredibly, in 2015, over sixteen years after Google started, "About one third of the original hundred hires" were still there.[15] That's remarkable.

Is Google able to treat employees this way because it's successful, or is it successful *because* of this approach to its employees? It's a feedback loop, but it would never have begun without a commitment from the leaders to serve the people. Though Google's parent company, Alphabet, now has 72,000 employees, they still grant stock to all of their employees.[16] If you run a company and these gestures are too out there for you, think about other ways you can show your people that you are there to serve them. A small action, if it's genuine and personalized, will go a long way.

Listening and Empathy

Serving means listening, interacting, and understanding. It also means adapting your approach to the various personalities in your organization. As I sometimes have to tell my kids, equal doesn't mean the same. In fact, treating everyone the same is an insult. It's not accounting for their individuality. *You don't know me,* they'll say. And they'll be right.

Being a servant leader requires truly knowing who your people are, how they're motivated, and what they want. How else can you serve them if you don't know these things? "You can't make great decisions by sitting in your office," Mike Smith warned in *You Win in the Locker Room First*. "You lead by leaving a footprint in every area of the building."[17] Tom Peters, a leadership expert who has studied some of the great US companies up close, calls it "managing by walking around."[18] It goes back to knowing everyone's Appreciation Language. A leader has to adapt and modify his communication style to each individual person who works for him. Remember: attempting to treat everyone the same means connecting with none of them. A spork isn't both a fork and a spoon. It's neither.

An integral part of servanthood is empathy and understanding. A true leader needs to get out there and get a sense of his employees'—and his customers'—experience. David Neeleman, cofounder of Jet-Blue, used to fly on his airline once a week—and sit in the back row. JetBlue actually doesn't have a first-class cabin and has long had a policy of never overbooking.

Neeleman would walk up and down the aisles to give out snacks and get feedback from passengers, talk to employees, help clean the plane, and even unload luggage.[19] After one particularly nightmarish holiday weekend, Neeleman wrote up a Customer Bill of Rights and released a public apology that blamed no one else or even the unique circumstances. "We let you down,"[20] he admitted. He extended his sense of servanthood to his customers: taking the blame and making a promise that it wouldn't happen again.

Different Strokes

I have thick skin. When I was a player, coaches could get up in my face, scream and cuss, and I was fine with it. I didn't take it personally. In fact, I used it as motivation: *I'll show you*. But some of my teammates were the opposite; when the coach got on them, they would almost cower and go back into their protective shell. They would just shut down.

Being a servant leader is figuring out that people are different and it's up to you to treat them as such. Learn what your people need and want and how to serve them in your capacity as their leader. Your people will develop trust and loyalty in you if they know you understand something about them. If they understand you're about serving them, they'll commit to you. They'll be there if they know they're getting paid first, they're going to eat first, and their needs are going to be met first. I guarantee they will respond to feeling purposeful and will react positively to feeling a part of something. Then, and only then, will you become part of something *worth* leading.

Key Point: A leader serves his people, not the other way around! Find ways to bring out the best in your people by understanding their needs, desires, and motivations.

Remember:

☞ Leaders understand that they work for their people.

☞ It is impossible to be both selfish and an effective leader.

☞ Leaders commit to adding value to everyone they come in contact with.

☞ Don't treat others the way you want to be treated. Treat others the way *they* want to be treated.

☞ Get to know your people so you can understand what that looks like.

CHAPTER NINE

Character

> Your reputation is what you're perceived to be; your character is what you really are.
>
> —John Wooden

While the previous chapter addressed the importance of *what you do*, character is about something even bigger: *who you are*. It is the raw material that is necessary to be an effective leader. A coach that preaches one thing and then behaves differently loses all credibility.

Character pays off. But here's the thing about acting with character: it doesn't *expect* the payoff. A person who acts with character isn't waiting around to be rewarded. He just commits to acting with integrity and trusting the world will fall in line. He works on himself.

As my longtime friend and mentor, former NBA assistant coach Kevin Eastman, likes to say, you earn your reputation through your repetitions. The example you set trumps the instructions you give. A leader's character is fundamental to earning others' respect; without their respect, they won't follow you anywhere.

As I write this book, the NCAA is being rocked by scandal. Stories are coming out about unsavory agents offering large and illegal payments to college players. Coaches, athletic directors, and other adults are involved in this and other misbehavior, and some careers and programs are at serious risk. As I read and watch these stories unfold, I always try to hold tight to the lesson. Character counts: who you are and who people think you are matter. They play an intimate role in what happens to you.

In the age of immoral and downright criminal stories coming out from the sports world to Washington DC, from Silicon Valley to Hollywood to Wall Street, we can never forget that character, ethics, and proper behavior come from the top. A leader is either modeling and encouraging one kind of behavior or sending a message that any other kind is acceptable. Remember: people follow *examples*, not advice.

Character is a way to let your team know that you can be trusted, which may be the most important quality a leader can bring. "Once a coach earns his players' trust," Jay Bilas wrote, "he can push them to new levels mentally and physically, where less trustworthy coaches might not dare tread."[1] Character is how you behave when no one else is watching. If you really want to earn a group's respect and dedication, show them you deserve it: act with integrity and demonstrate character.

You can easily judge the character of a man by how he treats those who can do nothing for him.

—Malcolm Forbes

Coach K's In-Box

The only thing more inspiring than meeting your idol is meeting him and finding out he is exactly as you'd expect him to be. Duke coach Mike Krzyzewski has always been one of my heroes. Coach K's former players universally sing his praises—and it's not just about wins, national attention, and NBA contracts. "He will always give every ounce of himself to help you become the best version of yourself," former Duke All-American Jay Williams wrote. "It doesn't stop when you're done playing for him. If you need him, he's there without your having to ask."[2]

When I was on staff with the basketball team at Montrose Christian High School, Coach K came to a practice because he was recruiting one of our players. I'd met him in passing at clinics before, but this time he was in our gym, watching our players. I knew I might never get the chance again, so I took it upon myself to sit down and talk to him.

Though he was there on Duke business, he was happy to chat with me. For the time that we spoke, he made me feel like I was the most important person in the gym. Through his eye contact, questions, tone, and body language, he showed he was clearly invested in the conversation. Though he had other things to do and a million things on his mind, he was never distracted, neither looking over my shoulder nor scanning the room. He was *present*.

I was so blown away that it was taking place that I realize now *I* was the one who wasn't present. Or rather, I wasn't as present as I would have liked to have been, as I don't remember many details of our conversation. But I do remember that he was inquisitive, asking me about the program at Montrose and my role with the team. As the conversation shifted to the player he was recruiting, he asked me about his character, work ethic, attitude, commitment, coachability, and respectfulness. Notably, he never asked anything about the player's athleticism or on-the-court skills. We also talked about my training philosophy and he shared what his strength coach—William Stephens—did with the Duke players.

I'm old school, so the next morning I hand-wrote him a thank-you note (yes, that means with pen and paper) to tell him how much I appreciated his time. "It may not have meant a lot to you, but you taking the time to talk to me was incredible," I wrote. "You're someone I've looked up to and admired for years and I really appreciate it. Thank you."

I put it an envelope, slapped a stamp on it, and sent it off to Duke, figuring that was that. It's not like I was expecting a response. It just felt like the right thing to do.

Three weeks later, to my surprise, I got a handwritten letter back.

Dear Alan:

Thanks for your note. I really enjoyed our conversation at Montrose. You have done a terrific job there and have obviously built a great national reputation. I'm happy for you.

Take care,
Coach K

I cannot communicate how blown away I was.

This man is the face of college basketball, and he took the time to show me a gesture of gratitude that got him nothing. That small gesture has had a massive impact on me and taught me a pivotal lesson: small things can make a big difference. Obviously, Coach K has a personal assistant who could've done it or he could've sent me an e-mail or had someone send a Duke T-shirt or a form letter. But he didn't. I was impressed with his kindness, but I was outright dumb-founded when it dawned on me, *Oh, he's like this with everyone.* This is just what he does! This is just who he is. I can picture Coach K's flooded in-box, and his commitment to answering each and every missive that comes in. That's character.

"Leaders show respect for people by giving them time,"[3] Coach K wrote in one of his books. His success is intimately tied to how he treats everyone. Coach K is the reason why I go out of my way to tell people how much I appreciate them. It is why I do my very best to return every e-mail, every text, and every voice mail as promptly as possible. I figure if one of the greatest coaches in college basketball history can make the time to hand-write me a note of gratitude, I can do the same.

Coach K once told an interviewer that he feels that character is the most important factor in recruiting,[4] and his track record backs it up. He lives by that standard, and he doesn't expect any less from his players. "Character drives everything," he has said. "A lack of it drives it downward; where you have a lot, it drives upward. Charac-ter is the foundation upon which you win."[5]

> Management is about authority. Leadership is about influence.
> —Joseph Rost, leadership scholar

How You Treat the "Nobodies"

Character means you don't view your relationships through the lens of what you can get out of them. You see people as people, not as avenues of gain or leverage. When current Golden State Warriors president Rick Welts was sixteen, he was a ball boy for the Seattle

Supersonics. In an interview he gave to Michael Gervais on his *Finding Mastery* podcast, Welts said that while everyone else treated him like part of the furniture, there were three athletes who went out of their way to be nice to him. And—not coincidentally, in my opinion—those three are the only three names any true basketball fan would recognize nowadays: Lenny Wilkens, who became a legendary coach; Rod Thorn, who became an NBA executive; and Thomas Meschery, who became a published writer and whose number was retired by the Warriors.[6] The only three people who gave a teenage ball boy any attention and respect lived *their lives* that way. Welts said that "people who are empowered and who don't treat people well inevitably fail. It may not be in a year, it may not be in five years, but inevitably [they'll] fail."[7]

Leaders live a life worth following. Their words, actions, beliefs, values, and behavior are all aligned. As Robert Sutton put it in *The No Asshole Rule*, "The difference between how a person treats the powerless versus the powerful is as good a measure of human character as I know."[8] It's true. When one day in the (far-off) future I meet my daughter's boyfriend and take the two of them out to a nice dinner, I know what I'll be watching: how he talks to the waiter and the coat check person and the valet. Of course he's going to put on a good face for me, but that won't tell me much. But his interactions with others—especially strangers—will tell me all I need to know about the kind of person he is.

It's about having a positive effect on people, adding value to every interaction. Babe Kwasniak once said to me, "It's not *who* you know, it's *who* knows you." These are wise words. There's a disproportional focus in business on contacts and shaking hands and the online currency of likes and follows. But those things don't really matter that much. It's not about whom you meet; it's about *who remembers meeting you* and what they remember about that interaction. Are you just accumulating paper-thin relationships that aren't really that consequential in the real world? Or are you making an impact? It's true that many people are drawn to enthusiasm and charisma. But *everyone* is drawn to character.

> People will forgive occasional mistakes based on ability...but they won't trust someone who slips in character.
>
> —John C. Maxwell

The Business of Character

Character is also good business because it creates a magnetic kind of loyalty. Employees want to get there early and stay late for a boss they respect. Customers want to feel like a company they patronize cares about them. A famous example: We think of Lexus as synonymous with premium luxury, but in 1989, when they were first launched by Toyota, they began with an all-time royal screwup. The first Lexus model had to be entirely recalled and repaired. It was a disaster, and it could have been the death knell for the product right out of the gate. As Galinsky and Schweitzer retell it in *Friend and Foe*, Lexus turned an absolute nightmare into a moment they would build their brand off of:

> Rather than simply sending out consumer notices and making a public announcement, Lexus called every single owner—yes, individually, on the phone. Then they tried to make repair as easy as possible; they even flew mechanics to customers if a dealership wasn't nearby...detailed every

car and gave it a full tank of gas. Within three weeks, Lexus emerged from the crisis with an enhanced brand—Lexus was no longer just about quality, they now were also known for their customer service.[9]

Lexus came out the other end of a crisis—a potentially company-killing one—looking even better. Today it is one of the most beloved brands in the world, and its customers are famously loyal. But it all began with a choice—to handle what could have been a meltdown with character and integrity.

Let's look at a new company, a "disruptor," and see how character still matters. In 2011, when Airbnb experienced its first (some would say inevitable) nightmarish experience between customers, CEO Brian Chesky didn't shy away from facing the problem. He ignored advisors who told him to take a measured stance or release a statement that had some version of, *Well, with thousands of strangers meeting up to live in each other's homes, something was bound to happen.* At the end of the day, he likely could've gotten away with this. The average consumer wouldn't judge the entire company because of one terrible incident.

But Chesky is playing the long game.

Instead, he publicly took full responsibility for the incident, releasing an apology that didn't mince words or offer the corporate-speak we are accustomed to. "We have really screwed things up," Chesky admitted about their initial handling of the incident. Then the company directly compensated the offended party and added a zero to the previous $5,000 insurance policy for hosts—making it a $50,000 policy.[10] Customers, and future customers, took notice. The CEO demonstrated that his company had integrity—at a time when it easily could've been focused on protecting its own ass.

Acting with character marks you as someone people can trust.

And trust is the kind of strong glue that will outlast all the other incentives. In 1988, at the time of Michael Jordan's second contract, agent David Falk offered to cut his firm's marketing fee, a move that Falk's partner thought was crazy. Jordan was about to be the most marketed player on the *planet*. Why offer to just give that money away? But Falk knew what he was doing. He was playing the long game, demonstrating to MJ what kind of person he was. Though Jordan turned down the offer, the fact that Falk made it no doubt left an impression.

As a result of Falk's offer, his relationship with Jordan "changed forever. For the first time, he knew he could completely trust me."[11] Jordan recognized Falk as a man of character, and thus, tied his career to his agent's—which turned out historically well for both of them. Jordan would spend his career as someone whom everybody wanted something from, but he had a strong relationship with Falk. He remembered his agent's moment of character, and it bonded the two for the rest of his career.

Getting Dirty

One sports tradition, a that's-the-way-things-have-always-been type of practice, is the idea that freshman and rookies need to pay their dues and do the grunt work. They carry the equipment, buy doughnuts for the team, and give up their aisle seat on the airplane. Basically they "serve" the veteran players. This strikes me as incredibly backward. It should be the *opposite*. Leadership isn't about lording power over others. The veterans and captains should be the ones doing the grunt work. They should be leading by example, demonstrating what the new players need to do for the good of the team. They are the ones who should be serving.

There's a famous story about the San Antonio Spurs, an NBA

team known for one of the most team-oriented cultures in sports. Not coincidentally, they also have the single highest winning percentage in history out of all the four major team sports.[12] When the Spurs were on the road, there used to be two buses from the hotel to the arena for practice time: the early bus and the late bus. The early bus was for rookies and younger players who needed to put in extra work. The late bus was for the veterans. But Tim Duncan, the team's star and leader (and a future Hall of Famer), *always* took the early bus.

Eventually, Coach Gregg Popovich took notice. He figured that if the team's best player felt it necessary to get to practice early, then everyone should. And they did—without complaint. Duncan was always the silent leader type, but this type of action proved his character more than a million locker room speeches could have.

At DeMatha High School, which has one of the premiere basketball programs in the country, Coach Jones still sweeps the floor before every practice. He doesn't have to, of course. He does it to remind himself, and to show others, that he is not too big or too important for any job. It's why Coach Jones's assistants and players look up to him. They recognize his character. And that kind of leader rubs off on everyone else.

Winning by Giving

Character means you understand that there are things beyond winning and losing. The workplace and the business world are not all zero-sum games. There can be more than one winner, and a workplace of battling egos inevitably suffers in productivity.

In his book *Give and Take*, Adam Grant highlighted successful businesspeople—not Mother Teresa types, but headstrong capitalists—who are what he calls "givers." "When people focus on others, as givers do naturally, they're less likely to worry about ego and minuscule details," Grant wrote. "They look at the big picture and prioritize what matters most to others."[13]

It reminds me of the late University of North Carolina head coach Dean Smith. Smith didn't convince every player to stay the full four years of college, though that would've made his job a whole lot easier. Smith famously encouraged his top players to leave for the NBA draft to secure their financial future. This seems like it was shooting himself in the foot, but Smith's choice to look out for his players' future became known—and that unselfish behavior ended up attracting top recruits to UNC. Players saw that Smith cared more about them than he did about himself or even winning.[14]

Decades after players left UNC, they still sing the praises of Smith, who seemed to truly be invested in his players as people. His approach to leadership, and his character, came through in his philosophy: "A leader should take the blame for the losses and give the players credit for the victories."[15]

The best story about Dean Smith didn't come out until he passed away in 2012. Every single player who had lettered as a member of one of his teams got a $200 check in the mail as prescribed in Smith's will. That's 180 players over thirty-six seasons! The money was for them to enjoy a nice meal out, on their coach.[16] That story just blows me away. There were players going back decades who got checks, from guys you never heard of to billionaire Michael Jordan. On top of that, Smith did it *after* he was gone. There was no way it could be transactional or even interpreted as anything other than a gesture of thanks—and servanthood.

Your Core

Character is the foundation of every aspect of your life. Ultimately that is going to be your default; it's what you do when you're not conscious of what people are thinking or who's peering over your shoulder. If you expect honesty from your employees, make sure you demonstrate it. If you want their loyalty, make sure they know they have yours first.

Any difference between what you say and what you do—which is hypocrisy, whether you're conscious of it or not—will harm your ability to guide, coach, and lead. The people I've met who are at the top in business or sports are the same in front of the camera, off camera, on their couch, in front of millions, and to their circle of friends. They are who they are to their core, and they don't put on any show.

Make a point of letting your employees know what you value: it's a way to ensure you will see more of it. Find someone in your organization who did the right thing, maybe even against his own interest, and highlight that. Your other employees will notice, and the behavior will spread. Remember: *that which gets praised gets repeated.*

At the end of the day, someone with low morals and weak integrity, no matter their talent in everything else, is not worth investing in. He is built on a weak foundation. When I'm looking to fill out any group or team, character is the first thing I look for. Everything else can be built up from there. It's one of the few things that you can't teach, so you're better off starting with it.

Facing the Tests

Character is about acting on your values. You might think you have character but believe that in the business world it has to be tucked away, that it's not an asset there. Maybe you've been told that the snake gets ahead, so you should bury your better instincts. This is simply not true. Character must be consistent, or else we call it something else.

We are constantly bombarded with situations that test our character. We're all human, and we all make mistakes. Character is not always black and white. It goes deeper than just not stealing money from someone's dresser. It's internal choices: if we're doing sprints at practice and I keep stopping two inches before the line—because no one sees me—that's a character issue.

Character is not about being a saint. It's the ability to acknowledge poor decisions and not repeat them. If not, what happens is that over time, it gets easier to act immorally, a process that slowly erodes your character. Are you a leader whose life is worth following? Do those who work for you know what you stand for?

When in doubt, follow the rule of former Google CEO Eric Schmidt: make sure you would work for yourself.

Key Point: Character is who you truly are, and it will show through. Lack of character and integrity undermines all of a leader's credibility.

Remember:

☞ Character is the foundation of how you get others behind you.

☞ People will be inspired by those with character and are more likely to go through the fire with someone they trust.

☞ Your team might not always be listening to what you say, but they're *always* watching what you do.

☞ Successful leaders magnetically pull people in the right direction by living with integrity and character.

☞ A good leader highlights and praises moments of character from others to communicate their value.

CHAPTER TEN

Empowerment

At Apple we hire people to tell us what to do, not the other way around.

—Steve Jobs

Empowerment is the last chapter of part 2 because it is the final piece. If you are a leader with **character** who **serves** his people, who has a healthy **culture** in place and a **vision** for what the team should be, then you have to take the last step: **empower them to action.** Like parenting, you do what you can to foster, nurture, and inspire, but then you have to let go.

Think back on Steve Kerr's Warriors team, a fully empowered group of players who are trusted by their coach. Leaders may set the destination, but not necessarily the path. A leader's primary job is to find out what each team member does really well and how to best utilize that skill set for the team's benefit. A coach—any kind of coach—must be comfortable giving his people a sense of independence, trusting that they will figure out the best way to get to where they need to go.

Empowering your people is a way of connecting with them,

building their confidence, and showing your belief in them. That feeling spreads. No matter the arena, people are happiest when they are growing, learning, and improving. Happiness, according to researchers, is about purpose and productivity.[1] Effective leaders give their people an opportunity to be of use and to matter. Then everyone wins.

Player-Coaches

In sports, the best coaches aren't those breathing down necks and they are never the micromanagers. They are leaders like Kerr and the Celtics' Brad Stevens, who carry themselves with confidence because they trust their system, the culture they created, and the people they have chosen. Empowerment is the natural extension of everything that has already been put into place.

Michigan State men's basketball coach Tom Izzo once told me, "A player-led team will always outperform a coach-led team." Coming from a coach, especially a coach of young men, that might give you pause. Wouldn't a coach *want* to be the focal point? Wouldn't he need to be? But of course, Izzo knows what he's talking about.

"If it's a player-coached team," he told me, "that means that they've taken ownership of themselves and their team, and your chances of success triple." Coming from one of the winningest coaches of all time, that's an impactful lesson. It doesn't mean he doesn't value his job or position; he just knows that the strongest thing a leader can do is empower his players to run their own team.

Izzo told me, "I think we spend so much time preparing for opponents, we don't spend enough time preparing for ourselves," which he called "self-scouting." Part of that process is knowing everyone. "You've got to spend time with kids to get them to trust you," he said. He makes a point of bringing back his star players to meet with his current team, and the concept hasn't left them. They return to "team-coach the culture of our team."

True leadership isn't about naked power; it's about being open to giving, spreading, and sharing that power. Leadership is not a one-way relationship; it requires buy-in from the other side—and people choose to buy in when they feel a sense of autonomy and control.

> Authority is the open heart; power is the closed fist.
>
> —Michael Foley, author[2]

Getting Out of Your Own Way

Empowerment is intimately tied to the very first trait discussed in this book: self-awareness. As a leader, you must know what you can and cannot do. You have the vision to hire others who can help you succeed, the character and commitment to serve them, and you've created the culture where they can thrive and lean on each other. Now it's time to let them do their thing. If you do everything else but then you don't let go, you are basically shooting yourself in the foot.

Virgin founder and CEO Richard Branson is a huge proponent of empowerment. He specifically relies on it so he can free up himself to focus on his vision. "People should delegate early on in their businesses, so they can start thinking about the bigger picture,"[3] he told an interviewer. When he meets with budding young entrepreneurs, he tells them to "go and take a week out to find somebody as good or better than yourself...let them get on and run your business day to day." Hire those who do what you can't, and let them do it. *If you could have done it all yourself, you would have.*

"Simply giving employees a sense of agency—a feeling that they are in control, that they have genuine decision-making authority—can radically increase how much energy and focus they bring to their jobs," wrote Robert Bruce Shaw, who assists executives in building teams.[4] Think about all the jobs you ever had. Which were the ones you liked the best? Weren't they the ones where you were free to do the most? Didn't that freedom make you enjoy the work?

Didn't that let you know your boss trusted you?

Weren't you *happier* at that job?

Trusting Your People

Delegation is something all kinds of coaches, even good coaches, struggle with. One reason is that they find it hard to trust that others can perform specific tasks as well as they can. They convince themselves that it will take longer to either teach someone else how to do it, or worse, have to fix it after they do. This is a very limiting belief system and one that can paralyze growth and infect the team culture.

Elite leaders understand the power of delegation from three vantage points:

1. Delegation unconsciously tells your people that you trust them. And trust is the glue to all relationships and cultures. Hovering over an employee's shoulder sends a message: I'm not sure I can depend on you.

2. The only way to learn is to do. Delegating gives people the vital reps they need to improve and grow. If you never give them an opportunity to do it on their own, they will never actualize their potential. Then their inability is not their fault. It's yours.

3. Delegating frees you up to do things that only the coach can do. The more time a coach spends doing work that other members of the team can do, the slower the progress of the entire team.

Taking Charge

The true test of a great leader is revealed not in what he does but what his people do without him. How does your team act when you're not there? How much slippage would there be if you took the week off? It takes tremendous security and confidence for a leader to hand off the reins. But it's vital.

In his book *Extreme Teams: Why Pixar, Netflix, Airbnb and Other Cutting-Edge Companies Succeed Where Most Fail*, Robert Bruce Shaw examined companies that make a point of empowering employees. He pointed to a study of a manufacturing plant where the productivity increased 20 percent in two months, a colossal jump. The radical idea? The company let its employees have agency over seemingly minor things like shift schedules and uniforms. That dose of freedom led to a happier and more productive workforce. And the numbers proved it.

Great companies, the visionary ones, have caught on to this idea. "Pick an area where your people are frustrated," wrote former Google VP Laszlo Bock, "and let them fix it. If there are constraints, limited time or money, tell them what they are. Be transparent with your people and give them a voice in shaping your team or company. You'll be stunned by what they accomplish."[5] Even in its early days, when Google was living in the gigantic shadow of Microsoft, the company practiced empowerment. Its founders were committed to "hiring the very best engineers we could and then getting out of the way."[6]

Micromanaging might give the boss a feeling of control, but it will suck away the employees' will to do their best. They will find somewhere else soon enough, a place that gives some autonomy with a boss who's comfortable giving it. If a coach truly wants the organization to thrive—and not just himself to thrive—then he should *want* free thinkers. He should seek out those who aren't afraid to challenge his point of view. As the saying goes: if everyone on your team is thinking alike, then someone isn't thinking. Allow for disagreements. Create an environment where subordinates are free to speak their minds.

Netflix's CEO, Reed Hastings, along with his executives, has consistently encouraged openness and honesty, with little concern for where someone is in the hierarchy. It has served the company well; Netflix accounts for about a third of the Internet bandwidth in the United States.[7] Former Netflix executive Patty McCord explained the company's mind-set in a *Forbes* interview: "All hiring should be based on starting with a problem you have to solve, and what it's going to take somebody to be great at solving it."[8]

Once the right people are on board, don't meddle and don't saddle them with unnecessary rules that do little but hinder them from shining. *Serve them by trusting them.* Orchestra conductors don't lead by playing every instrument; they lead by trusting everyone will properly play theirs.

> You can't force your will on people. If you want them to act differently, you need to inspire them to change themselves.
>
> —Phil Jackson

The Sage

Phil Jackson has eleven rings as an NBA coach, and though some (the haters and the misinformed) might think that having Michael

Jordan, Kobe Bryant, and Shaquille O'Neal just automatically produces championships, the players themselves know differently. Jordan had been a Chicago Bull for seven years before the team even made it to the Finals. But Jackson had been their head coach for only two.

In 1990, before the Bulls had won any championships, Jackson knew that Jordan would have to buy into the team concept if they ever were going to win a title. Instead of berating or lecturing Jordan on the importance of his teammates' success, Jackson let Jordan's own thinking do the work.

"I treated him like a partner," Jackson wrote, "and slowly he began to shift his way of thinking. When I let him solve the problem himself, he was more likely to buy into the solution."[9] That's the essence of empowerment. Jackson "discovered that the more I tried to exert power directly, the less powerful I became. I learned to dial back my ego and distribute power as widely as possible without surrendering final authority."[10]

He took control by releasing control—a Zen-like concept that Jackson brought to the rest of his coaching. For example, it is common practice that when the other team goes on a 6–0 run, the coach calls time out. But not Jackson. He liked letting his team figure their way out of trouble on their own—fostering a feeling that they *could*.[11] It's a formidable example of empowerment, the kind that leads to trust, self-confidence, and autonomy, all the things that a championship team needs. In 1999, after Jackson became head coach of the Lakers, he brought that same approach to Los Angeles in order to get a young, brash Kobe Bryant to trust and empower his teammates.

The empowerment that Jackson implemented with his teams spread all the way down the tree. He empowered Jordan, who empowered teammates Scottie Pippen, Horace Grant, the rest of the starters, and then all the way down the bench. Jackson empowered

Kobe, who empowered Shaq to make his own decisions and his Laker teammates to find their own roles in the system. At the top of the pyramid was a coach who was committed to not acting like he was on top of the pyramid. He let everyone feel on top of their own pyramid.

> If your manager knows what you're doing all the time, you're not doing your job and neither is he.
>
> —Hew Evans, Sony executive

The Soul-Sucking Meeting

We will continue to hold these meetings until we figure out why no work is getting done!

Sound familiar? Many businesses spend way too much time in meetings. There are people holding meetings to plan other meetings! And too many of them start late, run long, quickly go off topic, offer no value, or have no agenda. One way to empower your employees is to *respect their time*. Cut down on the meetings and limit them to who *needs* to be there.

An article in the *Harvard Business Review* noted: "Meetings have increased in length and frequency over the past fifty years, to the point where executives spend an average of nearly twenty-three hours a week in them, up from less than ten hours in the 1960s. And that doesn't even include all the impromptu gatherings that don't make it onto the schedule."[12] This is not an effective use of anyone's time. *HBR* surveyed 182 senior managers from a range of industries and concluded the following:[13]

- 65% said meetings keep them from completing their own work.
- 71% said meetings are unproductive and inefficient.
- 64% said meetings come at the expense of deep thinking.
- 62% said meetings miss opportunities to bring the team closer together.

Considering time is our most valuable resource, these meetings are being held at an astronomical price. Every minute spent in an unproductive meeting is a minute not being invested in purposeful work. With so much time being drained by meetings, most executives and employees feel they have to come to work early, stay late, and use weekends to get things done. Besides being a drain on productivity and morale, it builds resentment among the group.

Here are three tips for executives and managers to treat meetings like a seasoned basketball coach uses time-outs:

1. Only call them when absolutely necessary. College basketball coaches get a finite number of time-outs at the beginning of every game (four 75-second full time-outs and two 30-second time-outs), so they must use them strategically and call them only when they really need to. Choose your battles wisely. If you try to take everything on, your team will tune you out. The refrigerator in your kitchen always makes noise, so you no longer hear it. Don't become a refrigerator.

2. Be direct, purposeful, and time-conscious. When you have only 30 to 75 seconds to "meet"—you must be direct and purposeful. You don't have a choice! Give your team the necessary information and instruction they need to elevate their

performance. No fluff. Respect the fact that their time is just as valuable as yours.

3. Make sure they leave with confidence and direction. End every meeting in the emotional state you want your people in for whatever they are doing next, which should almost always be positive, optimistic, and confident. End meetings on a high note, as that is what they will remember and bring back to their work.

Who Are You Producing?

The job of a "coach" is not to compile a group of yes-men who will boost his ego and insulate him from criticism. The truly transcendent leader is interested in creating other leaders. It's not about manipulation or control or feeding one person's sense of self; it's about giving rise to independent thinkers and free actors and people who will develop the skills to one day be leaders themselves. If those working for you aren't constantly up for promotion or headhunted by other companies and competitors, then you're probably not developing your people.

Former San Francisco 49ers head coach Bill Walsh, pioneer of the "West Coast" Offense (still popular in the NFL), was a legend not just for the wins he produced but for the *people* he produced. According to *Superbosses* author Sydney Finkelstein, Walsh "dispensed with an authoritarian style of leadership and empowered individuals by teaching them to think independently." The evidence is inarguable, virtually unprecedented: Walsh produced other leaders at an astounding rate.

Walsh's "Family Tree" is unmatched in professional sports. In a span of thirty-six years (between 1979 and 2015), Walsh and head coaches that once worked under him had a total of 32 Super Bowl appearances and 17 championships.[14] His legacy continued long after he left the game: "As of 2008, the year after Walsh's death, coaches trained by Walsh led 26 of the league's 32 teams."[15]

There are parallels elsewhere, in business and in tech. One of the most famed groups of twenty-first-century entrepreneurs is jokingly referred to as the "PayPal Mafia." Early on, PayPal employed many future founders and CEOs, including Elon Musk, Peter Thiel, and Reid Hoffman, along with the founders of YouTube and Yelp and many others. Coincidence? Of course not. It's like saying the success of Walsh's protégés is a coincidence. PayPal famously had a culture of independent thinking and empowerment, one that encouraged its members to hold fast to their vision and ideas, and it paid off in the billions. What went on inside that company planted the seeds for the tech revolution we're still living in—and it's all because the members were *empowered.*

The Dad Perspective

Empowerment is one of those characteristics that spread from sports to work to our personal and family lives. As a father, empowering my children is always at the forefront of my mind. It is one of the primary pillars of my parenting philosophy. This stems from the age-old adage of "Give a man a fish and he will eat for a day. Teach a man to fish and he will eat for a lifetime." I teach my children certain skills and traits, model them, and then quickly empower them to use them and practice them on their own.

Even when they were very young, I empowered my children to make as many of their own decisions as possible—things like what to wear and what to eat. When we are at a store or at a restaurant, I empower them to ask the clerk what they are looking for or tell the waitress what they'd like to eat. It is my goal for them to feel comfortable making decisions, not to shy away from them. I want them to constantly feel, *I can do this*. This will only increase as they get older and they have to make bigger decisions (college, work, relationships). Hopefully, by that time, they will have had plenty of practice and will feel prepared to make the choices that are right for them.

Getting Back on D

Sports are a great vessel to teach empowerment because the "boss," the head coach, is literally not allowed in the game. He *has to* empower.

On a basketball court, the point guard, who is the court leader, takes the ball up the court and has it in his hands most of the time. It is imperative that he keeps the other four guys involved. If a player is not getting a chance to score on the offensive end, he loses motivation on the defensive end. It's such a fact of basketball that you can see it even at the professional level: more touches of the ball leads to more commitment on defense.

Vasu Kulkarni, CEO of sports analytics company Krossover and CourtsideVC, is one of the biggest basketball junkies I know. "As a point guard," Vasu told me, "I'm all about deferring. You'll never see me looking to score first, and I believe unconsciously the same thing happens when running a company. I try to defer every decision to another manager because it makes them feel involved, makes them think harder, work harder, because they have a say in how things go."

It comes down to giving your people a sense of ownership. Everyone needs to get a piece, and once they do, they'll commit.

The reason? Because their own success is intimately tied up with the group's. That's how a leader turns a collection of individuals into a team.

Key Point: Successful leaders trust the "car they built," and are comfortable delegating and letting others lead.

Remember:

☞ A measurement of a true leader is to see if he is producing other high-quality leaders.

☞ Empowering others creates "buy-in"—it gives them a vested interest in the mission.

☞ It takes tremendous security, trust, and confidence for a leader to hand the reins off. But it's vital.

☞ Empowerment is the opposite of micromanaging. Leaders grow by allowing others to lead, grow, and thrive.

Self-Test

Leadership Audit

Before moving on to part 3, complete this audit:

- Which of the five traits in this part would you most like to improve?

- Pick *either* one habit you can start maintaining *or* one habit you can rid yourself of to improve that specific trait.

- Focus on either starting the positive behavior or stopping the negative behavior for approximately sixty days.

- Ask three specific people to hold you accountable to doing so.

- At the end of sixty days, see if you have developed a new habit that effectively addresses this issue.

- Try it all again with another habit.

PART III

TEAM

Team, for our purposes, refers to any group, organization, or company that has to work together to achieve a common goal. Great teams are made up of individuals and coaches who possess the characteristics from the previous chapters. To put it all together: Successful teams are made up of **self-aware, passionate, disciplined, coachable,** and **confident** people, led by people with **vision** and **character** who have built a strong **culture** that **serves** and **empowers** each individual.

But there needs to be a third element, a collection of x factors, that defines the group as a whole. As I'll explain, the conditions need to be set for $1 + 1$ to equal 3. For a team to be successful, it must share certain characteristics, which are the focus of part 3.

*graphic designed by Jeremy Stein

CHAPTER ELEVEN

Belief

> The most effective way to forge a winning team is to call on the players' need to connect with something larger than themselves.
> —Phil Jackson

Good teams create buy-in. Great teams create believe-in.

While visiting a locker room once, I saw a poster that said, BELIEVE OR LEAVE. It has stuck with me all these years later because BELIEVE OR LEAVE is a binary option. You either believe in yourself, in your teammates, in your coaches, in your mission, in your culture, in your goals, in your standards—or you don't. And if you don't, you have to go. Collective belief is akin to a type of spell that everyone chooses to fall under—and it takes only one person to break it.

In sports, the players all wear the same uniform but that doesn't make them a team. Putting on the uniform is a starting point, not an endpoint. The jersey is a symbol—of unity and of commitment to a single goal. The adage in sports is that the name on the front of the jersey, the team name, is more important than the name on the back, the player's name. (Famously, the New York Yankees have never had the players' names on the jerseys, a tradition they've kept up for ninety years. You can draw your own conclusions about whether or not there's a connection there to their twenty-seven World Series titles, the most in American team sports.)

Skepticism and uncertainty, even inside one person, can cause huge problems for a team. The reason? Because it never stays there. It will spread, sap the group's spirit, and drain their belief in what they're doing. The nonbelievers have enormous power to destroy everything. Jon Gordon told me he calls these people "energy vampires," because they suck the positive spirit out of others. Doubt and negativity are incredibly contagious. Fortunately, so are enthusiasm and belief.

Holding the Scissors

Belief is the way we turn our goals, even our dreams, into something attainable. It all first happens in our minds. At the beginning of the 1999–2000 college basketball season, at the start of the very first day of practice, head coach Tom Izzo did something bold. He had a ladder brought out to be put under the hoop, handed out a pair of scissors, and asked each player to climb up those steps and cut one snip of the net, a ritual that is completed by the winners of the national championship each year. "The last night we play together as a team," he said, "we're going to do this again. So I want you to practice it. You have to believe we'll be cutting down the nets in March."

Some people might flinch at this ritual, thinking it would give Izzo's players a false sense of confidence. Others might say it was wrong for the coach to make a promise he couldn't guarantee. But I disagree: the coach was thinking about something bigger.

He was creating a moment of belief.

Izzo was interested in getting his young players to actually *feel* winning that last game. His goal was to create in them a visceral response—what it felt like to climb the ladder, hold the scissors, and cut that net. He wanted them to know in their bones how much he believed in them, and he wanted them to feel that belief in themselves. And at the end of that season the Michigan State Spartans indeed won a national championship and those same players got to cut down the nets for real at the RCA Dome in Indianapolis.

> Men will work hard for money. They will work harder for other men. But men will work hardest of all when they are dedicated to a cause.
>
> —Harry Emerson Fosdick, pastor

Bigger Than Self

Think about the jobs, tasks, internships, volunteer opportunities, or anything else you've ever had to wake up each day and do. Which did you enjoy the most? Why? I'm sure whether or not you believed in what you were doing was a huge factor in how you felt about it.

"Unless you give motivated people something to believe in, something bigger than their job to work toward," writes Simon Sinek, "they will motivate themselves to find a new job and you'll be stuck with whoever's left."[1] It's a sobering thought: if a leader doesn't give the group something to believe in, the only ones left will be those who believe in nothing. And try making a team out of that.

In *One Click: The Rise of Jeff Bezos and Amazon.com*, author Richard L. Brandt charts the growth of what will likely one day be the world's biggest company. At the heart of the company's success has been the focus on a belief in something larger. "One of his incredible talents," Brandt writes of CEO and founder Jeff Bezos, "has been to convince employees, from the highest manager to the lowest customer service rep stuck to her phone ten hours a day, that working at Amazon was not just a job—it was part of a visionary quest, something to give higher meaning to their lives."[2]

As Amazon expands—there are recent reports that they are moving into banking and health care—that philosophy becomes all the more important. Believing that your work has a larger purpose, that you are part of something bigger than yourself, that work is more than a paycheck, is always going to be the strongest motivator. Sure, people want money, promotions, and titles—but what they want even more? Something to believe in.

Belief and Others

Belief, in the way that I'm referring to it, is not the same as confidence. Confidence can happen alone. Belief happens in a context and within relationships. It involves multiple people and depends on the dynamic between those people.

After his improbable upset of the New England Patriots in Super Bowl LII, Eagles quarterback Nick Foles, whom virtually no one believed in, who had played backup all season to likely MVP Carson Wentz, gave an inspiring speech. What was most remarkable about it was that it wasn't at all about him, this quarterback who achieved the impossible, the man who proved all the doubters wrong.

"I think the big thing that helped me was knowing that I didn't have to be Superman," he said at the post-game press conference. "I have amazing teammates, amazing coaches around me. And all

I had to do was just go play as hard as I could, and play for one another, and play for those guys."

Take a second to read that over again. Foles's words might first sound like the typical post-game clichés, but they're not. Look carefully. What stands out? Notice he didn't go the traditional route—how his team believed *in him* and that's how he was able to pull off this stunning victory. It's the opposite. Foles talks about the belief that *he had in them*.

Let's take a look back at The Servant himself, Kevin Durant. During his famous MVP speech at the end of the 2015 season, which brought tears to the eyes of everyone in the room, KD thanked each of his teammates individually. In doing so, he used the same language and perspective that Foles used about his teammates. It was not about their belief in him, but about *his belief in them*. When he got to teammate Russell Westbrook, his #2, he thanked him for being "an emotional guy who would run through a wall for me." Having others believe in you is important. But being able to believe in them is the ultimate. That is what makes a team tighter than glue, stronger than steel, impossible to break.

Seeking Purpose

Belief is the thing that exists before anything else, before there's any evidence that an idea will work. It's like the sun—the force that first sparks the energy to trigger the food chain. As told in the book *The Accidental Billionaires* (and the film *The Social Network*), Mark Zuckerberg built Facebook out of a small, tight cadre of friends who *believed* that they were developing something important, revolutionary, and powerful.

That belief—more than the Harvard education, tech savvy, and early investment capital—is what shot Facebook into the strato-sphere. The other things no doubt helped, but they would all have been meaningless if they hadn't been built on a foundation of belief. Zuckerberg recognized this himself as he put together his company and looked for the right people to hire. "People can be really smart or have skills that are directly applicable," Zuckerberg has said, "but if they don't really believe in it, then they are not going to really work hard."[3]

There's a slew of scientific research backing this up: belief in something is a proven, powerful force. One of the most interesting studies on this topic comes from the research into recovering alco-holics. One of the first guidelines of recovery is that the alcoholic should believe in a "higher power," as he understands it. Not every-one is able to do this, but statistically, those who have given in to a higher power have a better overall sobriety rate.

Is this proof of a higher power? Nope. But it is proof that belief works. That belief can operate as that "higher power." For the recovering alcoholics, "it was belief itself that made the difference," researchers determined. "Once people learned how to believe in something, that skill started spilling over to other parts of their lives, until they started believing they could change." A big part of recov-ery programs' success is that the belief of the single participant is shared and expanded by the others in the program. As one scientist explained, "a community creates belief."[4]

That's a potent idea—*community creates belief*—and it's applicable across so many forums. When we are surrounded by others who believe, it makes our mission, its importance, and the possibility of its success, that much more real.

At their first practice of the year, each member of Izzo's Michi-gan State team got to cut down the net, but each player also got to *watch all his teammates do the same*. That was an equally important part of the exercise. "Change occurs among other people," a psychologist told author Charles Duhigg in *The Power of Habit*. "It seems real when we can see it in other people's eyes."[5] We look to others to determine our reality. When we are surrounded by believers, we can climb mountains. Sometimes, we can even move them.

Belonging

A community of belief and a sense of belonging are powerful tools. The epitome of this idea is the NCAA College Basketball Tournament, commonly known as March Madness. Turn on any game during the tournament and watch how invested all the players are. Look how hard they cheer, particularly the ones at the end of the bench, the ones who never get in the game. The best teams create a sense of mission and everyone—from the star player to the twelfth man—plays a part. They are bound by belief.

No matter how independent we may claim to be, we all require a feeling that we belong. It's in our nature. "At our core," Simon Sinek says, "we are herd animals that are biologically designed to find comfort when we feel like we belong to a group."[6] People respond to that feeling of belonging, and the strongest teams utilize these natural tendencies. It's not just in our heads; it's actually a chemical response. As Sinek goes on to explain: "Our brains are wired to release oxytocin when in the presence of our tribe and cortisol, the chemical that produces the feeling of anxiety, when we feel vulnerable and alone."[7]

In a study of high-performing organizations, Sinek found that "their cultures have an eerie resemblance to the conditions under which the human animal was designed to operate.... If certain conditions are met and the people inside an organization feel safe among each other, they will work together to achieve things none of them

could have ever achieved alone."[8] Belief operates not just as an emotional bonding tool. It goes all the way down to the chemical level,
to the literal makeup of who we are.

Back in the 1990s Stanford business professors James Baron and
Michael Hannan began a long-term study of different business cultures and tried to determine which were the most effective. They
ended up separating companies into five different groups and found
that the highest-performing companies have what they call a "commitment culture." The CEOs of these companies "believe that getting the culture right is more important than designing the best
product."[9] When the researchers examined the results, "commitment culture outperformed every other type of management style in
every meaningful way,"[10] including the firms that exclusively went
after the top talent. Belief is so powerful that it regularly trumps
skill, knowledge, and pedigree.

Cinderella Stories

The belief component is demonstrated in sports when underdogs—
whom *no one* else thinks can win—pull off seemingly impossible
victories. It's one of the reasons that March Madness is so fascinating.
When a high seed (a lower-ranked team) goes deep into the
tournament, it's a testament to the power of belief. As I write this,
an unheard-of school called University of Maryland, Baltimore
County (UMBC) just knocked off the number 1 ranked team in
the country, the University of Virginia. It is the first time in the
history of the tournament a 16-seed (the lowest-rated) has beaten a
1-seed. Fans and casual viewers alike are going insane because it taps
into something inside all of us: we want to believe. It moves us as
nothing else can.

The leading scorer on that historic UMBC team was DeMatha

graduate Jairus Lyles, who played under Coach Jones. Coach Jones would often reminisce with us fellow coaches and his players about his own playing days, including when he led a 14-seed Old Dominion over three-seed Villanova in triple overtime in 1995. Despite their seed, Jones's coach, Jeff Capel, told his Old Dominion players to make sure they packed for the entire weekend, for both the Villanova game and the next round after that. That simple act—*packing clothes for the entire weekend*—helped plant a belief in those players' minds. They would be staying in town after the Villanova game for another one. *Believe or leave.*

Smaller schools who pull off upsets are not intimidated by the Duke or Kentucky jerseys, bigger schools with larger stadiums and a wider reach. They know the score starts out at 0–0, that both teams put five players on the court and shoot at a 10-foot basket. They know the lower-seeded team doesn't automatically have the right to advance. They know there's a reason that they play the game.

When belief is shared in a group, it expands. It latches on to every member of the team and even on to those who are supporting that team. The more people add to that shared pool of belief, the more power it has. Everyone is responsible for carrying and exhibiting that belief, ensuring that it's always present in the group. When one person is having an off day, he can rely on the others' belief to power him through. It's a collective feeling that lifts everyone up.

The Immovable Wall of Standards

Belief has to exist across the board: from the coach, to the star player, all the way down to the end of the bench. There is a famous story where Bill Walton, the star of John Wooden's UCLA team in the early 1970s, didn't want to cut his hair or shave his beard, which he had grown over the summer. Coach Wooden had a strict policy about this and reminded Walton that he couldn't practice unless he adhered to it. Walton launched into a long speech about how he was an All-American (among the best players in the country), and he wanted to express himself and how he had the right to grow his hair however he wanted. Wooden listened attentively until Walton was done. Then he looked at his star player and said, "I understand you feel that way, Bill. We're sure going to miss you."

Walton sped off to get that shave and haircut before practice began.

Wooden stuck to his standards, understanding that if other players saw the star do what he wanted, the wheels were likely to come off the whole thing. And no one person—even the star, *especially* the star—could be allowed to make that happen.

Accountability

Is there anything more frustrating than peers getting away with negative behavior? Think about it: In the classroom, when you see students cheating without any punishment. At practice, if you see players not hustling after the ball. In the workplace, if you see people taking three-hour lunch breaks. If there's no accountability for one, then *there is no accountability at all.* The negative behavior will spread like a virus.

Belief arises out of accountability because it comes from a trust that others will fulfill their role. People are held accountable not just by the leaders, but *by each other.* "Most players believe accountability means blame," Jay Bilas wrote. "It doesn't. Accountability is being held to the standard you have accepted as what you want, individually and collectively."[11] It's why Bill Walton had to get that shave and haircut—otherwise the whole system broke down.

Holding someone accountable is something you do *for* them, not something you do *to* them. The same is true in business. Giant organizations like Netflix understand how things can slip through the cracks, so they call those accountable to a project "decision owners." It's not just a label; it's a reminder. The entire Whole Foods organization is designed as a series of teams, and a team has the ultimate say as to whether or not a new employee is hired, after a trial period, as a member of that team.[12] Ultimately, they all share in the bonuses the team receives. Google also uses this team-hiring format, which is becoming more popular with businesses.[13] The company asks the future employee's potential team members to weigh in on the hiring. It makes perfect sense: Go right to the source. Ask those who will have to hold the employee accountable if he is going to fit on that team. Of course they will know best.

A Culture of Belief

When I interviewed Chris Collins, head coach at Northwestern and son of the legendary NBA coach and broadcaster Doug Collins, he spoke openly about how belief comes after a tipping point. It took a couple of years for him to bring his team to the point where the belief that they would win carried them over the hump. "The common trait you see with all winning teams or winning businesses," he told me, "there's a swagger that those teams carry when they take the court. They believe they're supposed to win. I think that really shines through when you're in a close game...when you believe you're supposed to win, it can carry you through, it can will you to be successful."

Chris spoke to me about how his understanding of the power of belief arose out of the way his father raised him. Doug Collins never let his son win at anything—like another dad I know—because he wanted Chris to believe in his own abilities to will an outcome.

Once Chris finally did beat his dad, that belief was solidified internally and brought to every other game he played. Now he shares it with his players.

In their book *Tribal Leadership*, authors Dave Logan, John King, and Halee Fischer-Wright discussed their ten-year, 24,000-person study of effective workplace cultures. The winner, what they called a Stage Five culture, is made up of "pure leadership, vision, and inspiration"[14] and was found at places like Pixar and Apple. This type of culture was extremely rare, and made up less than 2 percent of the businesses they examined.[15]

What stood out the most was this explanation of how much Stage Five members are committed to their work: "People who have been part of a Stage Five tribe—or even seen one at work—often describe it in the same tone of reverence and gratitude they use *to tell stories of their kids*."*[16] Now, I'm not advocating that you should care more about work than your family; you shouldn't. The point is that the excitement, the sense of possibility, the positive energy that these people brought to their jobs shows what can happen if the key ingredient of belief is there.

One of the things I repeatedly emphasize in my talks to corporations is that businesses are made of people. It seems obvious, but it's something that is so basic, so foundational, that it gets missed. If we remind ourselves of this fact, many issues involving effort, care, and incentives that hurt businesses become easier to solve. People are driven by desires, fears, needs, and motivations. A tight-knit team regularly taps into the well of belief because they know it's the emotion—the engine—that powers everything else. Belief is when a group's positivity and confidence meet their trust and commitment.

---

* Emphasis is mine.

They think they can do it, and they put their minds and hands together to get it done. They will it into existence.

> **Key Point:** Though it's made up of different people, a team comes together over a collective belief in an idea and a mission.
>
> **Remember:**
>
> ☞ Success comes when commitment meets belief.
>
> ☞ Set goals that are both realistic and just out of reach—belief will help you cross the divide.
>
> ☞ The best leaders are able to cultivate a powerful feeling of belief within the team and tap into it consistently.
>
> ☞ Lack of belief from one player can pull everyone and everything down. Refuse to accept any holes or cracks in the group's sense of belief.
>
> ☞ An important aspect in creating a culture of belief is creating a sense of accountability. If a rule doesn't exist for one, it doesn't exist at all.

CHAPTER TWELVE

Unselfishness

> There is no limit to what a man can do so long as he does not care a straw who gets the credit for it.
>
> —Charles Edward Montague, author[1]

Society tends to propagate the idea that life is zero-sum, that in order for me to win, you have to lose. This happens with athletes battling for playing time and with employees fighting for the same promotion or carrying envy about someone else's success. We see it on a macro level in business and in the nature of capitalism itself. We see it in the tendency to seek status and material wealth in an effort to "keep up with the Joneses."

In my opinion, we are all born inherently selfish. As a father, I didn't have to teach my children to look out for themselves first; that came naturally to them. Before they could even speak, when crying was their primary form of communication, all they cared about was their own interest—to be fed, to take a nap, to have their diaper changed. Like most children, some of their first words were "No!" and "Mine!" Selfishness was wired in their DNA. Their mother and

I had to teach them to be unselfish, to share, and to give. Adults need to be reminded of this as well.

My longtime friend Matt King, who is a brilliant basketball coach and consultant with USA Youth Basketball, once told me, "You don't have to remind me each morning to look out for myself and to 'do me.' I do that naturally. We all do. What we all need to be reminded of us is that we are a part of something bigger and it's not about us."

When it comes to achievement, working together is more efficient and productive than everyone doing his own thing. Any of the players that sit on the end of the bench at a high school like DeMatha or a college like Duke could absolutely have a larger role somewhere else. They would get a lot more playing time—and attention—at other schools, but they choose to give up personal accolades for collective success. These players opt for the smaller role to be part of something much bigger than themselves. We often call these types "team players," and they are the glue that keeps groups together.

The Art of the Backup

Swen Nater is a rarity. He is the only college basketball player in history selected in the first round of the NBA Draft who never started a college game. He is also the only player to have led both the NBA and the ABA in rebounding. An accident? A fluke? Neither. It was all about whom Nater spent his college career playing under—and with.

As the reserve center at UCLA in the 1970s, Swen Nater played backup to Hall of Fame legend Bill Walton for two championship teams under John Wooden. I was a bit in awe when I spoke to him, as I would argue that Nater is the epitome of unselfishness. Not only did he never start a single game for those UCLA teams, but there was never even a moment when that seemed possible. He had the option of leaving UCLA—other teams wanted him—but he didn't take it. In fact, he told me, "I never thought twice about leaving."

Nater came to basketball late in life; he didn't play high school ball, and only had a couple of junior college years on the court before transferring to UCLA. Maybe it was because he came to basketball later than most players that he approached it with a unique unselfishness. That attitude likely made his career. He wanted to become a professional and figured "practicing against Bill Walton and UCLA every day was a good step in that direction," as he told me. Would he have made it to the NBA as a dominant center on another team? Maybe. Or maybe not. Perhaps he wouldn't have developed his game and gotten any better because he wouldn't have had a reason to.

This chapter was originally called "Selflessness," but when I interviewed Swen, he said the word sounded too much like taking your self away, which wasn't the goal at all. Unselfishness is not losing yourself, he told me: "It's almost the opposite. It's taking your talents, the ones that are needed, and using those to benefit the team…the ones that the coach decides that you should use." So I changed the name of this chapter.

Swen understood the place where unselfishness and success intersect: he didn't sacrifice a career because of unselfishness—he *built* one off it. As Coach Wooden told him: "The best thing you can do for the team is to improve yourself." When I asked him what made him choose to spend his college career as a backup, when he could have transferred anywhere to be a starter, likely raising his profile and his draft prospects, he answered thoughtfully:

That's not an instant decision. That's something you decide upon because the culture at UCLA was such. That was the culture of Coach Wooden—he never took credit for any victories or good play, he always gave credit to the players and publicly. And mostly, not the scorers, the other guys who did the little things: rebounds, great passes, stopped a great opponent defensively... by example the culture was set and he enforced it, in practice and in games.

Swen emphasized that, under Wooden, he didn't develop an interest in self-glory. "It's all about the group," he told me, "and what's needed for them to run productively and effectively." Though a lot of players say that—it's become something of a sports cliché— I took it at face value because Nater actually lived it. And he was rewarded for it.

Wooden saw his backup center's unselfishness, knew he wanted to go pro, and did what he could to help. He continually reminded Nater that being coached by him and going up against Walton every day in practice was the best thing for his game. Wooden even did what he could to help get the professional scouts to notice his un-selfish backup center. "Part of the reason we won was that I made Bill Walton better," Nater says now.

In his post-basketball life, as an executive, he continues to emphasize the importance of the same principles. He preaches get-ting rid of the ego that wants to be fed and putting that energy back into the collective. "Immediately recognize the people that helped you, whatever success that was," he says. "I make a point to include others so I can give credit if something good happens." As a twenty-year-old kid, it's not that Nater didn't have the same selfish desire that most have. He just chose not to develop that part of himself, and over time, it drained away. What was left was an unselfishness that laid the groundwork for his future—and inspired others, includ-ing me.

> I was the most egotistical player they would ever meet. My ego is not a personal ego, it's a team ego. My ego demands—for myself—the success of my team.
>
> —Bill Russell

Team Ego

Winning athletes understand how to operate and succeed within the team structure. That kind of leadership trickles down to everyone else. Unselfishness doesn't mean not being competitive or committed. It means that those personality traits are channeled into the team's mission and not toward one's own acclaim.

Hall of Famer Bill Russell didn't just preach unselfishness. The winningest player in NBA history—he won eleven titles in thirteen years with the Celtics—walked the walk. Russell's commitment to the defensive end of the court, where accolades are less common, is what made him a legend. Though he was clearly the alpha male on every one of his teams—and the best player in the league for more than a decade—it was his reputation as a loyal teammate that made him one of the most respected players to ever step onto the court. In fact, his unselfishness stretched so far that he even declined his induction into the Pro Basketball Hall of Fame. The reason? He told a reporter he wanted to be celebrated for "team play, not individual accomplishment."[2]*

---

* Russell has given others reasons over the years for declining, including racial inequality in the Hall and in the league during his playing days.

Self-Test

Teammate Audit:

- Fifteen index cards: Write the name of a colleague on each card.
- Every workday, send one of them one of three things:
    - Someone you know who may benefit them (and ask if they'd like an introduction)
    - Something you know that may add value to them (a book recommendation, an article, or a video)
    - An inquiry to see how they are doing and what you can help with ("How are things in your world?")

Unity

Strive to be the best *for* the team, not the best *on* the team. Instead of looking around and belittling those under you and being jealous of those above you, find a way to work with them. It will behoove everyone, including yourself. The old saying is that a rising tide lifts all boats—being part of a successful team will ultimately burnish your own career. Demonstrate your unselfishness by making a point to credit others and take the blame when appropriate.

Pat Riley, who as head coach for both the Los Angeles Lakers and the Miami Heat has five championship rings stretching over twenty-five years, has seen what it takes to build and sustain a championship team. (Riley also has another two rings as team president for the Heat). Because of that, he has also had a front-row seat to what can tear one apart. Riley famously coined the term the "Disease of Me"[3] to describe what happens over the course of a championship team's trajectory. In the beginning, everyone is in it for the team and for that ring. But once success arrives, people start looking out for themselves, bemoaning the credit or attention or money they aren't getting, forgetting what made them winners in the first place. The Disease of Me is a sickness of selfishness, and it ultimately destroys a winning culture. The glue that keeps a team together is eroded, and the chemistry that is lost doesn't just reappear.

In his book *The Ideal Team Player*, management expert Patrick Lencioni explains that team players need to be "humble, hungry, and smart"[4] (he clarified that he means *people* smart). "They share credit, emphasize team over self, and define success collectively rather than individually."[5] Inevitably, the snake who's only looking to climb the corporate ladder will infect everyone else on the team. Decades ago, that personality might have been rewarded, but times and culture have changed significantly. Even top talent is not enough to overcome a selfish attitude. For instance, Netflix openly advertises the fact that they don't hire "brilliant jerks" because "the cost to effective teamwork is too high."[6] No one, in any industry, is good enough at what he does to get a pass for being selfish.

1+1 = 3

Studies show that virtually all of us want to be part of something bigger than ourselves, a member of a tribe, group, or team. It's in our animal nature. Though that's true, it is also true that we are born selfish beings. We all come out of the womb looking out for ourselves and doing what's in our own best interest. It's only natural.

For a team to be great, on some level, that instinct has to be unlearned and that mind-set has to shift. You need to care about the team's needs, vision, and mission as much as your own personal agenda. That's not easy. Swen Nater didn't become an unselfish player overnight; it took working with and buying into a team system for him to get it. *It's not you versus me; it's you plus me.* With that mind-set, there's exponential growth. My friend's dad used to say that on good teams 1+1 = 2, but on great teams 1+1 = 3.

Think about a basketball team. It's natural for the backup point guard to feel he is in a competition against the starting point guard. But that's a toxic mind-set, and it erodes the team fabric. A point guard can't succeed on his own anyway—he is usually measured by how much better he makes his teammates. (In fact, all players are now measured by this criteria.) His success is tied directly to the success of the other four players on the court.

The backup's mentality needs to be: *what can I do to make the starter even better?* That doesn't mean the backup shouldn't want that starting job; he should hustle his butt off and, like Tom Brady, be in a position to take over if the opportunity ever arises. It just means he shouldn't be ruled by that outcome. Don't be so self-directed that you miss the point of being a member of a team. *A rising tide lifts all boats.*

One Ball in Houston

Unselfishness is most acutely required when there is more than one "star" on a team or in a group. Two or three stars don't double or triple a team's chances of winning by their mere presence. There needs to be a commitment to unselfishness or else some of the star power just starts to cancel itself out.

In the summer of 2017, when Chris Paul was traded to the Houston Rockets, the doubters took to the streets (or more accurately, to social media). There was no way in the world this would work. It was going to be a disaster! How would Chris Paul, who needed to have the ball to play his game, coexist with James Harden, who needed the ball even more! The previous season Harden led the NBA in possession time and Paul was seventh. And as the saying goes, there is only one ball. The naysayers made some noise, but Houston ended the season with the best record in the league—by a healthy margin.

How did that happen? "You do what you have to do on the team that you're on," Paul told a reporter. "That's the way games work."[7] (This is a sneaky brilliant quote by the way. That's *exactly* how games work.) Of course, players are media trained to say unselfish things, but the statistics—and the Rockets' record—bear this out. Not only that, but Harden won league MVP that year, proving he didn't have to lessen his game to work with Paul. They didn't each take a step back to win; they took a step *toward each other*.

First, both stars knew there were plenty of possessions and shots to feed two scorers. Second, when a team adds another threat, opportunities open up, and the Rockets capitalized on this. Before Paul joined the Rockets, defenses could plan and scheme to shut down Harden and make him the focal point. When the Rockets added another legitimate scorer in Paul, teams couldn't focus solely on Harden or Paul would torch them. As someone who wants to play alongside other great players, Paul is empowered, not threatened, by pairing up with Harden.

Two superstar players on the same team chose to raise each other's level of effort and focus. Of course, all this *could* be true of any one-two punch, but it took Harden and Paul to both buy in, to unselfishly embrace the other's presence, for it to work. According to the NBA's all-important Plus/Minus statistic (which measures how effective a team is when an individual is on the court), Paul and Harden currently rank numbers 1 and 2 in the league. More proof: *1 + 1 = 3*.

The Quiet Alpha

In the world of basketball, it is nearly impossible to preach the power of unselfishness without touching on the king of unselfishness, the

San Antonio Spurs' Hall of Famer Tim Duncan. Duncan's attitude goes way back. While at Wake Forest, Tim Duncan actually coauthored an academic paper called: "Blowhards, Snobs, and Narcissists: Interpersonal Reactions to Excessive Egotism"[8] It was an early peek at Duncan's attitude, which would help him claim the title as the most unselfish Hall of Famer in NBA history.

Duncan came into the league as a highly touted rookie and the number 1 overall pick. However, unlike more than a handful of top picks who put up impressive numbers for a limited amount of years and then vanish, Duncan became one of the all-time greats. Talent? Of course. But all those guys were extremely talented. Those who flame out never quite lose their feeling that, as the number 1 pick, they deserve to be treated like a number 1 pick. But Duncan didn't seem interested in that at all.

As a young player, Duncan responded to the mentoring of veteran David Robinson, flourished under the team concept instilled by coach Gregg Popovich, alternated his position constantly depending on the team's makeup, wasn't a top-ten scorer though he easily could have been, played off the ball, took less money so there was room under the salary cap to sign other talent, and never said a word about his retirement until the season was over, avoiding the goodbye tours that most legends embark on during their last season. He is the quietest Alpha Dog the sport has ever produced and, as most argue, the greatest power forward of all time.[9] "[B]y lowering himself," Sam Walker wrote in *The Captain Class*, Duncan "was able to coax the maximum performance out of the players around him."[10]

Did some people give Duncan a hard time because he was an introvert, not interested in self-glory? Sure. But he made a decision that to achieve the pinnacle in a team sport, he had to focus on what mattered: collective success. Even though he is retired, it's obvious that his shadow looms large. The Spurs' culture—with obvious credit to Coach Popovich, who's still there—continues to be among the healthiest and most team-oriented in professional sports.

The Myth of the Taker

There's a misconception—in business and in sports—that unselfish people get trampled on, that if you don't look out for yourself, you're bound to get burned. But it's a myth—and a poisonous one at that.

As I discussed in chapter 9, in his book *Give and Take*, researcher Adam Grant demonstrates how the highest performers—across the board—are actually givers. "Their generosity earns them deep and lasting respect,"[11] he wrote. The team supports givers, helping them reach their full potential. Givers are recognized as such and get lifted by a group that recognizes and values that giving.

"There's something distinctive that happens when givers succeed: it spreads and cascades....Givers succeed in a way that creates a ripple effect, enhancing the success of people around them."[12] Grant also noted that, on a practical level, givers keep themselves out of the rat race: fewer people are gunning for them. Because of this, colleagues are more likely buy into the giver's ideas because he has been established as not being motivated by self-interest. People are attracted to the giver; they trust the giver; they want to assist the giver and work with the giver. The giver is the one who *endures*.

I think of them as the opposite of Jon Gordon's energy vampires. The givers fill and feed the culture instead of detracting from it. The "negative impact of a taker is double or triple the positive impact of a giver," Grant calculated. "With one taker on a team, you begin to notice that paranoia spreads and people hold back out of fear that they'll be exploited."[13]

All of us are givers—to some extent, I hope—in our personal lives. But we feel a need to take, or at least balance our giving and taking in the workplace like it's a profit and loss statement. Maybe we don't want to be seen as too generous because then we'll be perceived as soft or pushovers. Maybe we're worried what people would think or how we might be taken advantage of.

If we fight through those stereotypes, we'll recognize that unselfishness and generosity in the workplace build success. You can be assertive and ambitious but still be a team player by channeling those drives into the group's success—not just your own. Giving and winning are not mutually exclusive. Just ask Swen Nater. And Tim Duncan. And Chris Paul and James Harden. And Bill Russell.

Key Point: What makes or breaks a team—all teams—is how much each member is willing to sacrifice self-interest and self-glory for team success.

Remember:

☞ A team is a group of people who each put the group's needs ahead of his own. Every act of selfishness erodes the team's fabric.

☞ Each of us has an instinctive drive toward self-interest. A team chooses to put this aside in service of a larger goal.

☞ A group will be find success if they scrap you versus me and replace it with you plus me. With that mind-set, 1+1=3.

☞ Unselfishness is not about charity or just basic kindness; it has been proven as an effective approach to achieving and succeeding.

CHAPTER THIRTEEN

Role Clarity

> Many players I've coached didn't look special on paper, but in the process of creating a role for themselves, they grew into formidable champions.
>
> —Phil Jackson[1]

Of course, talent is important in any field, but there's not a single industry where it exists in a vacuum. People can excel only when they are allowed to do so, when they are put in a position to succeed, when they are in a place where their role—and the roles of those around them—is clearly defined. This is an underrated but hugely important aspect of teamwork. In some ways, it is the very *definition* of teamwork. It's literally how teams work.

Clear roles function as a map, keeping team members on track, ensuring they don't walk all over each other, and trusting that important issues don't get missed. Team sports are a perfect illustration of this: the roles are clearly identified, and analyzing what went right or wrong on any given play or game can be isolated to figure out who's responsible. That doesn't mean blame. That means making the necessary adjustments and figuring out how to fix it for next time.

Role clarity is a big picture idea. It means a team understands what the person to his left and to his right is responsible for. He knows how what he does affects those two team members, as well as everyone else. It's understanding *how the machine works*. A team is a jigsaw puzzle, and the only way for that puzzle to be completed is if each part sits properly together with the others. The picture won't make sense any other way. A leader must examine every person on the team, what their strengths and weaknesses are, and what motivates or demotivates them. Remember: the right role isn't always what a player wants to be; it's what he *needs to be* for the puzzle to come together.

The best coaches bring this out in their weaker players so that the unit stays strong and invested. The worst coaches spend all their energy on the stars, missing an opportunity to motivate and utilize their other players. The strongest teams are made up of people who know exactly what their and everyone else's role is—and there's a mutual trust that everyone will execute their function. No one can be his best if he has to worry about other people's responsibilities, if he can't trust that those things will get done.

Victor Finds His Role

NBA All-Star Victor Oladipo is a shining example of a player who, in various situations, has flourished by understanding and maximizing his role. I've known Victor since he was in high school, and he has always worked as though he was trying to make the team. "I'm still in a situation where I feel like I haven't accomplished anything," he told me on my podcast. When you realize how far he's already come, how few people make it to the NBA at all and lead their team to the playoffs, that's an amazing statement. It's also the attitude that leads to greatness.

I began working at DeMatha during Victor's senior year. When the high school basketball season ended, and his obligation to attend off-season workouts ceased, he still chose to come. Yep. That was his work ethic. As an eighteen-year-old nearing graduation—with the season over(!)—he still came to school for every 6 a.m. morning workout. Suffice to say, even at DeMatha, this was not something seniors typically did.

Victor took pride in leading by example and serving as a mentor to the younger, returning players. He knew his role as a veteran and recognized how much his attitude and actions impacted the others. The fact that this was a team that Victor would never again play for only proves the point. He understood his role and fulfilled it long after he was required to do so.

Victor has always been a team-first guy. I think it's because he didn't experience individual success—and the attention that comes with it—until his later years of high school. He began as a role player, alongside guys getting more shots and more attention. When he left DeMatha for Indiana University, he knew the transition—and the role change—was not going to be easy. He admitted to me that he knew he was a late bloomer at DeMatha and that "My work ethic is the one [thing] that kept me going."

It was not until his breakout junior year at Indiana that Victor elevated himself again—in his own eyes and in the eyes of NBA scouts—this time to be one of the NCAA's top prospects. He told me that it was, "how I affected my team, how I helped them win, that's when I realized I could play at the next level." That's key. It's not that his shooting or passing or defense got better—although they all did. Victor's rise to the upper echelon of college basketball hinged on how well he could play as one-fifth of a team on the court. That's what NBA scouts want to see. And unless your name is LeBron James, working as part of a cohesive unit is the only way to succeed in the NBA. (Actually, it's true for LeBron, too.)

I've followed Victor's career closely and have admired his willingness to accept a variety of roles, at DeMatha, at Indiana University* as an All-American and *Sporting News'* Player of the Year, as the number 2 overall pick in the NBA draft, and in his stints with the Orlando Magic, Oklahoma City Thunder, and now with the Indiana Pacers. It has been a pleasure to watch Victor come into his own with the Pacers—stunning the league, becoming 2018's Most Improved Player, and making the once-forgotten squad a legitimate playoff threat. It has also been a validation for him.

In Oklahoma City, Oladipo was stifled in his role, and a big part of that was that it didn't exist. He was stuck playing second fiddle to that year's MVP, Russell Westbrook, perhaps the most ball-dominant guard of the modern era. With no clear role for Oladipo in the backcourt with Westbrook, there was no way for him to show what he could do. Consequently, Oladipo plateaued. He didn't whine, complain, or point fingers; he simply couldn't flourish in that environment. It took the right situation for Victor to thrive, and the right role for him to shine. He blossomed once he found a team that knew what to do with him. Both his leadership and his team-oriented play have come to the forefront. Since joining the Indiana Pacers, Victor has flourished for three reasons:

1. He has worked relentlessly on his game. He's spent countless hours in the gym raising his strengths and tightening up his

---

* He graduated from Indiana University in three years after taking 19 credits in his final semester.

weaknesses, even totally revamping his body in the off-season to develop bulk and muscle.

2. He is the ultimate team player, willing to do whatever the team needs him to do to be successful. Victor won't let pride or ego get in the way of doing what his coaches and teammates require. He learned this at DeMatha and carried it to Indiana University and the NBA.

3. He found a better fit with his current team. Not a better team necessarily, a better *fit*. His strengths aligned perfectly with what the Pacers needed. His talents were not being utilized with the Magic and the Thunder; the role they needed him to play didn't factor in his strengths. Victor has more freedom and opportunity with the Pacers and is on his way to becoming the best player he can be.

Though Oladipo had once been written off in some circles, he has recently opened everyone's eyes. It reminded the basketball world of one of its most enduring truths: *you have to put the player in a position to succeed.* Give him a role that matches his strengths and give him room to grow.

MJ Before MJ

The legend of Michael Jordan by now is well known, but the story of his Chicago Bulls team has somehow gotten lost, buried in the myth of Michael and his transcendent play. People forget—or don't even know—that the Chicago Bulls were not immediate champions when he joined the team. Or even a couple years in. The Bulls were regularly shut down in the playoffs, often by the Detroit Pistons. In fact, Jordan did not make the NBA Finals until his seventh season. Did Jordan improve in those years? Yes, of course, but he was pretty dominant by year three. The Bulls did not win their first championship because of any big leap Jordan made. It had to do with everyone else around him.

Once the role players' positions were filled—and Jordan *accepted them* in those roles—the Bulls finally rolled over the Pistons on their way to the Finals (and subsequently rolled over everyone in the Finals as well). It wasn't just about Jordan's teammate, All-Star and all-defensive stalwart Scottie Pippen, elevating his game either. It was about all his teammates knowing how they fit in the grand scheme: Horace Grant, John Paxson, Bill Cartwright, B. J. Armstrong, and everyone down the line. It was up to coach Phil Jackson to find a way for each player to know, embrace, and then *make the most of* his individual role. They each had to accept where they fit, and Jordan had to let them succeed in those roles.

There's a famous story that illustrates this so well. During a time-out in the close and decisive Game 5 of the 1991 Finals, Jackson screamed at Jordan, "Who's open? Michael, who's open!"

"Pax," Jordan reluctantly admitted, meaning outside shooter John Paxson.

"Get him the fucking ball!"[2] Jackson replied. It is a pivotal moment in Bulls' lore and for good reason. Once Pax could prove he could knock down his shots, and Jordan trusted he would, everything gelled.

Steve Kerr, who played with Jordan and for coach Phil Jackson during the Bulls' second string of championships, felt Jackson was "exceptionally gifted in keeping everyone involved and letting every player know he had a role,"[3] Kerr told David Halberstam in *Playing for Keeps*. Jordan's role was a given, but according to Kerr, "The players also knew that if they did not do their parts and were not ready at all times, nothing good would ever happen either."[4]

The fact that Kerr then went on to become one of the top coaches in the league—finding a way to make all the alphas in Golden State coexist—is not a coincidence. He learned from the master. As he told an interviewer:

> What struck me about Phil was just the inclusion, making everybody feel important, 1-15 on the roster, every guy felt like he had a role to play. [Jackson] emphasized that the way he went about his business....the fifteenth man matters. That's good advice in any setting, whether you're running a business or a classroom. You can make the people who may not think that they matter...feel like they do. It's an incredibly powerful force. That's what leadership is to me, galvanizing, empowering, making people feel good about themselves, but also that everything they do matters.[5]

Great teams understand the feedback loop: every person is responsible for his own role, and every person is accountable to the team's mission. *We can't win without your doing your part, but you can't win without all of us doing ours.*

Among all the legendary teams Jackson has been a part of, perhaps the greatest was the 1995–96 Chicago Bulls, whose sixty-nine regular season wins was a record at the time.

"One thing I loved about this team," Jackson wrote in his book, "was that everyone had a clear idea about their roles and performed them well. Nobody groused about not getting enough playing time or enough shots or enough notoriety."[6] Jackson had a sixth sense about how to get his players to find, understand, and shine in their role.

The most effective thing you can do on the court is know, embrace, and fulfill your role to the best of your ability. That's what builds championship teams. Many teams have the right people in the wrong positions, which is fixable. It's important for teams to take stock of whether or not they are utilizing people in a way that capitalizes on their strengths.

And don't forget, if you're on the bench—and we're all on the bench in some capacity—you also have a role to play. Here are the three traits you must exude while you wait to "get in the game."

- **Be engaged:** care about what is going on around you.

- **Be enthusiastic:** *show* that you care about what is going around you; try to bring infectious and positive energy to those who are "playing."

- **Be ready** for the moment when your name is called and make the most of the opportunity.

The Challenge of the Big Three

Clear roles also become necessary when there is an overabundance of talent at the top. Accumulating the most qualified people doesn't just automatically generate success. The group needs to operate in harmony—and when strong personalities are each used to being the number 1 guy, a lack of role clarity becomes a problem.

When LeBron James and Chris Bosh joined Dwyane Wade's Miami Heat in 2010, the anticipation was electric and the hype was through the roof. Three superstars on one team, way back in 2010, was a rarity. But few remember that the "Big Three" were not as immediately successful as many had predicted. For one thing, they dropped far too many close games.

Some analysts understood the problem: Wade, LeBron, and

Bosh had all been the leader on their respective teams. But when they joined up, they couldn't figure out who would play what role. It was not just about ego or self-perception; it had on-the-court consequences. With seconds remaining in a game, when a last shot has to be set up, not knowing who does what is a very big deal.

It wasn't just the eye test either—the numbers back it up. "In late-game situations, the Heat's execution and coordination were disastrous," wrote *Friend and Foe* authors Adam Galinsky and Maurice Schweitzer. "Their record in close games was the second worst in the league."[7] Considering their talent and the fact that they made it to the Finals that year, this statistic really drives home the importance of having clear roles. "At a certain point, adding more top talent caused teams' winning percentages to go down rather than up," the authors determined. "These teams had *too much* talent."[8]

Without clear roles, adding talent doesn't do anything; it might even drag a team down. This idea is universal and transfers elsewhere. Studies have shown that when there's an excess of talent at a Wall Street company, it backfires. "[T]op talent was beneficial for performance…" according to Galinsky and Schweitzer, "but only up to a point: The effect of more talent turned negative and started to harm performance. When there is too much talent, the stars and high-status individuals compete among themselves to establish who the alpha dog is."[9] A team doesn't come together once some overall talent threshold is reached. A team becomes a team when each piece is locked into place and each player is accepting of and comfortable with that place.

The Puzzle

Part of the credit to the Heat's figuring it all out should go to head coach Erik Spoelstra, who proved to be an exceptional leader. Like

Spoelstra, the premiere college basketball coaches lean heavily on role clarity. The head coaches have to get through to players who have been the best players on the court for most of their lives. When these players arrive at a top program like Duke or Villanova, they have to learn how to fit in a lot more than they did in high school.

When I asked Villanova's coach Jay Wright what the key was to getting these players to buy into their roles, he told me, "They have to believe that the role that you're giving them is really best for them in the long run. I think guys will sacrifice in the short term for their team, if they believe... that it is going to pay off for them."

With two titles in three years, Wright has obviously found a way to keep everyone involved—from his stars all the way down to his practice squad. In fact, Nova's leading scorer for the 2018 championship game was sixth-man Donte DiVincenzo, who scored 31 *off the bench*, a record for a bench player in the title game. It led to looks from NBA scouts and getting drafted seventeenth overall—because he thrived in his role in Wright's system, a huge plus for prospective NBA players.

With full credit to this young man for his big-time performance, I can't help but think that Wright's philosophy of treating everyone as valuable in their respective roles gave Donte the confidence to shine. Wright clearly developed a system throughout the season where each player accepted his role. With each season, he had an instinct for how to get buy-in from each of them. "Your instincts can grow with your experience," Wright told me in our interview, "combining that, that's your wisdom."

Superstar Nova player Mikal Bridges began as a role player, then moved to sixth man, and became the team's leader in his third year, obviously impressing Wright with how he fulfilled each role he was given. He, too, is headed for the NBA, as are two other players from that championship team (Omari Spellman and Jalen Brunson). Succeeding in their roles under Wright's system made these players attractive to the NBA, where no one can do anything alone.

Star in Your Role

In basketball a lot of players want to be the primary offensive weapon. That's what's sexy and gets the attention. When we're young and imagining ourselves in the final seconds of a big game, no one imagines themselves getting a key rebound or setting a killer pick. *We picture ourselves taking the final shot.* But as we mature, we understand that winning is not just about who gets lifted up on everyone's shoulders. That's for the movies.

Success is not about being the star. It's about *starring in your role.* Over time, people will notice and that role will expand. If you're not a team's three-point shooter now, make 200–300 after practice from game spots at game speed. Then you'll earn your way to becoming the team's three-point weapon in crunch time. A leader's primary job is to find out what each team member does really well and how to best utilize that skill set for the team's benefit. Then he must get everyone on the team to understand, embrace, and star in his role.

Roles on any team must be clearly communicated by the leader. This needs to be explicit and consistent. Players must have the humility to accept their role; however, it's up to the coach to make sure that role—and the reasoning behind it—is properly communicated. If there's an employee who is always stepping out of his role and throwing off team chemistry, ask yourself this: Does he know what his role is? Are you sure? Go find out.

Steps to Clarifying Roles

- Clearly establish and communicate each individual's role.
- Create buy-in and believe-in with their role.
- Praise those who star in their role, regardless of what that role is.

That third step is extremely important. It's up to leaders to communicate each teammate's value. For example, a coach needs to sit down with the tenth man, who rarely gets in to play the game, and say, "Look, I know you don't get a lot of minutes but your ability to push our starting point guard in practice is invaluable to this team. If you didn't do that every single day, he wouldn't be the player he is, and if he wasn't, we wouldn't be this successful."

Ideally, the leader needs to acknowledge this point in front of others as well, so the role player can feel recognized for his contribution in a group setting. If you have someone who works under you who is unmotivated, or annoyed that he's not getting recognition or a bigger role, give this a try—praise him both privately and in front of others. I guarantee you'll see a difference in his attitude and his output.

The Power of Role Players

The great NBA and college basketball teams are not successful just because of their stars. There are lots of stars in the league, and up to a certain point, they cancel each other out in head-to-head matchups. Every team in the playoffs has a star; that's just how the league works. Team A's star gets his points and Team B's gets his, and it's the role players that end up making the difference.

The Spurs of the past decade and the Warriors of the present decade consist of stars, but those guys alone are not what makes them champions. The defensive specialists and spot-up shooters and locker room "glue" guys, along with the stars, all have to buy in to their respective roles. For the operation to run smoothly, they each have to be happy to serve the whole.

If you watch a Warriors game, you'll see MVP-level play from Kevin Durant and Steph Curry, but you won't see isolated stars grinding out their points. You'll see a high-level machine firing on all cylinders. In 2018 the Spurs were without their only star, Kawhi Leonard, for just about all season, and their record still put them atop the playoff picture. It doesn't mean Kawhi isn't amazing; it means the rest of the team bought in to their new roles and learned how to function without him.

The same goes for college powerhouses like Duke and Kentucky. Coaches Mike Krzyzewski and John Calipari recruit and mold players who are happy to serve a function, not just put up stats and end up on highlight reels. They convince the players that serving the whole by playing their role is important. That not only will this approach get them a national championship, but it'll also put them in a position to be a lottery pick in the NBA draft.

NBA phenom Jeremy Lin built his game by doing what needed to be done along the way. He was undrafted out of college at Harvard, waived multiple times, and bounced around to a few teams before catching the NBA world by storm for the New York Knicks in 2012 in what was dubbed Linsanity. At that moment, in New York, the energy and heroics that Lin brought were exactly what the team (and the town) needed.

But he couldn't do that everywhere. If he'd tried, he would've been out of the league by the next year. He figured out how to approach each situation and locate his role. Then he executed the hell out of it.

"When I was on the Charlotte Hornets," Lin told me in an interview, "I took a lesser role to fill a void on the team—playmaking off the bench. We ended up doing much better than all the preseason polls predicted, and it was one of the most fun seasons I've ever had playing basketball." Wait, *what*? Read that again. Jeremy Lin, who for a couple of weeks, as a twenty-four-year-old, was the absolute king of New York, had more fun playing a smaller role in Charlotte than he did during his time at the top of the mountain. That is the definition of someone who is happy to fill his role. That's a true team player. Lin is now with the Atlanta Hawks serving a different role there as well—his success is a testament to this openness and adaptability.

I think of clear roles like a pit team changing the tires on a race car. They are in lockstep—each person knows his task and executes it with precision to get that car back on the track in minimal time. It's one of the finest examples of people fulfilling their roles I have witnessed, and it gets me every time I see it.

Self-Test

Think about the most important responsibilities you are expected to fulfill in your role. Can you list them? How can you do each better?

Have you met with your boss to discuss how you could better fulfill your role? Have you done outside work, conducted research, or found other ways to improve how you fulfill your role?

Why not?

Where You Stand

Understanding and buying in to your role requires a mix of humility and confidence. Humility is necessary so you understand that you are not operating alone, that you're a necessary, but not the *only,* piece on a team. Confidence is required to take that role and absolutely crush it. Maximize what can be done in that position, and very often it will expand or lead to newer and bigger roles. Then you can do it all over again.

Key Point: A team needs to understand that it is an interlocking puzzle where each shape and size is distinct, necessary, and valuable to the whole.

Remember:

☞ Role clarity comes from the leader; accepting and embracing that role is up to the individual.

☞ Begin with fulfilling your current role. Do what your team needs you to do, not what you want to do, what you feel like doing, or what is convenient for you.

☞ If possible, spend extra time earning an expanded or new role.

☞ It is vital that leaders acknowledge the so-called role players—those who don't get "highlights and headlines."

☞ Don't assume that a collection of top talent will automatically generate success. Becoming a unit involves an understanding and acceptance of roles.

CHAPTER FOURTEEN

Communication

> My father told me that it doesn't matter who is doing the selling or who is doing the buying; it's the human connection that counts.
>
> —Tim Draper, venture capitalist

An effective player, coach, or teammate is interested in connection. He learns how to connect and is constantly looking to hone these skills, building bridges to those above, below, and across from him. Communication requires learning the subtle art of breaking down walls, not building them higher. It reminds me of a saying I've heard a few times which rings absolutely true: Don't call people out; *call them in*. Successful teams talk *to* each other, not *at* each other.

Communication is essential for any team—and it's not just about the information imparted from one person to another. It's much larger than that. It's about stepping outside yourself, your own needs and wants, and seeing the bigger picture. How we communicate is literally how we interact with the world around us. It's how people know who we are, and how we know who they are. It's so basic that we forget it:

I only know how you feel if you tell me.
You only know how I feel if I tell you.

Misunderstanding

Our words are incredibly powerful, so we must choose them
carefully.

One word that is often used to help strengthen a connection is
understand.

I understand how you are feeling.
I understand what you are going through.
I understand why you did that.

But I actually believe it does the opposite. No matter how well
intended, telling someone you understand a feeling is condescending
and patronizing. It causes the listener to put up walls, creating the
very separation it's trying to bridge. Saying you understand is usually
an effort to express empathy, but it doesn't. It often comes off as dis-
ingenuous. You can understand facts, but you can't truly understand
a person's feelings. Even if you've gone through something similar, the context and details will always be different. Respect them
enough to give them their individual experience and impressions.

So instead of telling them you "understand" how they are feeling, tell them you can "appreciate" how they are feeling or "respect"
what they are going through. They will respond to your honesty
and be grateful for what they will see as genuine sympathy.

Getting Outside Ourselves

Though we all learn to talk at a young age, effective communication
is a skill that develops over time. Like any skill, it can be learned
and improved with proper practice and repetition. And once you

learn how to do it, it can open up doors to you that you always thought were closed. This goes for relationships and it goes for the workplace.

For this book I interviewed former NBA player and current ESPN college basketball analyst Jay Williams, one of the most impressive professionals and people I have ever met. Growing up, Jay learned how to dribble using a flat basketball. He couldn't ask his hardworking mother for a new one, so he learned on what he had. As it turned out, this gave him a huge benefit in the long run. It was those hours of practicing with a flat ball that helped him become an enormously skilled dribbler.[1]

It's a fitting story: Throughout his life and career, Jay has found a way not just to bounce back from adversity, but to bounce back *stronger*. Twice in his life, after major setbacks, he has had to build himself up and has reached the top of his field: as a National College Player of the Year and champion at Duke, as the number 2 pick in the NBA draft, and now one of the premiere college basketball analysts in the business.

After Jay's NBA rookie season, a motorcycle accident almost took his leg and ruined his career; Williams had to learn how to walk again. In his book *Life Is Not an Accident: A Memoir of Reinvention*, he wrote openly about the emotional toll that the grueling surgeries and therapies had on him. It took nine operations for him just to able to lift his foot off the ground. After a series of setbacks and getting lapped by old ladies in the swimming pool, Jay was ready to give up. He hit rock bottom and went into a spiral of addiction and suicidal impulses.

It took over three years to build himself back, in body, mind, and spirit. Though he made it far enough back for a cup of coffee with the Nets, he was never the same player. But dealing with adversity is what Williams was built for. He's a personal inspiration to me because of his ability to overcome what he needed to and subsequently excel in multiple fields. The wisdom Jay carries today is made up of the kind of diamonds that come only from heavily pressured coal.

When I interviewed Jay, he zeroed in on one quality above all else that helped him make him who he is. He admitted he had trouble finding his voice when he was younger and credits his success with his ability to get outside of himself and connect with others. In a word: communication.

Jay admitted to me that he was a "horrible communicator" when he was younger, and when he got to Duke, "Coach K forced me to get outside of myself. It was the best learning experience I ever could've gone through because it forced me to convey my thoughts even when times were difficult." Coach K has long been a huge promoter of honest and consistent communication. His players always had to say each other's names during drills as they passed the ball, which instilled the behavior into their brains and into their game.

Not only was communication necessary at Duke, but Coach K framed it as an attitude issue. When a player was too quiet or introverted on the court, Coach K would attribute it to *selfishness*. Think about it: when you are not communicating with your team, who is in the dark? You always know what you're thinking so it may not matter to you. But to those around you? It's poison.

"When you do not communicate, you internalize everything," Williams told me. "You focus all of your internal attention on yourself and what you did wrong in that moment, and that's a very selfish mentality." Williams learned that there were times at Duke that he would get caught up in a blown play, lost in his head, when the right thing to do would have been focusing on the next play. He should have been communicating with his teammates and paying attention to what *they* wanted to accomplish, not what he wanted for himself.

Jay credits Coach K for sitting him down and showing him these things on tape. When Jay watched footage from his game, he noticed how after a turnover his body language would show he was focused on himself to the detriment of the team for the next possession. On the court, it created a negative cycle. However, seeing himself do it, and understanding how it hurt the team, helped Jay turn things around.

The lessons Jay learned about communication apply off the court as well, to business and to life. "The ability to communicate to somebody regardless of the situation is what business *is*..." Jay told me. "You're actually taking the time to assess the person you work with and recognize their strengths and their weaknesses and then cater what you have to say through that particular lens."

Jay also brings heart to all his interactions. It's important that our relationships—even in business—are not just "transactional," as he explained to me. "When you meet somebody," he asked, "are you instantly going to a place of *what can this person do for me and what can I do for this person?* And that's the limit of the relationship. Or is it personal? Are you taking a second to understand what this person is going through? Those moments when you come back to that person in time.... They'll then go to an extra length to help you with what you need. That's business 101." Jay reiterated what I firmly believe: business—all business—is not about the service or the product. It's about people.

Finally, communication acts as a necessary and healthy release valve. Whether in relationships, at the office, or in the public eye, Jay told me, when we're not communicating, we are letting our frustration build and spill over into the next interaction, and then into the next. Communication is a way of checking in with those around us, but also with our own feelings. It's a way to make sure they don't get bottled up, ignored, and left to fester. When we communicate with our team, we open ourselves up: to their insight, to their empathy, to their support. Our thoughts create our reality, but we have to remember that this isn't an objective reality. We spend all of our lives inside our own heads, but we forget that no one else knows what's going on in there.

Talking on the Court

Good teams talk. Great teams communicate. Hall of Fame coach Bob Hurley often closes his eyes for a minute in the middle of practice so he can hear what is going on. He wants to hear shoes squeaking and players talking because it tells him things that his eyes can't always see. The key is making successful communication a habit. For basketball players, I have developed a rating system to help evaluate and improve communication:

0—Silent (unacceptable at any time)
1—Noise (players who clap their hands)
2—Contact (players who give high fives and fist bumps)
3—Generic talk (players who shout phrases like "Good job!" and "Pick it up!")
4—Specific talk (players who use names and examples like "Nice cut, James!")
5—Directing (players who are "coaches on the court"—they constantly say it all)

Coaches should rate the five players on the court with the goal of the total reaching at least 20, and strive to get all players to a level 4 or 5. They should encourage players who talk on both ends of the floor and reward players who vocally encourage teammates when they make a great play and correct teammates when they make a mistake. Putting concrete measurements on a team's communication is one way to make sure it's happening—at a rate and intensity that is fruitful. Otherwise, you're just assuming that your team is communicating enough, which is a common way for it to slip through the cracks.

Open Communication

Effective communication isn't always pleasant. Getting along just to get along can actually backfire. If issues that are causing problems are left unaddressed, the team is not being served at all. Those unspoken matters are going to grow and expand while they sit in the dark.

Great teams do not hold back from one another and are unafraid to air their dirty laundry. Think about it: How else is it going to get clean? They admit their mistakes, their weaknesses, and their concerns without fear of reprisal. "It is only when team members are truly comfortable being exposed to one another that they begin to act without concern for protecting themselves," management expert Patrick Lencioni wrote in *The Five Dysfunctions of a Team*.

Communication is not just about support and kindness; sometimes it's about progress and productivity. A study of executives from various industries found that when they were asked "whether they had ever had issues at work that they had *not* voiced, fully 85 percent said that they had, at some point, felt unable to discuss their concerns."[2] Almost 9 out of 10 employees are afraid to voice their issues? That is a huge problem.

Ray Dalio, who manages the world's largest hedge fund, Bridgewater Associates, and is one of the 100 richest men on earth, practices what he calls "radical honesty" and "radical transparency."[3]

It's the philosophy behind a company that has become astoundingly successful. "Radical truthfulness is just, put everything on your table and get past it," he explained to an interviewer. It's a way to ensure that people know who is getting ahead or not, and why. This strategy conserves energy for the things that truly matter, rather than creating an environment of suspicion, insecurity, and confusion.

Imagine a workplace you've been (or are still) a part of: How much time and energy was spent on what the boss was thinking about your performance, what this colleague was saying behind your back, and so on? Think about what a drain on morale that was. Think about how open and honest communication would have given you peace of mind, while also conserving your time and energy.

In a visionary move, Dalio has decided to knock down those walls in an effort to set up and expand communication lines. A company should be committed to keeping everything out in the open, lest employees feel more like passive cogs than active members of an organization that values them. Remember: people crave that feeling of being wanted and needed.

What Needs to Be Said

Hearing what people think of us is not always the easiest thing to sit through, but it is absolutely essential for our own growth as well as the team's. Recently, I went through something of a boot camp in this very skill. I participated in a CEO Mastermind Retreat in Vail, Colorado. Part of the retreat was an exercise where each participant had to spend time on what was called "The Hot Seat." The goal of the exercise was for each person to be as open and as vulnerable as possible. Whoever was in the hot seat had to share his biggest current challenge—personal or professional. The other members of the group were tasked with listening empathetically and offering honest feedback, creating a safe environment for the person in the hot seat. Once he was done, he was allowed only two responses to the feedback: "Thank you" or "Can you please clarify that?" He was not allowed to respond, defend, justify, or dismiss.

During my session in the hot seat, I had an incredibly difficult time. We all naturally want to deflect, explain, and protect ourselves from harm. That is our instinct. But I gained so much more by not being able to do any of that. It was like having my hands tied behind my back: rather than being a handicap, it actually gave me better balance. I was far more open than I would have been in a regular conversation. The practice was incredibly powerful and provided the kind of fertile environment for personal breakthroughs.

Another powerful team exercise we learned to bring back to our respective workplaces: Everyone on the team is given a handful of index cards and a pen. On the front of each card, they write down specific traits. Some positive ones: hardest worker, most talented, mentally toughest, and most coachable. Some negative ones: laziest, most selfish, and most distracted. Then, on the back of each card, they write down one teammate's name that they feel epitomizes the trait.

Again, the writing is done in private and is 100 percent anonymous. When it's over, someone collects the cards and tallies the stats to reveal the results. If nine out of twelve players think you are the most selfish, guess what? If your most talented is your laziest and most selfish, you're going to have a problem. If the team's hardest worker is also the most talented and most coachable, things are looking good. An exercise like this is actually forward-looking. So much of our behavior is actually changeable—often we just need the push or the spark. An exercise that lays out what our coworkers really think of us may just be what we all need.

> Confrontation is simply meeting the truth head on.
>
> —Coach K

Six Steps to Mastering Tough Conversations

Effective coaches and leaders stand firm in telling their people what they *need* to hear, not necessarily what they *want* to hear. Trust and truth go hand in hand and feed each other. You have to tell the truth to earn trust. And you must have trust that the person is going to tell you the truth. Remember: *Time never makes tough conversations easier.* Confront issues early and directly.

Step 1: Create a Safe Environment

This is an ongoing process, and it's mandatory if there is going to be the necessary trust required for a tough conversation to be productive and smooth. Think about the difference in food quality between something cooked in an oven and something given a minute in a microwave. Real relationships take time.

Step 2: Keep It Professional

It's important not to swerve into the personal. Confront issues and behavior, not people. Trust they can handle it and don't assume you know what their responses will be. Never initiate when angry, frustrated, or disappointed as you are more likely to lose your professionalism in these emotional states.

Step 3: Be Respectful

Remember: in person > phone > e-mail > text.

Give the person the respect they deserve. Be honest and direct, but with respect and tact. Reduce innate barriers and defensiveness through word choice, such as

Can I bounce something off you?
We need to discuss something important because I care about you.
This feedback is to help you.

Step 4: Watch Your Language

Feelings are always valid; actions are not. Just because something is understandable doesn't mean it's acceptable. Never assign blame— use "I" statements ("I'm feeling" > "you make me feel").

Step 5: Empathize and Clarify

Ask for their perspective and then listen. Do not interrupt; allow them to have a full response. Specifically ask for clarification if needed. Affirm and validate their feelings and intentions without judgment.

Step 6: End Strong

Thank them and acknowledge them for having the conversation. Don't forget to take adequate time to process and let emotions settle.

After an appropriate length of time, formally follow up to resolve and move forward.

Positive Communication

Here's another valuable exercise that you can implement with your organization. At the end of a meeting, everyone goes around the room and signifies something specific they appreciated about a colleague. *Jodi, you were an empathetic listener today, and I appreciate it.*

Then each person says something they feel they did well. *I feel I did a nice job with breaking down our team's task into manageable parts.*

Finally, they share something the team did as a whole. No generalities: be specific in your comments. *The team communicated effectively about the standards needed to get this project done.*

The key to this working is that the communication is genuine and detailed. Whoever leads the session cannot let anyone off the hook if they say, "Alan did a good job." Ensure everyone is digging deep and offering specific feedback.

There are a few reasons why this exercise is so effective:

1. When you praise someone specifically in front of his peers, it's a great **bonding** mechanism.

2. With a brush of humility, it gives you the **confidence** and **opportunity** to acknowledge something you're proud of. It is not conceited or arrogant to acknowledge something you did well. Be proud of the work you do.

3. This type of behavior feeds and supports the **collective**.

Mismatch

Keep in mind the power of negative communication. There is something called Gottman's Ratio, named for the psychologist who coined it: a negative interaction has *five times* the impact of a positive interaction.[4] That's a wildly uneven match, so keep in mind the power of your negative communication and how it will throw your relationships out of balance.

You don't have to like everyone with whom you work. But you do have to care about them. Caring is an act of will. It is a choice. You can choose to help, assist, and serve someone that you may not particularly like. That is a standard of which elite teams are made.

The three most powerful things you can say to a colleague or teammate:

1. *I got your back.*
2. *I believe in you.*
3. *I care about you.*

Thermostats

Communication helps to set and maintain the tone of an organization's culture. As legendary motivational speaker Les Brown used to say, "It's the difference between a thermostat and a thermometer." A thermostat sets the temperature, and a thermometer simply reads it. A thermostat *dictates* the environment while a thermometer just *reacts* to it.

In his prime, NBA Hall of Famer Steve Nash was a thermostat. His energy and enthusiasm were every bit as valuable as his shooting and passing skills, which were considerable. In 2004, the year Nash won the first of two back-to-back MVP awards, he led the league in two statistical categories: assists and touches. Yes, *touches*. He led the league in high fives, fist bumps, and pats on the back. How do I know? Because some researchers at UC Berkeley kept track.[5] They were conducting a formal study to see if there was a correlation between showing enthusiasm and winning. The Suns even had an intern count Nash's touches during one game. The number of times Steve Nash touched a teammate as an act of enthusiasm in a 48-minute game? Two hundred and thirty-nine.

Nash credits his father for his team-oriented approach because he had a "different reward system." Nash Sr. instilled a teamwork mentality in Steve as a young athlete, valuing his passing over his scoring, and sometimes letting him and his brothers score if they passed back and forth—but never if someone tried to take it in on his own.[6]

Jay Bilas told me it was Dean Smith at UNC who first instituted the "point to the passer" gesture. It was a way, after a made basket, for the scorer to show appreciation to the passer. It's something you now see all over basketball courts, as common as a high five or a fist bump. It even led to what UNC called the "Bobby Jones Rule"—even if you miss an easy shot, when the pass is good, thank the passer.

Businesses that have taken a cue from the "point to the passer" approach have had remarkable success. For instance, Zappos has taken interpersonal communication to an impressively high level in their offices. It is one of their core values, and their actions and reward systems reflect that. Each month employees are encouraged to single out a colleague for a $50 "coworker bonus award."[7] In addition, the physical headquarters itself is designed to encourage communication between colleagues. CEO Tony Hsieh closes the side doors of headquarters during office hours to create "collisions" among employees, unplanned encounters that he feels are necessary to create a tight group.[8] Remember that *community* and *communication* derive from the same root word; they feed each other.

Squad Goals

Another benefit of communication is that it acts as a collective form of motivation. Scientists recommend that when you're going on a diet or trying to quit smoking, you should tell others. Putting it out there creates a motivating environment in which you are setting yourself up for success. Daniel S. Schwartz, chief executive of Restaurant Brands International (which owns Burger King, Popeye's, and others), posts his own goals on the wall in his office, along with his progress, for all his employees to see. He asks his employees do the same.[9] There is a power in simply stating what you—individually or as a team—hope to achieve. It brings it to life, gives it a name and a presence, making it all the more real and possible. It's a version of Tom Izzo's ritual of practicing cutting down the nets.

Author Daniel Coyle has written bestselling books on team culture and currently works as an advisor for the Cleveland Indians. In *The Culture Code*, Coyle used examples from business to sports to the military to pinpoint the three characteristics that help a group cohere. He found them to be: a feeling of safety, a sharing of vulnerability, and a clear understanding of a larger goal.[10] Not surprisingly, all three of these traits share a common denominator: they require communication.

If companies don't intentionally open the lines of communication, they are effectively keeping them closed. Most employees' default position is not to speak up to their boss—for obvious reasons. So unless this kind of behavior is clearly encouraged, it is being discouraged. If you're in charge, you might be thinking, *But my people always know my door is open for them to talk to me! I don't need to tell them that.*

Guess what? You're wrong. Let them know.

At Pixar a few years back, President Ed Catmull started to notice that "employees seemed to be censoring themselves more and more" around the bosses, which he felt was both a symptom of a larger problem and a drag on the company's mission. A creative environment simply cannot function without free-flowing communication, and creativity was Pixar's bread and butter. So Catmull did something about it. He brought together the whole company for what was called "Notes Day," a session where everyone was free to weigh in on *everything*.[11] The airing out of employees' pent-up thoughts and feelings was so productive that soon the meetings became regular occurrences.[12]

Don't mistake communication for constant agreement. In fact, if there isn't some conflict in your team's communication, you're probably holding things back, being inauthentic, or not doing it right. According to entrepreneur and author Margaret Heffernan, we should see conflict as a type of thinking.[13] Great teams are comfortable with clashes, as long as they're respectfully communicated, productive, and not personal.

Conflict itself isn't negative: it depends on what kind it is and how it is handled. Patrick Lencioni, who studies what makes businesses work and fail, echoed this: "All great relationships, the ones that last over time, require productive conflict to grow."[14] It's not really about the conflicts that you have—it's how those conflicts are resolved and whether or not hashing them out solves their initial cause.

Size Matters

No matter how hard you try, the size of a group can reach a point where it's impossible to connect and communicate. Where you can, keep the groups and the meetings small. At Amazon, Jeff Bezos famously has something called the two-pizza rule: no team should be bigger than one that two pizzas can feed. The main reason? The small size serves communication.[15] Think about how large meetings stifle open communication and why that is. How much time is spent off-topic? How many side conversations inevitably get going? How effective can a large group actually be? Is anything ever really decided?

Under Steve Jobs, Apple had a similar concept for meetings, called the "small group principle." No one was allowed in the meeting who wasn't necessary. Steve Jobs wasn't the kindest person about this rule, and he frequently kicked people out of rooms when he felt they didn't need to be there. Though the method might be harsh, and I can't subscribe to Jobs's approach, the intention was correct: it's not like letting them stay in those meetings was any better. It doesn't value them, since they could be doing something else.[16] It's why Steve Jobs continually called Apple "the biggest startup on the planet." The small group principle remained, even as it became one of the most influential companies in the world.

> Listen to learn. Don't listen to reply.
>
> —John C. Maxwell

Listening Skills

As I've stated, communication is not just about talking. In fact, I'd argue that a more important component is listening. But not just listening. *Active* listening. *Attentive* listening. Most people simply pretend to listen while they are formulating their response. You need to actively listen, with an empathetic ear, to clearly understand the person's perspective and point of view. Is this how you listen? How often are you just waiting to talk?

World-class leaders and elite sales professionals have mastered the art of active listening. They know that "telling is not selling" and that, nine times out of ten, the best answer they can give is actually another question. A question that dives deeper and refines clarification.

Communication goes far beyond words. There is tone, eye contact, body language, and all kinds of nonverbal clues that we unconsciously share in our conversations. But just because it's unconscious doesn't mean we can't work on it. Remember to listen with your eyes: Lock in your feet, hips, shoulders, and head. Let your colleagues know that their thoughts and feelings are important by giving them your time and attention.

Hearing is involuntary. If someone claps their hands or blows a whistle, you hear that. You don't have choice. But listening is voluntary. You choose whether or not to be present and to actively listen to what someone is communicating to you. Listen to their words, but also follow their nonverbal cues.

Listening is a skill. And how do you get better at any skill? Purposeful, consistent practice. You get reps. Thankfully there is no shortage of opportunities to practice listening in this world: Your kids love to talk. Your spouse loves to talk. Your friends love to talk. Your coworkers love to talk. So take advantage and practice active listening every chance you get.

The Incredibly Shrinking Attention Span

No matter who we are, we all want to feel genuinely listened to—and in recent years, that innate desire has gotten that much harder to fulfill. In 2002, before the handheld device and social media revolution had taken hold, the human attention span was 12 seconds. In 2018 it is now hovering around 8 seconds.[17] And it's only going to get shorter. A major pillar of teamwork is being able to transfer a thought, idea, or emotion to someone else and get them to understand clearly how you're feeling and what you're thinking. It's not as easy as it used to be, but it's essential.

Former NBA coach and current TV analyst Jeff Van Gundy has said that good teams have ELO communication: *early, loud, and often.* Consistent communication is the key—thoughts and feelings are constantly fleeting and in flux. The more you can communicate, the more you ensure everyone's on the same page. The more open the communication, the more cognizant you will be of dissent, role conflict, and disunity. It's how you find that poisonous stuff and nip it in the bud.

Communication brings issues to the surface—sometimes intentionally and sometimes unintentionally, but both are valuable. One of the most dangerous things an organization can have is mixed messages. Think of the old game of telephone you played as a kid. If I tell you something and you misinterpret and run with it, the problem multiplies: that many more people have no idea what I actually said. It happens all the time, and it's an example of a how a single incident of miscommunication can cause havoc.

College coaches often tell me that that the biggest difference between college and high school players is not skill level or athletic build: it's their ability to communicators. Most high school players are nowhere near the type of effective communicators they need to be for a successful college basketball career. They have to learn to talk often and with purpose. It takes practice. Watch any clip of a game where LeBron James is miked and you'll hear a constant running commentary that will make you realize what a phenomenal floor leader he is. (It's practically exhausting to watch.)

Phil Jackson once ran an entire practice scrimmage with the Lakers where the players were *forbidden* to talk. The team was having communication issues so he instituted the no-talking rule and came down hard, sidelining or giving wind sprints to anyone who spoke. He wanted them to see how hard basketball is when you don't talk. A million little things go wrong for a team who can't talk to each other. When a player can't warn a teammate "Screen coming!" or "Switch!" or yell out who he's guarding, it's like playing with a hand tied behind his back. The players quickly got Jackson's message.

Communicating with Legends

One of the highlights of my career was having dinner with legendary coach Bobby Knight after a Nike Championship Basketball Clinic where we were both speakers. I've always been a fan of Knight's and have read all of his books, so it was an unbelievable experience to actually dine with him. He is a brilliant storyteller with a remarkable memory. He remembered incredibly specific details like the name of the referee who made a crucial call during a game from over forty years ago! Knight continually beat the drum on the importance of listening and communication.

At any point during practice, he suggested, call a time-out. Huddle the players and give them four or five specific instructions. Then send them back on the court. Wait fifteen seconds and then call them back in: ask them to write down the things you asked them to do. It is scary how little they will recall. Players must be able to carry out simple instructions from the bench to the court. If they couldn't, then they couldn't play for Knight.

Until 2008 Bobby Knight had the most wins in NCAA men's basketball history. That was when he was overtaken by Coach Don Meyer.* Meyer is one of the winningest coaches of all time, yet most fans have never heard of him—because he chose not to coach at the Division 1 level.

Before he passed away in 2014, I spoke alongside Coach Don Meyer on two different occasions. I had the privilege to watch him speak and to talk privately with him, which was a real honor. Though he had been slowed down by cancer toward the end of his life, Meyer was the epitome of a servant leader, overwhelmingly humble, genuine, and authentic. A lot of the key things he preached in his talk came down to communication. "A scared team is a quiet team," he said. "Great teams are vocal and communicate." His advice to young coaches? "Let your players know these two things every day: here is one thing you are doing well (and why), and here is one thing you can do better (and how)."

Coach Meyer was a coach's coach. While he absolutely loved his players, he was always a tremendous resource to other coaches—at every level and at every point in their careers. He was such a powerful speaker, blending humor with wisdom with tangible X's and O's. My hand was cramped from taking so many notes during his talk.

But what really blew me away was that during my talk later in the day he sat in the front row and took notes throughout. At that point in time, he had been coaching longer than I had been breathing, yet he was giving me the full attention and regard he expected of others. As successful as he was, he knew there was still more to know, and he loved learning. It also communicated to me that I was

---

* Mike Krzyzewski became the wins leader in 2012.

worth his time and respect. At his level, if he could still do that, then we all can.

> The best way to persuade is with your ears.
> —Dean Rusk, former US secretary of state

Custom Communication

We don't know what we're saying until we know how someone hears it. Communication is also about feedback—making sure there is a two-way exchange of ideas, perceptions, and feelings. Otherwise it's like screaming down a well. Steve Kerr,* former Goldman Sachs executive and a researcher on leadership development, once offered a fantastic metaphor. He told author Geoff Colvin that, "practicing without feedback is like bowling through a curtain that hangs down to knee level. You can work on technique all you like, but if you can't see the effect, two things will happen: You won't get any better, and you'll stop caring."[18]

Customize how you talk to each person. Determine what type of communication is most appropriate for the situation and the individual. When is a private chat the right way, or when is addressing the team as a whole more effective? When is it appropriate to send out a mass text, and when should you talk to each person individually?

Today's technology allows us to communicate any way we want, so it's important, especially for young people, to develop interpersonal skills: Look people in the eye, have face-to-face conversations. Don't hide behind text messages. People defer to the easiest

---

* This is not Golden State Warriors' coach Steve Kerr.

method of communication instead of the most appropriate. It's easy to text a coach and say you can't make practice—because it's one-sided. You don't have to deal with the other person on the end of the exchange. I'd argue that it's not communicating at all.

Someone once told me that if you find yourself saying, "I've told you a hundred times" and the person you're talking to is still causing the problem, maybe consider that you are the problem. Take ownership of the issue. Maybe the problem is on your end. Why else would you have to say something a hundred times? The proof is in the pudding: your message isn't getting through. The communication issue is on your end; make sure you adjust so that the next time you say it, the 101st, is the last.

Key Point: A team doesn't know what it doesn't share with each other. Whether through positive reinforcement, constructive criticism, or tone and body language, great teams understand the value of communication.

Remember:

☞ Communication ensures that teams will catch dissent, role conflict, or disunity before it becomes unmanageable.

☞ Our ideas and emotions are constantly in flux. The best communication is open, honest, and consistent.

☞ Don't forget that communication is about TRUST.

☞ The most important, and most often forgotten, form of communication is listening. Listen with empathy and purpose.

☞ Think about the most appropriate form of communication for a given person or situation rather than the most convenient. Customize and individualize what you say and how you say it.

CHAPTER FIFTEEN

Cohesion

> A company is ultimately going to be what its people are.
>
> —Phil Knight

Cohesion is the final chapter of part 3 because it brings together the four previous qualities: belief, unselfishness, role clarity, and communication. It's the end result of those pieces fitting together. An organization that is made of people who **believe** in the mission, who are willing to **unselfishly share** credit and take blame, who each play their **specific roles**, and who **communicate** effectively will operate cohesively. Cohesion is the sound of the machine humming along because all the parts are in working order.

Team sports are a useful example of cohesion because the execution is on such a public stage. Professional sports teams are organizations whose workplace is out in the open (televised and studied nightly), whose roles are clearly understood, whose contributions are (mostly) logged and accounted for, and whose dynamics and interactions are visible to the naked eye.

Championship coach Phil Jackson described the cohesion of a team on the court working "like five fingers on a hand,"[1] which is the perfect image. Each finger has its own characteristics and role, but the whole hand is what gets most things done—and it operates as a unit on an unconscious level. We don't think about typing or gripping or grabbing a fork as the merging of five or ten individual units. But that's exactly what it is.

The Collective

It's important to note that not all teams even look like teams. Sometimes there's one person at the top who is the face of the organization, but there's an entire network of people operating right beneath the surface. That's the case with Colin O'Brady.

When I met Colin, I was struck by the fact that he looks like a normal guy, but I wasn't fooled: he's a triathlete, an endurance athlete, and one of the greatest mountain climbers on earth. I'd call him a superman, but that would make it sound like he was born this way. And of course, he wasn't. He brought himself to where he is through an almost incredible level of dedication, focus, and endurance.

O'Brady has set two world records—he has climbed the highest summit on each continent in record time (131 days) and completed the Explorers Grand Slam in the fastest time, which is climbing the seven highest peaks along with reaching the North and the South Poles.* Yet, O'Brady has earned every power he has.

Colin's story is inspirational. After an accident left his feet and

---

* Incredibly, it only took Colin an extra *eight* days to achieve this record. As I write this, I just found out that Colin recently set a third world record by climbing the tallest peak in each of the fifty states—in twenty-one days! (He beat the old record by twenty days.)

legs severely burned, doctors told him that he might never be able to walk again. But after years of excruciating pain and effort, along with eight surgeries, Colin began to participate in (and win) triathlons. He then moved on to the ultimate physical endurance test, climbing mountains.

In a testament to Colin's generosity of spirit, he has linked up his adventures with a charity (Beyond 7/2) while also working as a motivational speaker. Though Colin can push himself to unparalleled discomfort, when I met him, he struck me as an engaging and relaxed guy. He is also enormously humble, refusing to take all the credit for his mammoth accomplishments. Colin emphasized to me in our interview that his name might be the one in the record books, but none of his ventures were done solo. There was simply no way that he could complete these amazing feats alone. "The truth behind the success has been building high-functioning teams to support my audacious goals," he told me. "Without a cohesive team, progress breaks down quickly when the going gets tough."

When I asked him the key to cohesion, he tied it back to communication. "The best teams allow everyone to have a voice and to really be heard," he explained to me. "Safe, fluid, and honest communication enables this cohesion and unlocks the potential for growth." Under the frigid and dangerous conditions with which Colin and his team operate, communication is an absolute necessity. He is dealing with issues of life and death on these peaks, and one misunderstanding could be fatal.

Summiting the granddaddy of them all—Mount Everest— "required a very strong team of people," Colin humbly noted. "Although technically I was just climbing with my partner, Sherpa Pasang Bhote, we relied on many other people to reach the top of the world. From base camp support to logistics getting in and out of the country, to porters and other teams collaborating to fix the ropes on the mountain, it was a huge team effort. Without cohesion we would most certainly have failed." We don't always think of all the men and women behind the men and women, but if those people didn't cohere, the "star" couldn't achieve anything. Colin's example is important, especially in today's economy when you might work for a nontraditional organization or in an independent capacity. You are still part of a team. If you don't think so, break down how you effectively achieve any of your goals. Ask yourself: Who else is involved? That is your team.

In our interview Colin told me that he defined cohesion as when "everyone feels the same urgency and desire to succeed together." The language he uses here is important—especially in his job—because it's not just about what people think; it's about what they *feel*. If his people don't feel the excitement or danger, then it's likely they are not as invested as he is. And that is a problem.

There's a sense of pride and commitment that specifically arises when no one's contributions are treated as worthier than any other's. "I think often we live in a top-down society where people feel marginalized in group settings," he maintained. "Hierarchical structures do not always get the best work out of the collective whole. Cohesion needs to be more emphasized."

The fact that this is coming from a guy who has climbed the world's tallest mountains only drives the point home further. The "flattening" of any workplace, team, or organization makes each member feel integral to the whole. A team coheres only when everyone feels like they matter—as individuals and as contributors to the mission, whether that's climbing Mount Everest, executing a play on the basketball court, or landing a new client.

> When you first assemble a group, it's not a team right off the bat. It's only a collection of individuals.
>
> —Mike Krzyzewski

Filling Their Cups

When you watch a cohesive organization at work, it's enough to make you jealous—even when things aren't going its way. I don't think I'm alone in saying I'd rather lose on a team that worked together and cared about each other than win in a group where everyone was out for themselves.

Few coaches in professional sports have had the longevity and success of the San Antonio Spurs' head coach Gregg Popovich. An incredible stat courtesy of Bloomberg: "Since Gregg Popovich took over as head coach of the NBA's San Antonio Spurs 21 years ago, the rest of the league's teams have replaced their leaders a total of *228* times. No other coach has held his current job for more than a decade."[2] Even with some long-term players like Tim Duncan and Manu Ginóbli, Popovich still has had to maintain cohesion through various retirements, trades, injuries, free-agent signings, and the regular turnover that is a normal part of the NBA. As the rest of the league and fans of the game know, when an NBA player becomes a Spur, he (or she*) becomes part of Pop's cohesive unit.

An illustrative story: In 2013 the Spurs were on the road, up 3–2 against the Miami Heat in the NBA Finals. The Spurs were

---

* In 2014 Becky Hammon was hired as a Spurs assistant coach, the first full-time female coach in any of the four major team sports. In the summer of 2018 it was reported that she had been interviewed for an NBA head coaching job with the Milwaukee Bucks.

one win away from the championship, and in case it happened that night, Popovich booked a reservation to celebrate at his favorite Italian restaurant in Miami. Though the Spurs nearly had the game in hand, Ray Allen's famous three-pointer from the corner buried San Antonio in a crushing loss. Of course, everyone assumed the reservation would be canceled as the Spurs regrouped and prepared for game 7. But Popovich insisted they keep it. In fact, the loss was all the more reason to keep it.

"They sat and ate together," Daniel Coyle wrote in *The Culture Code*. "Popovich moved around the room, connecting with each player in turn.... In a moment that could have been filled with frustration, recrimination, and anger, he filled their cups."[3] Popovich understood that more than in victory, those players needed to feel part of a team that night. They needed to come together as people. Popovich cared about each of his players as individuals, with their own fears, emotions, and need to belong. As onetime Spur Will Perdue once said about Popovich: "He saw you as a human being first and a basketball player second."[4]

The most successful people I've been around have a cohesive inner circle. Members of your inner circle play a huge role in your performance and development. As it's been said, "You are the company you keep." (As I like to say, you can't hang with jackasses and expect to be a racehorse.) I believe your inner circle should include people you trust; people you respect; and people of varying ages, backgrounds, and life experiences. Members of your inner circle should

1. Tell you the truth.
2. Hold you accountable.
3. Be supportive.
4. Challenge you.
5. Want to see you happy.

Self-Test

Personal Audit:

- Who are the five people that most positively influence you?
- Who are the five people you actually spend the most time with?
- Compare lists.

Remember: We are the company we keep. Be intentional with whom you invest your time in.

Ten Assists

Our most valuable currency is our attention. No matter what we say or promise, our attention—because it is finite—reveals who and what we truly value. My friend and mentor Rich Sheubrooks taught me a team cohesion exercise called "Ten Assists." Every morning, start by putting ten pennies in your left pocket. And every time you throw a teammate "an assist," you transfer one penny from your left pocket to your right pocket. An assist can be anything you do to serve a colleague, from bringing them coffee to rescheduling a conference call to helping them meet a deadline. Here's the catch: you cannot leave the office until you've dished out ten assists.

The Greatest Game I Ever Saw

Perhaps the greatest example of cohesion I have ever participated in, and been witness to, was an epic high school basketball battle in March 2006. I have been around elite-level basketball for almost twenty years, and that game was, hands down, the most electric experience I have ever been a part of. I still get goose bumps every time I think about it. (It's not just me: Ten years later, *The Washington Post* revisited it, calling it "One of the Greatest High School Games in D.C. History."[5])

At the time, Oak Hill was on a 56-game winning streak and was 40–0, ranked number 1 in the nation by every publication. Before a sell-out crowd of 4,000, our team, Montrose, rallied from being down 16 in the fourth quarter to hit a game-winning put-back, as time expired, to win 74–72. In addition to the buzzer-beater finish, the reason that game will go down in history as one of the most memorable ever was the high-caliber players who participated. Oak Hill featured current NBA players Tywon Lawson (Wizards) and Michael Beasley (Knicks), and Montrose was led by MVP and NBA champion Kevin Durant.

Montrose was able to do the impossible and rally from what appeared to be an insurmountable lead against the best team in the nation because of team cohesion, which came from the same four traits that have made up the final part of this book.

Communication: In environments where communication is difficult, it's *particularly* necessary. That gym was standing room only with a DJ spinning records at every dead ball. It was so deafening our players couldn't hear Coach Vetter from the sideline, but they still found a way to communicate effectively with each other. Hand signals, eye contact, and extra tight huddles before every free throw kept our guys on the same page at all times.

Belief: Strong communication helped strengthen our belief in ourselves and our ability to do what many thought wasn't possible. But it's important to note that our belief began much earlier than that. It began during the previous off-season and was reinforced every single day. True belief is attained only through demonstrated performance. Our guys put in work for the months leading up to that game to earn their belief. *Believe or Leave.*

Unselfishness: It's essential that when you look at your teammates you *feel* that they want it as badly as you do. The primary turning point in the game came in the fourth quarter when point guard Taishi Ito (5 feet 9, 155 pounds) stepped in and took an offensive charge from Michael Beasley (6 feet 7, 230 pounds). Beasley had a full head of steam on a fast break and was coming on like a runaway freight train. Taishi sacrificed his body by stepping on the tracks and drawing an offensive foul that completely swung the momentum in Montrose's favor. The play didn't just give Montrose the ball; it sparked the team like a jolt of electricity. Taking a charge is one of the most unselfish plays a player can make because they are the ones receiving physical pain for the good of the team. And it doesn't show up on the stat sheet.

Clear Roles: One of the main reasons we were able to make such an improbable comeback was because our players stuck to the plan. They didn't panic. They stayed on script. Each player knew and embraced his function; no one tried to play the hero. Each team member homed in on his role and executed it. Durant was clearly our number 1 offensive option and each player fulfilled their role, one of which was to get him the best looks at the basket. If Montrose players started doing what they wanted to do instead of what the team needed them to do, the wheels would have come off. While KD received most of the headlines, we won because everyone fulfilled their roles.

I can't emphasize enough that the aspects that gave us victory weren't built that night. They were simply demonstrated, maybe even *actualized*, that night. Montrose's cohesion had been built, brick by brick, for the years, months, weeks, and days leading up to that game. Comebacks like that, against teams of that caliber, do not happen without thousands of unseen hours building a team's cohesion.

Start with the Hire

Cohesion means "the action or fact of forming a united whole."[6] It means unity and togetherness, but as the definition states—*it is an active thing*. It's something a team has to work on. It's something that is done, not something that is.

If you're building an organization, cohesion starts with the hire. It's easier to pick pieces than to change pieces. Hire complementary people and those who are happy to fit into the puzzle. *What drives you needs to be good for us. What drives us needs to be good for you.*

In the world of basketball, recruiting is enormously important to team cohesion. Whether it's college coaches recruiting a high school player, or an NBA GM evaluating a college or overseas player, the depth they go to determine whether someone is a team player is astounding: they go back to sixth grade teachers to find out if you were a jerk or not.

I will have GMs reach out to me when players I know and have worked with are going through this process. Though I was the players' high school performance coach, the first bunch of questions will have nothing to do at all with athletic ability. They'll ask about his attitude, what kind of guy he was, and how he treated others. They ask about promptness, accountability, listening skills, work ethic, and unselfishness. The litmus test is this: "Alan: Would you let him date your daughter?"

They can watch the tapes for all their games. By the time they start asking me about his coordination, his balance, and his strength, we're on to the ninth or tenth question. The best teams, organizations, and companies have a tight and strenuous filter to make sure they get the best people. Cohesion will not come about with a random assortment of individuals. They have to have the attitude and willingness to cohere.

Four Cohesion Killers

1. Entitlement—those who think they deserve more
2. Arrogance—those who act as though they are better
3. Selfishness—those who are out for themselves
4. Complacency—those who simply don't care

Filling Gaps

Cohesion is also about filling in the blanks. College head coaches need charisma to recruit, motivate, and push people beyond their comfort level. They have to know their X's and O's and be able to get everyone integrated to feel part of the team and the culture. But even the best coaches are not going to be the best in their field at *each* of these. So they find others who are.

"It's important for me that everyone I hire have a certain seat on the bus," Kentucky coach John Calipari wrote. "In other words, I won't hire the same type of person for five different positions. We need everybody on the bus to do something different—to be put to their best use, what they're better at than anyone else on staff."[7] *Make sure there's a seat for everyone on the bus.*

Balance your staff out. University of South Carolina coach Frank Martin has a reputation for being energetic and volatile, but he makes sure he has coaches on staff who can play good cop and have a softer edge, so he's not subjecting his players to a bench of drill sergeants. The best leaders know they don't need to be great at everything; they need to be great in some things and assemble a team that fills in the other pieces.

Every team and organization needs "glue guys," those who are willing to do the little things that need to be done for everything to work. Glue guys do the jobs that are not really spelled out or explicitly assigned. The little things that might otherwise get missed or overlooked.

A glue guy in basketball takes a charge, sprints in both directions, dives for loose balls, and when on the bench, stands up and cheers for a great play or high fives a teammate coming off the floor. No one is assigned that role, their contributions aren't on the stat sheet, and they're never the stars, but their importance to team cohesion is enormous. A glue guy lives by the mantra that "Nothing here is someone else's job."

Self-Test

Think about your team or organization.

1. Who is the "star"? In what way?
2. Who are the role players? How do they serve the star and the mission?
3. Who is the glue on your team? Who holds your team together?
4. Who does all the little things to make your team successful?
5. Who picks up the slack when others are down?
6. Who doesn't seem to care about recognition or praise?
7. How do you specifically contribute to your team's cohesion?

What Championship Teams Do for Each Other

1. *Lead* their teammates.
2. *Love* their teammates.
3. *Elevate* their teammates.
4. *Respect* their teammates.
5. *Trust* their teammates.

6. *Discipline* their teammates.
7. *Back* their teammates.
8. *Challenge* their teammates.

> All of us is smarter than one of us.
>
> —Japanese proverb

The Cohesion of Children

Cohesion might just be something that we know how to achieve instinctually. Maybe we end up destroying it as we age because we develop egos and high opinions of the "right way" to do things. Design expert Peter Skillman once conducted a famous experiment that elegantly explains how cohesion works. A group of kindergarteners were pitted against a group of business school students in a design challenge: In a subscribed time period, each group had to build a tower with uncooked spaghetti, tape, string, and a marshmallow. Over and over again the kindergarteners won the challenge—by a huge margin.[8]

The reason? According to author Daniel Coyle, adults get caught up in questions of status and power instead of the larger goal. Though they *appear* organized, "their underlying behavior is riddled with inefficiency, hesitation, and subtle competition."[9] Meanwhile, kindergarteners may *look* like a five-alarm fire but "they are not competing for status.... They experiment, take risks, and notice outcomes, which guides them toward effective solutions."[10]

At UNC, coach Dean Smith was so committed to team cohesion that he valued it over winning! Smith was willing to lose games if it meant giving his players greater freedom, "because in the long run he believed that you went further by working as a team, by sacrificing individuality to team effort."[11] If a player committed a team infraction, Coach Smith would sometimes punish everyone else to emphasize cohesion, to show that "everything was built around the concept of team and against the idea of individuality and the danger of individual ego."[12]

Of course, teams can't always agree on everything, but they have to believe the others are all in. Teams at Amazon use the phrase "disagree and commit." It's an innovative way for team members to voice their opinion but then let the idea move forward. That's how you maintain cohesion without the minority voices feeling shut out. Respect them enough to hear their objection. Then let them decide to join the group.

The Big Picture

High school basketball taught me so much about how teams operate, why some fail and why others succeed. At DeMatha, Coach Jones used to teach that no player is bigger than the team, and no team is bigger than the program. "It doesn't matter who scores," he would say. "It just matters that *we* score."

A few years ago, when I was still a performance coach there, DeMatha was in the conference championship game. With seconds left, the game was tied and we came up with a big steal. Our best player—an All-American—got fouled with no time on the clock. He was a great free throw shooter and had to make only one and, bless his heart, he missed both. We went to overtime, and the team was so dejected that we got killed. With about 30 seconds left, and the other team up by 8, Coach Jones called a time-out.

Everyone was wondering why, and the assistants and players were all looking at each other in confusion. We couldn't win. That ship had sailed. But Coach Jones had something else on his mind besides winning.

"Look, guys," he said in the huddle, "We are going to lose this game. But thirty seconds from now, when you lose, you're going to lose with class, lose the right way because the name on the front of your shirt has been building a reputation for the last sixty years. And you're not going to do something in a couple of seconds that is going to diminish that. I know you're upset, but this is not only about you. There's something bigger than each of us out there." Then he sent them back out on the court.

It's the mind-set all organizations ought to have—the giants, the ones trying to be giants, and the ones just getting their feet wet. Once you've decided to be part of a team, you have to accept that the team is bigger than you. That's the whole point.

Take the Time to Celebrate

The final element of a cohesive team is simple: celebrate victories. Make sure that those are group victories and that the celebration is inclusive and about the group. Two-time national champion coach Jay Wright doesn't care for self-directed celebrations. "If you're excited, you have a lot of energy; turn and give that energy to your teammates," Wright has said.[13] It's a good rule of thumb: if you are the only one cheering, then there's nothing to cheer about.

Celebration is also about bringing a level of enjoyment to the work, the camaraderie, and the environment itself. External rewards are no substitute for intrinsic motivation, but they can go a long way toward making people feel appreciated. When the company is rewarded together, it can be incredibly unifying. During a successful month at his first company, Micro-Solutions, Mark Cuban walked around handing out hundred-dollar bills to the sales force, a way to celebrate jobs well done that I'm sure were appreciated.

"Athletes take time to celebrate their victories," author and performance development consultant Graham Jones wrote in *Forbes*. "It helps remind them why all the hard work and commitment is worthwhile. At a time when survival is the priority of so many organizations, don't forget to spend time celebrating successes, however small they may be."[14]

Teams will hit highs and lows together, and making the most of each—celebrating one and learning from the other—ensures and solidifies cohesion. In the end, businesses are made up of people who want praise and recognition, who want to feel part of something, and who want to take a moment to feel good about what they have achieved.

Key Point: A cohesive unit operates in sync and as a single unit, through a combination of the previous four traits: unselfishness, belief, clear roles, and communication.

Remember:

☞ Cohesion is the glue that secures everything together.

☞ The best teams are like a puzzle; different but complementary pieces creating the final picture—one missing or out-of-place piece and the puzzle is incomplete.

☞ Great teams suffer and celebrate together.

☞ There are few things in life and business more satisfying than a team coming together to achieve something they could not do individually. It's a feeling you'll want to seek again and again.

Self-Test

Team Audit

Select a team that you are a part of:

1. Which characteristic in part 3 do you feel the team exhibits strongly? How so?

2. Which characteristic do you feel your team needs to work on?

3. What specifically can you and your team members do to elevate their performance in this area?

4. Set up a schedule to check in and evaluate your team's progress on these specific fixes.

CONCLUSION

The First Step

> If you do not change your direction, you will end up exactly where you are headed.
>
> —Chinese proverb

There's a reason that LeBron James, Kevin Durant, and Kobe Bryant have already successfully bridged into the media and business worlds. They are bringing their commitment to preparation, their instincts as leaders, and their understanding of team dynamics into other industries, where the same principles apply.

Success originates from a single point: *commitment.* There is never an excuse to let someone outwork you. *Never.* Don't let all the talk of hacks and shortcuts convince you otherwise. Nothing of value ever comes without effort. Everyone wants success, but few are willing to make the necessary sacrifices. *Are you?*

If you are not happy with your current work or life situation, start addressing the things you can change. If it's a drastic change that's needed, find the courage to make that first step. If it's a minor change within your current situation, start planning out the ways to execute it. If it's an attitude change, decide what you care about and how that will inform your approach moving forward.

Each day is literally a new beginning. "Although we can't always determine when we start, we can exert some influence on beginnings," wrote bestselling author and behavioral scientist Daniel Pink. "In most endeavors, we should be awake to the power of beginnings and aim to make a strong start. If that fails, we can try to make fresh start. And if the beginning is beyond our control, we can enlist others to attempt a group start."[1] Pink simplifies it this way: "Start right. Start again. Start together."[2]

Jenny Blake is a career strategist (formerly with Google) and the author of *Pivot: The Only Move That Matters Is Your Next One*. When I interviewed her for this book, Blake and I talked about the meaning of the word "pivot," which is applicable in basketball as well as business. In basketball, a pivot is when you plant one foot and you move the other so you can scan your options. Pivoting gives you open angles and vantage points. The right pivot can help you notice something—a cutting man, an open passing lane—that maybe wasn't in your vision beforehand.

It comes down to an immutable fact: If you are not growing, you are shrinking. In our careers, Blake told me, "That's how you stay agile, by pivoting continuously." She defined pivot as "change without starting from scratch," which I appreciated. It recognized that not everyone needs to wake up tomorrow and quit their jobs. There are gradations of changes we can all make in our current situations.

I think it's incredibly revealing that we don't talk about the life we "have" or the life we "got." We talk about the "life we lead."

The life we *lead*.

We are in charge.

Can you make the necessary changes in your life and work? Do you want to? Think about the language you use, even the words in your internal monologue. Researchers have determined that those who use the phrase "I don't" instead of "I can't" have a much higher success rate at changing their habits.[3] The change in language will help "give yourself a psychological edge." The reason? *Choice.*

Once you accept that you are making a choice—to start a good habit, improve a skill, or execute steps toward your goal—you are unconsciously moving the impetus onto yourself. You are reminding yourself that the decision to care, to develop good habits, and to put in the effort is up to you. And it starts with a single step.

When three-time volleyball gold medalist Karch Kiraly was asked how he prepared to win gold at the Olympics. "I never did," he replied. "I only prepared to win the next play."[4] It reminds me of a moment from an event I participated in called Hell on the Hill, which was exactly what it sounded like. Organized by Jesse Itzler, the event required that we run up and down an eighty-yard hill, on a slope that averaged a forty-degree angle, *100 times.* In total, it came out to over eight miles.

The terrain was neither straight nor smooth, there were tons of bumps and ripples along the way, and the gradation varied throughout. This sporadic terrain made it so much more challenging. Like a seasoned golfer trying to access the lay of the green, each of us soon found the "easiest" path to the top (and I use that term loosely). But the problem with that collective discovery was that this path became contested and crowded, and we all quickly wore its grass to mud. A light rain fell on and off throughout the day, and the wet grass made it incredibly challenging to even go *down* the hill. At around the seventieth climb, I hit a wall. I was struggling—physically, mentally, and emotionally spent. I was just about ready to quit.

Among the people participating in Hell on the Hill was Steve Wojciechowski, former Defensive Player of the Year at Duke and currently the men's head basketball coach at Marquette. He and I were at about the same pace the whole time, and we had met before, when he was a guest on my podcast. When Wojo came up alongside me, I asked him, "How many more reps do you have?"

"One rep."

"Wait, what?" I asked. "One?" There was no way this guy only had one rep. I was almost pissed off.

But then he said, "Yep. Just one rep. *Thirty more times.*"

I smiled because it was the perfect attitude. It was a lesson in living present, in focusing on the single step, in blocking out everything else and zeroing in on only what needed to be done.

As you look out on your own personal and professional landscape, I hope you have the courage and determination to take that first single step. Have belief in yourself, in your coach, and in your team, and I know you will make it to the next one.

ACKNOWLEDGMENTS

> Don't delay gratitude.
>
> —Skip Prosser

I wake up every morning with the goal of telling as many people as I can, every single day of my life, that I appreciate them. I aim to consistently model an attitude of gratitude.

From start to finish, writing this book was a thoroughly enjoyable experience.

But this page is without question the hardest to write.

That's because there are so many people who deserved to be thanked, recognized, and acknowledged.

There is a widespread emotional disorder called FOMO (fear of missing out). It has reached levels of epic proportions with the rise of social media. It's an anxiety caused from the feeling that somewhere, something amazing is happening and you are missing it.

At the risk of sounding overly dramatic, when it came time to write this page, I started to experience a similar and related disorder called FOMS (fear of missing *someone*).

I started to worry I would (inadvertently) forget someone.

I have worked with, worked for, befriended, studied, observed, listened to, and learned from hundreds of amazing people, who have in one way or another contributed to this book. Some more recently and directly than others, but all of whom have helped shape the man I am today and therefore shape the contents of this book.

That list is simply too exhaustive to even attempt to name.

So to my family, friends, associates, colleagues, partners, teammates, agents, mentors, teachers, coaches, trainers, advisors, counselors, consultants, clients, supporters, and followers, please know...

I appreciate you.

NOTES

Introduction

1. David Halberstam, *Playing for Keeps: Michael Jordan and the World He Made* (New York: Random House, 1999), 165.

Chapter One

1. http://www.espn.com/nba/story/_/id/22812774/kevin-pelton-weekly -mailbag-next-victor-oladipo.
2. Geoff Colvin, *Talent Is Overrated: What Really Separates World-Class Performers from Everyone Else* (New York: Penguin, 2008), 118.
3. Adam Galinsky and Maurice Schweitzer, *Friend and Foe: When to Cooperate, When to Compete, and How to Succeed at Both* (New York: Crown Business, 2015), 132.
4. Simon Sinek, *Leaders Eat Last: Why Some Teams Pull Together and Others Don't* (New York: Portfolio, 2014), 199.
5. Tom Rath and Barry Conchie, *Strengths Based Leadership: Great Leaders, Teams, and Why People Follow* (New York: Gallup Press, 2008), 2.
6. Interview with Howard Schultz, *How I Built This*, with Guy Raz https:// www.npr.org/2017/09/28/551874532/live-episode-starbucks-howard -schultz; and Howard Schultz with Joanne Gordon, *Onward* (New York: Rodale Books, 2012), 3–7.
7. Interview with Howard Schultz, *How I Built This*, with Guy Raz.
8. Tasha Eurich, *Insight: Why We're Not as Self-Aware as We Think and How Seeing Ourselves Clearly Helps Us Succeed at Work and in Life* (New York: Crown Business, 2017), 7.

Chapter Two

1. Jesse Itzler, *Living with a SEAL: 31 Days of Training with the Toughest Man on the Planet* (New York: Center Street, 2005), 65.

2. Tim S. Grover, *Relentless: From Good to Great to Unstoppable* (New York: Scribner, 2013), 39.

3. Interview with Steve Nash, *Suiting Up*, with Paul Rabil, https://suitinguppodcast.com/episode/steve-nash-nba-star-entrepreneur/.

4. Mark Cuban, *How to Win at the Sport of Business* (New York: Diversion Books, 2013), 3.

5. Interview with Jason Stein, *The Bill Simmons Podcast*, https://www.theringer.com/the-bill-simmons-podcast/2017/8/4/16100290/smart-guy-friday-cycle-ceo-founder-jason-stein-and-bills-dad-on-game-of-thrones.

6. Interview with John Mackey, *How I Built This*, with Guy Raz, https://one.npr.org/?sharedMediaId=527979061:528000104.

7. Eric Schmidt and Jonathan Rosenberg, with Alan Eagle, *How Google Works* (New York: Grand Central Publishing, 2014), 5.

8. Ryan Holiday, *Ego Is the Enemy* (New York: Portfolio, 2016), 55.

9. Ibid.

10. http://www.espn.com/nba/truehoop/miamiheat/columns/story?page=Spoelstra-110601.

11. Holiday, *Ego Is the Enemy*, 57.

12. Grover, *Relentless*, 11.

13. http://www.espn.com/blog/new-england-patriots/post/_/id/4801190/tom-bradys-passion-comes-through-with-talk-of-ambassador.

14. Brett Ledbetter, "How to Stop Comparing and Start Competing," TEDxGatewayArch. https://www.youtube.com/watch?v=bU09Y9sC7JY.

15. Galinsky and Schweitzer, *Friend and Foe*, 35.

16. http://faculty.chicagobooth.edu/devin.pope/research/pdf/website_losing_winning.pdf.

17. Ryan Holiday, *The Obstacle Is the Way: The Timeless Art of Turning Trials into Triumph* (New York: Portfolio, 2014), 4.

18. https://deadspin.com/thousands-of-gymnasts-are-sharing-videos-of-their-best-1825963309.

19. https://hbr.org/2012/07/how-leaders-become-self-aware.

20. Amy Wilkinson, *The Creator's Code: The Six Essential Skills of Extraordinary Entrepreneurs* (New York: Simon & Schuster, 2015), 115.

21. Maury Klein, *The Change Makers: From Carnegie to Gates, How the Great Entrepreneurs Transformed Ideas into Industries* (New York: Times Books, 2003), 186.

Chapter Three

1. Cal Newport, *Deep Work: Rules for Focused Success in a Distracted World* (New York: Grand Central, 2016), 14.

2. Richard L. Brandt, *One Click: Jeff Bezos and the Rise of Amazon.com* (New York: Portfolio, 2011), 23.

3. Newport, *Deep Work*, 71.

4. Ibid., 40.

5. https://news.harvard.edu/gazette/story/2010/11/wandering-mind-not-a -happy-mind/.

6. I first read this story on the Facebook page for Mark C. Crowley, *Lead from the Heart: Transformational Leadership for the 21st Century* (Bloomington, Ind.: Balboa Press, 2011, and then found more accurate details from Leda Karabela at http://yhesitate.com/2011/08/07/no-madam-it-took-me-my-whole-life/.

7. https://www.forbes.com/sites/neilpatel/2015/01/16/90-of-startups-will -fail-heres-what-you-need-to-know-about-the-10/#4f25a2526679.

8. Tony Schwartz, *The Way We're Working Isn't Working: The Four Forgotten Needs That Energize Great Performance*, 33.

9. Cuban, *How to Win*, 15.

10. This idea originated with Jim Rohn's work.

11. http://www.investors.com/news/management/leaders-and-success/ basketball-player-larry-bird-grit-and-discipline-helped-him-lead -championship-teams/.

12. "The Champ," *Readers Digest*, January, 1972, 109.

13. Jeff Bezos, commencement speech at Princeton University, May 30, 2010.

Chapter Four

1. This is in a variety of places but I read it in Jeff Jarvis's *What Would Google Do?* (New York: Harper Business, 2009), 20.

2. https://www.forbes.com/100-greatest-business-minds/person/arthur -blank.

3. http://money.cnn.com/2018/03/06/news/companies/dominos-pizza -hut-papa-johns/index.html.

4. Carol Dweck, *Mindset: The New Psychology of Success* (New York: Random House, 2006), 21.

5. Halberstam, *Playing for Keeps*, 66.

6. Adam Bryant, *Corner Office: Indispensable and Unexpected Lessons from CEOs on How to Lead and Succeed* (New York: Times Books, 2011), 15.

7. Ibid., 12–13.

8. Ibid, 13.

9. Leigh Gallagher, *The Airbnb Story: How Three Ordinary Guys Disrupted an Industry, Made Billions . . . and Created Plenty of Controversy* (Boston: Houghton Mifflin Harcourt, 2017), 164.

10. Ibid., 167.

11. Wilkinson, *The Creator's Code*, 39.

12. Daniel Coyle, *The Culture Code: The Secrets of Highly Successful Groups* (New York: Bantam, 2018), 78.

13. John Wooden and Steve Jamison, *The Essential Wooden: A Lifetime of Lessons on Leaders and Leadership* (New York: McGraw-Hill Education, 2007), 18.

14. https://www.businessinsider.com/the-blakely-family-dinner-table -question-2015-3.

15. "Research Reveals Fear of Failure Has Us All Shaking in Our Boots This Halloween," Linkagoal's Fear Factor Index, October 14, 2015.

16. Charles Duhigg, *The Power of Habit* (New York: Random House, 2014), 282.

17. Brandt, *One Click*, 88.

Chapter Five

1. Cuban, *How to Win*, 71.

2. Interview with Perry Chen, *How I Built This*, with Guy Raz, https:// www.npr.org/2017/09/05/540012302/kickstarter-perry-chen.

3. Ibid.

4. Dan McGinn, *Psyched Up: How the Science of Mental Preparation Can Help You Succeed* (New York: Portfolio, 2017), 151.

5. "Mental Preparation Secrets of Top Athletes, Entertainers, and Surgeons," *Harvard Business Review* June 29th, 2017, https://hbr.org/ideacast/2017/06/

mental-preparation-secrets-of-top-athletes-entertainers-and-surgeons
.html

6. https://www.history.com/shows/the-selection-special-operations
-experiment.

7. Bob Rotella, *How Champions Think: In Sports and in Life* (New York: Simon
& Schuster, 2016), 15.

8. Ibid., 113.

9. Shawn Achor, *The Happiness Advantage: The Seven Principles of Positive
Psychology That Fuel Success and Performance at Work*, (New York: Currency,
2010), 98.

10. The ideas behind this cycle were inspired by Jim Rohn's work.

Chapter Six

1. http://www.espn.com/nba/story/_/id/22045158/chris-paul-pursuing
-passing-perfection-houston-rockets-nba.

2. Ibid.

3. https://www.sbnation.com/2017/4/13/15257614/houston-rockets-stats
-winning-james-harden-daryl-morey.

4. Coyle, *The Culture Code*, 229.

5. Robert Bruce Shaw, *Extreme Teams: Why Pixar, Netflix, Airbnb and Other
Cutting-Edge Companies Succeed Where Most Fail* (New York: AMACOM,
2017), 104.

6. Brandt, *One Click*, 101.

7. Shaw, *Extreme Teams*, 35.

8. Eurich, *Insight*, 250.

9. http://variety.com/2013/biz/news/epic-fail-how-blockbuster-could
-have-owned-netflix-1200823443/.

10. Wilkinson, *The Creator's Code*, 2.

11. http://www.businessinsider.com/steph-curry-worth-14-billion-to-under
-armour-2016-3.

12. Wilkinson, *The Creator's Code*, 3.

13. Ken Segall, *Insanely Simple: The Obsession That Drives Apple's Success* (New
York: Portfolio, 2012), 3.

14. Ibid., 2.

15. https://www.forbes.com/100-greatest-business-minds/person/brian
-chesky.

16. Interview with Lewis Howes, "The Mask of Masculinity," *Art of Charm,* with Jordan Harbinger, https://theartofcharm.com/podcast-episodes/lewis -howes-the-mask-of-masculinity-episode-688/.

17. Angela Duckworth, *Grit* (New York: Scribner, 2016), 98.

18. https://www.medicaldaily.com/i-hate-my-job-say-70-us-employees -how-be-happy work-319928.

19. https://www.forbes.com/sites/keldjensen/2012/04/12/intelligence-is -overrated-what-you-really-need-to-succeed/#26f49bf2b6d2.

20. Charles Duhigg, *Smarter Faster Better* (New York: Random House, 2017), 6.

21. Klein, *The Changemakers*, 97.

Chapter Seven

1. http://www.espn.com/nba/story/_/id/23016766/how-brad-stevens -navigated-boston-celtics-injury-woes-nba.

2. https://www.si.com/nba/2017/05/16/steve-kerr-nba-playoffs-golden -state-warriors-injury-leadership.

3. Ibid.

4. Mike Krzyzewski and Donald T. Phillips, *Leading with the Heart: Coach K's Successful Strategies for Winning in Basketball, Business, and Life* (New York: Warner Business Books, 2001), 14.

5. Interview with Jay Williams, *Suiting Up*, with Paul Rabil, https:// suitinguppodcast.com/episode/jay-williams-nba-espn-analyst-and -entrepreneur/.

6. Jay Williams, *Life Is Not An Accident: A Memoir of Reinvention* (New York: Harper, 2016), 58–59.

7. Laszlo Bock, *Work Rules! Insights from Inside Google That Will Transform How You Live and Lead* (New York: Twelve, 2015), 155.

8. Astro Teller, "The unexpected benefit of celebrating failure," Ted Talk, https://www.ted.com/talks/astro_teller_the_unexpected_benefit_of _celebrating_failure.

9. Bock, *Work Rules!*, 126.

10. Ibid., 147.

11. http://fortune.com/2015/03/05/perfect-workplace/.

12. Robert I. Sutton, *The No Asshole Rule: Building a Civilized Workplace and Surviving One That Isn't* (New York: Business Plus, 2007), 2.

13. Ibid., 81.

14. Ibid., 36.

15. Coyle, *The Culture Code*, 81.

16. Wooden and Jamison, *The Essential Wooden*, 30.

17. Jay Bilas, *Toughness: Developing True Strength on and off the Court* (New York: Berkley, 2013), 2.

18. Tony Hsieh, *Delivering Happiness: A Path to Profits, Passion, and Purpose* (New York: Grand Central Publishing, 2013), 2.

19. Interview with Tony Hsieh, *New York Times*, http://www.nytimes.com/2010/01/10/business/10corner.html.

20. David Burkus, *Under New Management: How Leading Organizations Are Upending Business as Usual* (Boston: Houghton Mifflin Harcourt, 2016), 59.

21. Interview with Tony Hsieh, *How I Built This*, with Guy Raz, https://www.npr.org/2017/01/23/510576153/zappos-tony-hsieh.

22. Ibid.

Chapter Eight

1. https://www.inc.com/mareo-mccracken/with-1-sentence-this-nba-champion-coach-teaches-everything-you-need-to-know-about-emotional-intelligence.html.

2. http://www.espn.com/nba/story/_/id/22048880/lamarcus-aldridge-san-antonio-spurs-asked-traded-gregg-popovich-reveals.

3. John Calipari and Michael Sokolove, *Players First: Coaching from the Inside Out* (New York: Penguin, 2014).

4. http://news.gallup.com/businessjournal/193238/employee-recognition-low-cost-high-impact.aspx.

5. Anthony Tjan, *Good People: The Only Leadership Decision That Really Matters* (New York: Portfolio, 2017), 108.

6. Achor, *The Happiness Advantage*, 58.
    (Note: He didn't write two books with that title—it's the same book and they changed the sub.)

7. Howard Schultz, with Joanne Gordon, *Onward* (New York: Rodale Books, 2012), xiii.

8. Joseph A. Michelli, *Leading the Starbucks Way: 5 Principles for Connecting with Your Customers, Your Products and Your People* (New York: McGraw-Hill Education, 2013), 70.

9. Ibid., 5.

10. Simon Sinek, *Start with Why: How Great Leaders Inspire Everyone to Take Action* (New York: Portfolio, 2011), 88.

11. Sinek, *Leaders Eat Last*, 178.

12. http://archive.fortune.com/magazines/fortune/fortune_archive/2007 /09/17/100258873/ index.htm.

13. Kim Scott, *Radical Candor: Be a Kick-Ass Boss without Losing Your Humanity* (New York: St. Martin's Press, 2017), 101.

14. Tony Schwartz, *The Way We're Working: The Four Forgotten Needs That Energize Great Performance* (New York: Free Press, 2010), 118.

15. Bock, *Work Rules!*, 77.

16. Ibid., 21.

17. Jon Gordon and Mike Smith, *You Win in the Locker Room First: The Seven C's to Building a Winning Team in Business, Sports, and Life* (New York: Wiley, 2015), 58.

18. Achor, *The Happiness Advantage*, 194.

19. Wilkinson, *The Creator's Code*, 125.

20. Tjan, *Good People*, 104–5.

Chapter Nine

1. Bilas, *Toughness*, 25.

2. Williams, *Life Is Not an Accident*, 25–26.

3. Krzyzewski and Phillips, *Leading with the Heart*, 132.

4. https://hbr.org/2017/03/mike-krzyzewski.

5. Interview with Brett Ledbetter, *What Drives Winning*, https://whatdrives winning.com/speaker/coach-k/.

6. Interview with Rick Welts, *Finding Mastery*, with Michael Gervais, https:// findingmastery.net/rick-welts/.

7. Ibid.

8. Sutton, *The No Asshole Rule*, 25.

9. Galinsky and Schweitzer, *Friend and Foe*, 196.

10. Gallagher, *The Airbnb Story*, 54.

11. David Falk, *The Bald Truth: Secrets of Success from the Locker Room to the Boardroom* (New York: Gallery Books, 2009), 61–63.

12. http://espn991.com/all-time-winners-losers-by-winning-percentage-in -the-four-major-sports/.

13. Adam Grant, *Give and Take: Why Helping Others Drives Our Success* (New York: Penguin, 2014), 114.

14. Ibid.

15. Dean Smith and Gerald D. Bell, with John Kilgo, *The Carolina Way: Leadership Lessons from a Life in Coaching* (New York: Penguin, 2004), 17.

16. https://www.msn.com/en-us/sports/ncaabk/dean-smith-willed -dollar200-to-each-of-his-former-players/ar-AAa3482.

Chapter Ten

1. https://medium.com/darius-foroux/the-purpose-of-life-is-not-happiness -its-usefulness-65064d0cdd59.

2. Michael Foley, *The Age of Absurdity: Why Modern Life Makes It Hard to Be Happy* (London: Simon & Schuster UK, 2011), 44.

3. http://freakonomics.com/podcast/richard-branson/.

4. Shaw, *Extreme Teams*, 151.

5. Bock, *Work Rules!*, 149.

6. Schmidt and Rosenberg, with Eagle, *How Google Works*, 8.

7. Victor Luckerson, "Netflix Accounts for More Than a Third of All Internet Traffic," Time.com, May 29, 2015, http://time.com/3901378/netflix-inter net-traffic/.

8. https://www.forbes.com/sites/kevinkruse/2018/02/19/netflix-culture -deck-co-creator-says-leaders-need-to-explain-context/#72929413590c.

9. Phil Jackson and Hugh Delehanty, *Eleven Rings: The Soul of Success* (New York: Penguin, 2013), 96.

10. Ibid., 12.

11. Ibid., 13.

12. https://hbr.org/2017/07/stop-the-meeting-madness.

13. Ibid.

14. Sydney Finkelstein, *Superbosses: How Exceptional Bosses Master the Flow of Talent* (New York: Portfolio, 2016), 4.

15. Ibid., 4.

Chapter Eleven

1. Sinek, *Start with Why*, 103–4.

2. Brandt, *One Click*, 162.

3. Mark Zuckerberg speech, "Entrepreneurial Thought Leaders Seminars," Stanford University speaker series, October 2005.

4. Duhigg, *The Power of Habit*, 85.

5. Ibid., 89.

6. Sinek, *Leaders Eat Last*, 61.

7. Ibid., 50.

8. Ibid., 14–15.

9. Duhigg, *Smarter Faster Better*, 148.

10. Ibid.

11. Bilas, *Toughness*, 25.

12. Burkus, *Under New Management*, 119.

13. Ibid., 129.

14. http://www.triballeadership.net/media/TL-L.Excellence.pdf.

15. Dave Logan and John King, *Tribal Leadership: Leveraging Natural Groups to Build a Thriving Organization* (New York: Harper Business, 2011), 241.

16. Ibid.

Chapter Twelve

1. Charles Edward Montague, *Disenchantment: Essays [Thoughts on the First World War]*, 1922 (Ithaca NY: Cornell University Library, 2009).

2. http://www.nytimes.com/2011/02/13/sports/basketball/13russell.html?mcubz=3.

3. Holiday, *Ego Is the Enemy*, 133.

4. Patrick Lencioni, *The Ideal Team Player: How to Recognize and Cultivate the Three Essential Virtues* (San Francisco: Jossey-Bass, 2106), x.

5. Ibid., 157.

6. http://knowledge.wharton.upenn.edu/article/how-netflix-built-its-company-culture/.

7. https://www.youtube.com/watch?v=tVw8d3azOyk.

8. Sam Walker, *The Captain Class: A New Theory of Leadership* (New York: Random House, 2018), 138.

9. http://bleacherreport.com/articles/2083645-tim-duncan-is-the-best-power-forward-of-all-time-and-its-not-close.

10. Walker, *The Captain Class*, 140–42.

11. http://www.slate.com/articles/business/psychology_of_management/2014/05/adam_grant_s_give_and_take_a_theory_that_says_generous_people_do_better.html.

12. Grant, *Give and Take*, 10.

13. http://www.slate.com/articles/business/psychology_of_manage ment/2014/05/adam_grant_s_give_and_take_a_theory_that_says _generous_people_do_better.html.

Chapter Thirteen

1. Jackson and Delehanty, *Eleven Rings*, 14.
2. http://www.complex.com/sports/2011/05/the-greatest-moments -in-chicago-bulls-playoff-history/game-5-1991-nba-finals.
3. Halberstam, *Playing for Keeps*, 48.
4. Ibid.
5. Interview with Steve Kerr, *Pod Save America*, https://crooked.com/podcast /indictments/.
6. Jackson and Delehanty, *Eleven Rings*, 159.
7. Galinsky and Schweitzer, *Friend and Foe*, 73.
8. Ibid., 74.
9. Ibid., 75.

Chapter Fourteen

1. Williams, *Life Is Not an Accident*, 39.
2. E. W. Morrison and F. J. Milliken, "Speaking Up, Remaining Silent: The Dynamics of Voice and Silence in Organizations," *Journal of Management Studies* 40 (2003): 1353–58, https://www.inc.com/margaret-heffernan /encourage-employees-to-speak-up.html.
3. Ray Dalio, *Principles: Life and Work* (New York: Simon & Schuster, 2017).
4. https://www.gottman.com/blog/the-magic-relationship-ratio-according -science/.
5. M. W. Kraus, C. Huang, and D. Keltner, "Tactile Communication, Cooperation, and Performance: An Ethological Study of the NBA," *Emotion*, 2010, 10:745–749.
6. Interview with Steve Nash, *Suiting Up*, with Paul Rabil.
7. https://www.forbes.com/sites/danpontefract/2015/05/11/what-is-happening -at-zappos/#37ffb2ac4ed8.
8. Coyle, *The Culture Code*, 66.
9. https://www.nytimes.com/2017/09/08/jobs/corner-office-daniel -schwartz-restaurant-brands-international.html.

10. Coyle, *The Culture Code*.
    (Note: No page number because the entire book is organized into those sections.)

11. Eurich, *Insight*, 237–41.

12. See Ed Catmull and Amy Wallace, *Creativity, Inc.* (New York: Random House, 2014), for more on "Notes Day."

13. Margaret Heffernan, "Dare to Disagree," Ted Talk, https://www.ted.com/talks/margaret_heffernan_dare_to_disagree.

14. Patrick Lencioni, *The Five Dysfunctions of a Team: A Leadership Fable* (San Francisco: Jossey-Bass, 2002), 202.

15. https://www.cnbc.com/2017/08/16/how-jeff-bezos-two-pizza-rule-can-lead-to-more-productive-meetings.html.

16. Segall, *Insanely Simple*, 26.

17. https://www.nytimes.com/2016/01/22/opinion/the-eight-second-attention-span.html.

18. Colvin, *Talent Is Overrated*, 70.

Chapter Fifteen

1. Jackson and Delehanty, *Eleven Rings*, 220.

2. https://www.bloomberg.com/news/features/2018-01-10/the-five-pillars-of-gregg-popovich.

3. Coyle, *The Culture Code*, 59.

4. https://www.bloomberg.com/news/features/2018-01-10/the-five-pillars-of-gregg-popovich.

5. https://www.washingtonpost.com/news/recruiting-insider/wp/2016/03/04/montrose-christian-vs-oak-hill-a-look-back-at-one-of-the-greatest-high-school-games-in-d-c-history/?noredirect=on&utm_term=.7a081a499cce.

6. https://en.oxforddictionaries.com/definition/cohesion.

7. https://coachcal.com/news/2013/8/7/it-takes-a-village-to-create-the-kentucky-effect_23216.aspx?path=fromcoachcal.

8. Coyle, *The Culture Code*, xv.

9. Ibid., xvii.

10. Ibid.

11. Halberstam, *Playing for Keeps*, 75.

12. Ibid.

13. https://www.gq.com/story/jay-wright-villanova-the-anti-coach.
14. https://www.forbes.com/2009/11/02/athletes-lessons-executives-leadership
-managing-sports.html#2e2bef42152a.

Conclusion

1. Daniel H. Pink, *When: The Scientific Secrets of Perfect Timing* (New York: Riverhead, 2018), 89.
2. Ibid.
3. https://medium.com/the-mission/3-scientifically-proven-ways-to
-permanently-break-your-bad-habits-307182fc8fa8.
4. https://www.si.com/more-sports/2010/01/01/volleyball1001.

ABOUT THE AUTHORS

ALAN STEIN JR. is a corporate performance coach and world-renowned speaker. He spent more than fifteen years working with the highest-performing basketball players on the planet. Alan delivers high-energy keynotes, interactive workshops, and impactful full-day trainings to help organizations improve performance, cohesion, and accountability. He inspires and empowers everyone he works with to take immediate action and improve mind-set, habits, and productivity. Alan teaches how the same strategies that elite athletes use to perform at a world-class level can be utilized in business to build a winning culture. He is an amicably divorced father of twin sons (Luke and Jack) and a daughter (Lyla) and lives just outside of Washington, DC.

JON STERNFELD is the coauthor of *A Stone of Hope: A Memoir*, with Jim St. Germain; *Strong in the Broken Places: A Memoir of Addiction and Redemption through Wellness*, with Quentin Vennie; and *Crisis Point: Why We Must—and How We Can—Overcome Our Broken Politics in Washington and Across America*, with Senators Tom Daschle and Trent Lott. He lives in New York.